Bloom's Major Literary Characters

Bloom's Major Literary Characters

Nick Adams

Edited and with an introduction by
Harold Bloom
Sterling Professor of the Humanities
Yale University

CHELSEA HOUSE
PUBLISHERS
A Haights Cross Communications Company

Philadelphia

8/24/10
Lan
 # 40 —

10 9 8 7 6 5 4 3 2 1

Library of Congress Cataloging-in-Publication Data applied for.

ISBN 0-7910-7885-X

Contributing editor: Pamela Loos

Cover design by Keith Trego

Cover: ©Ewing Galloway / Index Stock Imagery Inc.

Layout by EJB Publishing Services

Chelsea House Publishers
1974 Sproul Road, Suite 400
Broomall, PA 19008-0914

www.chelseahouse.com

Contents

HAROLD BLOOM

The Analysis of Character

"Character," according to our dictionaries, still has as a primary meaning a graphic symbol, such as a letter of the alphabet. This meaning reflects the word's apparent origin in the ancient Greek character, a sharp stylus. *Charactēr* also meant the mark of the stylus' incisions. Recent fashions in literary criticism have reduced "character" in literature to a matter of marks upon a page. But our word "character" also has a very different meaning, matching that of the ancient Greek *ēthos*, "habitual way of life." Shall we say then that literary character is an imitation of human character, or is it just a grouping of marks? The issue is between a critic like Dr. Samuel Johnson, for whom words were as much like people as like things, and a critic like the late Roland Barthes, who told us that "the fact can only exist linguistically, as a term of discourse." Who is closer to our experience of reading literature, Johnson or Barthes? What difference does it make, if we side with one critic rather than the other?

Barthes is famous, like Foucault and other recent French theorists, for having added to Nietzsche's proclamation of the death of God a subsidiary demise, that of the literary author. If there are no authors, then there are no fictional personages, presumably because literature does not refer to a world outside language. Words indeed necessarily refer to other words in the first place, but the impact of words ultimately is drawn from a universe of fact. Stories, poems, and plays are recognizable as such because they are human utterances within traditions of utterances, and traditions, by achieving authority, become a kind of fact, or at least the sense of a fact. Our sense that literary characters, within the context of a fictive cosmos, indeed are fictional personages is also a kind of fact. The meaning and value of every character in a successful work of literary representation depend upon our ideas of persons in the factual reality of our lives.

Literary character is always an invention, and inventions generally are indebted to prior inventions. Shakespeare is the inventor of literary character as we know it; he reformed the universal human expectations for the verbal imitation of personality, and the reformation appears now to be permanent and uncannily inevitable. Remarkable as the Bible and Homer are at representing personages, their characters are relatively unchanging. They age within their stories, but their habitual modes of being do not develop. Jacob and Achilles unfold before us, but without metamorphoses. Lear and Macbeth, Hamlet and Othello severely modify themselves not only by their actions, but by their utterances, and most of all through *overhearing themselves*, whether they speak to themselves or to others. Pondering what they themselves have said, they will to change, and actually do change, sometimes extravagantly yet always persuasively. Or else they suffer change, without willing it, but in reaction not so much to their language as to their relation to that language.

I do not think it useful to say that Shakespeare successfully imitated elements in our characters. Rather, it could be argued that he compelled aspects of character to appear that previously were concealed, or not available to representation. This is not to say that Shakespeare is God, but to remind us that language is not God either. The mimesis of character in Shakespeare's dramas now seems to us normative, and indeed became the accepted mode almost immediately, as Ben Jonson shrewdly and somewhat grudgingly implied. And yet, Shakespearean representation has surprisingly little in common with the imitation of reality in Jonson or in Christopher Marlowe. The origins of Shakespeare's originality in the portrayal of men and women are to be found in the *Canterbury Tales* of Geoffrey Chaucer, insofar as they can be located anywhere before Shakespeare himself, Chaucer's savage and superb Pardoner overhears his own tale-telling, as well as his mocking rehearsal of his own spiel, and through this overhearing he is emboldened to forget himself, and enthusiastically urges all his fellow-pilgrims to come forward to be fleeced by him. His self-awareness, and apocalyptically rancid sense of spiritual fall, are preludes to the even grander abysses of the perverted will in Iago and in Edmund. What might be called the character trait of a negative charisma may be Chaucer's invention, but came to its perfection in Shakespearean mimesis.

The analysis of character is as much Shakespeare's invention as the representation of character is, since Iago and Edmund are adepts at analyzing both themselves and their victims. Hamlet, whose overwhelming charisma has many negative components, is certainly the most comprehensive of all literary characters, and so necessarily prophesies the labyrinthine complexities of the will in Iago and Edmund. Charisma, according to Max Weber, its first codifier, is primarily a natural endowment, and implies a primordial and idiosyncratic power over nature, and so finally over death. Hamlet's uncanniness is at its most suggestive in the scene of his long dying, where the audience, through the mediation of Horatio, itself is compelled to meditate upon suicide, if only because outliving the prince of Denmark scarcely seems an option.

Shakespearean representation has usurped not only our sense of literary character, but our sense of ourselves as characters, with Hamlet playing the part of the largest of these usurpations. Insofar as we have an idea of human disinterestedness, we tend to derive it from the Hamlet of Act V, whose quietism has about it a ghostly authority. Oscar Wilde, in his profound and profoundly witty dialogue, "The Decay of Lying," expressed a permanent insight when he insisted that art shaped every era, far more than any age formed art. Life imitates art, we imitate Shakespeare, because without Shakespeare we would perish for lack of images. Wilde's grandest audacity demystifies Shakespearean mimesis with a Shakespearean vivaciousness: "This unfortunate aphorism about art holding the mirror up to Nature is deliberately said by Hamlet in order to convince the bystanders of his absolute insanity in all art-matters." Of *Hamlet's* influence upon the ages Wilde remarked that: "The world has grown sad because a puppet was once melancholy." "Puppet" is Wilde's own deconstruction, a brilliant reminder that Shakespeare's artistry of illusion has so mastered reality as to have changed reality, evidently forever.

The analysis of character, as a critical pursuit, seems to me as much a Shakespearean invention as literary character was, since much of what we know about how to analyze character necessarily follows Shakespearean procedures. His hero-villains, from Richard III through Iago, Edmund, and Macbeth, are shrewd and endless questers into their own self-motivations. If we could bear to see Hamlet, in his unwearied negations, as another hero-villain, then we would judge him the supreme analyst of the darker recalcitrances in the selfhood. Freud followed the pre-Socratic Empedocles, in arguing that character is fate, a frightening doctrine that maintains the fear that there are no accidents, that overdetermination rules us all of our lives. Hamlet assumes the same, yet adds to this argument the terrible passivity he manifests in Act V. Throughout Shakespeare's tragedies, the most interesting personages seem doom-eager, reminding us again that a Shakespearean reading of Freud would be more illuminating than a Freudian exegesis of

Shakespeare. We learn more when we discover Hamlet in the Freudian Death Drive, than when we read *Beyond the Pleasure Principle* into *Hamlet.*

In Shakespearean comedy, character achieves its true literary apotheosis, which is the representation of the inner freedom that can be created by great wit alone. Rosalind and Falstaff, perhaps alone among Shakespeare's personages, match Hamlet in wit, though hardly in the metaphysics of consciousness. Whether in the comic or the modern mode, Shakespeare has set the standard of measurement in the balance between character and passion.

In Shakespeare the self is more dramatized than theatricalized, which is why a Shakespearean reading of Freud works out so well. Character-formation after the passing of the Oedipal stage takes the place of fetishistic fragmentings of the self. Critics who now call literary character into question, and who proclaim also the death of the author, invariably also regard all notions, literary and human, of a stable character as being mere reductions of deeper pre-Oedipal desires. It becomes clear that the fortunes of literary character rise and fall with the prestige of normative conceptions of the ego. Shakespeare's Iago, who wars against being, may be the first deconstructionist of the self, with his proclamation of "I am not what I am." This constitutes the necessary prologue to any view that would regard a fixed ego as a virtual abnormality. But deconstructions of the self are no more modern than Modernism is. Like literary modernism, the decentered ego came out of the Hellenistic culture of ancient Alexandria. The Gnostic heretics believed that the psyche, like the body, was a fallen entity, mechanically fashioned by the Demiurge or false creator. They held however that each of us possessed also a spark or pneuma, which was a fragment of the original Abyss or true, alien God. The soul or psyche within every one of us was thus at war with the self or pneuma, and only that sparklike self could be saved.

Shakespeare, following after Chaucer in this respect, was the first and remains still the greatest master of representing character both as a stable soul and a wavering self. There is a substance that endures in Shakespeare's figures, and there is also a quicksilver rendition of the unsettling sparks. Racine and Tolstoy, Balzac and Dickens, follow in Shakespeare's wake by giving us some sense of pre-Oedipal sparks or drives, and considerably more sense of post-Oedipal character and personality, stabilizations or sublimations of the fetish-seeking drives. Critics like Leo Bersani and René Girard argue eloquently against our taking this mimesis as the only proper work of literature. I would suggest that strong fictions of the self, from the Bible through Samuel Beckett, necessarily participate in both modes, the sublimation of desire, and the persistence of a primordial desire. The mystery of Hamlet or of Lear is intimately invested in the tangled mixture of the two modes of representation.

Psychic mobility is proposed by Bersani as the ideal to which deconstructions of the literary self may yet guide us. The ideal has its pathos, but the realities of literary representation seem to me very different, perhaps destructively so. When a novelist like D. H. Lawrence sought to reduce his characters to Eros and the Death Drive, he still had to persuade us of his authority at mimesis by lavishing upon the figures of *The Rainbow* and *Women in Love* all of the vivid stigmata of normative personality. Birkin and Ursula may represent antithetical and uncanny drives, but they develop and change as characters pondering their own pronouncements and reactions to self and others. The cost of a non-Shakespearean representation is enormous. Pynchon, in *The Crying of Lot 49* and *Gravity's Rainbow*, evades the burden of the normative by resorting to something like Christopher Marlowe's art of caricature in *The Jew of Malta*. Marlowe's Barabas is a marvelous rhetorician, yet he is a cartoon alongside the troublingly equivocal Shylock. Pynchon's personages are deliberate cartoons also, as flat as comic strips. Marlowe's achievement, and Pynchon's, are beyond dispute, yet they are like the prelude and the postlude to Shakespearean reality. They do not wish to engage with our hunger for the empirical world and so they enter the problematic cosmos of literary fantasy.

No writer, not even Shakespeare or Proust, alters the available stock that we agree to call reality, but Shakespeare, more than any other, does show us how much of reality we could encounter if only we retained adequate desire. The strong literary representation of character is already an analysis of character, and is part of the healing work of a literary culture, which implicitly seeks to cure violence through a normative mimesis of ego, *as if it were stable*, whether in actuality it is or is not. I do not believe that this is a social quest taken on by literary culture, but rather that we confront here the aesthetic essence of what makes a culture *literary*, rather than metaphysical or ethical or religious. A culture becomes literary when its conceptual modes have failed it, which means when religion, philosophy, and science have begun to lose their authority. If they cannot heal violence, then literature attempts to do so, which may be only a turning inside out of the critical arguments of Girard and Bersani.

I conclude by offering a particular instance or special case as a paradigm for the healing enterprise that is at once the representation and the analysis of literary character. Let us call it the aesthetics of being outraged, or rather of successfully representing the state of being outraged. W. C. Fields was one modern master of such representation, and Nathanael West was another, as was Faulkner before him. Here also the greatest master remains Shakespeare, whose Macbeth, himself a bloody outrage, yet retains our imaginative sympathy precisely because he grows increasingly outraged as he experiences the equivocation of the fiend that lies like truth. The double-natured promises and the prophecies of the weird sisters finally induce in Macbeth an apocalyptic version of the stage actor's anxiety at missing cues, the horror of a phantasmagoric stage fright of missing one's time, of always reacting too late. Macbeth, a veritable monster of solipsistic inwardness but no intellectual, counters his dilemma by fresh murders, that prolong him in time yet provoke him only to a perpetually freshened sense of being outraged, as all his expectations become still worse confounded. We are moved by Macbeth, however estrangedly, because his terrible inwardness is a paradigm for our own solipsism, but also because none of us can resist a strong and successful representation of the human in a state of being outraged.

The ultimate outrage is the necessity of dying, an outrage concealed in a multitude of masks, including the tyrannical ambitions of Macbeth. I suspect that our outrage at being outraged is the most difficult of all our affects for us to represent to ourselves, which is why we are so inclined to imaginative sympathy for a character who strongly conveys that affect to us. The Shrike of West's *Miss Lonelyhearts* or Faulkner's Joe Christmas of *Light in August* are crucial modern instances, but such figures can be located in many other works, since the ability to represent this extreme emotion is one of the tests that strong writers are driven to set for themselves.

However a reader seeks to reduce literary character to a question of marks on a page, she will come at last to the impasse constituted by the thought of death, her death, and before that to all the stations of being outraged that memorialize her own drive towards death. In reading, she quests for evidences that are strong representations, whether of her desire or her despair. Such questings constitute the necessary basis for the analysis of literary character, an enterprise that always will survive every vagary of critical fashion.

Editor's Note

My Introduction centers upon a Nick Adams fragment of fifty printed pages, not published until *The Nick Adams Stories* (1972), eleven years after Hemingway's suicide in July, 1961, a few weeks short of turning sixty-two. The rather beautiful fragment, "The Last Good Country," concerns Nick and his tomboyish young sister, Littless, with whom he has a repressed quasi-incestuous relationship.

Philip Young, a Hemingway biographer, reminds us that Nick Adams is the Hemingway hero, essentially Hemingway himself, while Horst H. Kruse establishes the aesthetic independence of "The End of Something," but also situates it in Nick's saga.

"Big Two-Hearted River" is judged by Joseph M. Flora as being religious in its tonality, after which Nicholas Gerogiannis finds in "The Bather" an analogue for the incest theme in "The Last Good Country."

Kenneth G. Johnston employs "A Way You'll Never Be" as a prophecy of Hemingway's eventual suicide, while Lawrence Broer reads "On Writing" as an overt fusion of Hemingway and Nick Adams.

"Big Two-Hearted River" is sensitively handled by Kenneth S. Lynn as a struggle within a wounded self, after which Paul Smith assigns the authorship of *In Our Time*, by implication, to an older Nick Adams.

Paul Wadden paradoxically sees Nick Adams, after his first love turns to another man, as being himself a betrayer, while David J. Ferrero fends off feminist critics of Hemingway and Nick.

In an essay closing this volume, Howard L. Hannum sums up Nick Adams as caught between sonship and fatherhood, unable to resolve the contest between past and present.

HAROLD BLOOM

Introduction

Where, in Hemingway, can we best locate the work in the writer? As with Lord Byron, Oscar Wilde, Norman Mailer, there is never any problem locating the writer in the work, in Hemingway's instance. More people have a recognition of the Hemingway myth than have ever read Hemingway. He lives on in the public imagination as Papa, the hard-drinking big-game hunter, war correspondent and pugilist (he literally knocked down Wallace Stevens, and figuratively hoped he could go fifteen rounds with Leo Tolstoy). We associate him with Paris in the 1920s, Madrid in the 1930s, and after that a blend of Havana and Key West, until he went home to emulate his father's suicide.

It is in *The Nick Adams Stories*, collected as a single volume in 1972, eleven years after Hemingway's death, that I think we encounter must fully the work in the writer, the influence of the poet upon himself. I say "poet" deliberately, echoing Wallace Stevens, for whom Hemingway was essentially a poet, whose subject was "extraordinary actuality." I do not mean that we are to read the Nick Adams stories as prose-poems, though the strongest among them are stylistic masterpieces: "The Light of the World," "The Killers," "In Another Country," "Big Two-Hearted River," and "The End of Something." But these are also sustained visions, which is rare in short stories. They, even "The Killers," are Hemingway's portraits of the artist as a young man, Nick Adams.

1

Eight—mostly unfinished—Nick Adams stories, that Hemingway did not publish, are marvelous revelations both of the writer's stylistic art, and the sometimes invidious effects of Hemingway's own work upon him. In a clear sense, he was his own worst influence, as here in "On Writing," where something unruly breaks loose:

> Talking about anything was bad. Writing about anything actual was bad. It always killed it.
>
> The only writing that was any good was what you made up, what you imagined. That made everything come true. Like when he wrote "My Old Man" he'd never seen a jockey killed and the next week Georges Parfrement was killed at that very jump and that was the way it looked. Everything good he'd ever written he'd made up. None of it had ever happened. Other things had happened. Better things, maybe. That was what the family couldn't understand. They thought it all was experience.
>
> That was the weakness of Joyce. Daedalus in *Ulysses* was Joyce himself, so he was terrible. Joyce was so damn romantic and intellectual about him. He'd made Bloom up, Bloom was wonderful. He'd made Mrs. Bloom up. She was the greatest in the world.
>
> That was the way with Mac. Mac worked too close to life. You had to digest life and then create your own people. Mac had stuff, though.
>
> Nick in the stories was never himself. He made him up. Of course he'd never seen an Indian woman having a baby. That was what made it good. Nobody knew that. He'd seen a woman have a baby on the road to Karagatch and tried to help her. That was the way it was.
>
> He wished he could always write like that. He would sometime. He wanted to be a great writer. He was pretty sure he would be. He knew it in lots of ways. He would in spite of everything. It was hard, though.
>
> It was hard to be a great writer if you loved the world and living in it and special people. It was hard when you loved so many places. Then you were healthy and felt good and were having a good time and what the hell.

"In the presence of extraordinary actuality, consciousness takes the place of imagination" is one of the *Adagia* of Wallace Stevens. Who judges what is extraordinary? I know nothing either of trout-fishing or of bullfighting, but sometimes when Hemingway writes about trout-fishing, I am persuaded of what Emerson linked as "the transcendental and extraordinary." Bull-fighting, doubtless a skill, a sport, an art to entire national cultures, is the center of Hemingway's *Death in the Afternoon*, which I assume gratifies a special taste I cannot share. As a literary critic, Hemingway is properly defensive; the short stories of *Dubliners* share an eminence with Hemingway's, Chekhov's, and only a few others. But you are ill-advised to reread even *The Sun Also Rises*, the best of Hemingway's novels, side-by-side with rereading *Ulysses*. Stephen wanes is the presence of Leopold Bloom, but Jake Barnes is only a name upon a page when compared with Dedalus. Joyce had and hadn't made Poldy up; Poldy was the Portrait of the Artist as a Middle-aged Man, as Richard Ellmann demonstrates in his biography of Joyce. Whether Molly "was the greatest in the world" is rather disputable, but beyond argument her substance is more an achieved representation than is that of Lady Brett Ashley. One isn't using Joyce as a club against Hemingway; the point is to surmise why Hemingway goes so bad whenever he goes bad. Joyce parodies an aspect of himself in the Stephen of *Ulysses*; Hemingway's self-parodies are involuntary, as in the passage quoted above.

Much more interesting because it is so poignant is the long, puzzling "The Last Good Country," where the work in the writer, Nick Adams in Ernest Hemingway, traps the reader into seventy pages that alternate between narrative incoherence and stylistic brilliance. The incoherence has little to do with the status of incompleteness scholars defensively assert for "The Last Good Country." Plot isn't the problem; an incremental tension or inconsistency between character and style is troublesome, and may account for Hemingway's abandonment of what could have been a remarkable novella, closer to *The Adventures of Huckleberry Finn* than anything else by Hemingway, even the marvelous "Big Two-Hearted River."

Two game wardens, one of them potentially dangerous, come after Nick Adams because he has killed a deer out of season. Hemingway is not much interested in the wardens, and so they bore us at some length, in the middle part of the story, taking up pages 92–107 of *The Nick Adams Stories*. The life of "The Last Good Country" is the adventures out in the open woods of Nick and his twelve-year-old youngest sister, called Littless. In the mode of Shakespearean pastoral comedy, Littless has cut off her hair to look like a boy, in order to join Nick in his flight from the law. Alas, both Nick and Littless have been reading Hemingway, and their conversational exchanges can be charmingly improbable:

"I like it," Nick said. "The hell with everything. I like it very much."

"Thank you, Nickie, so much. I was laying trying to rest like you said. But all I could do was imagine things to do for you. I was going to get you a chewing tobacco can full of knockout drops from some big saloon in some place like Sheboygan."

"Who did you get them from?"

Nick was sitting down now and his sister sat on his lap and held her arms around his neck and rubbed her cropped head against his cheek.

"I got them from the Queen of the Whores," she said. "And you know that name of the saloon?"

"No."

"The Royal Ten Dollar Gold Piece Inn and Emporium."

"What did you do there?"

"I was a whore's assistant."

"What's a whore's assistant do?"

"Oh she carries the whore's train when she walks and opens her carriage door and shows her to the right room. It's like a lady in waiting I guess."

"What's she say to the whore?"

"She'll say anything that comes into her mind as long as it's polite."

"Like what, brother?"

"Like, 'Well ma'am, it must be pretty tiring on a hot day like today to be just a bird in a gilded cage.' Things like that."

"What's the whore say?"

"She says, 'Yes indeedy. It sure is sweetness.' Because this whore I was whore's assistant to is of humble origin."

"What kind of origin are you?"

"I'm the sister or the brother of a morbid writer and I'm delicately brought up. This makes me intensely desirable to the main whore and to all of her circle."

Littless is not only Hemingwayesque, but amiably incestuous in desiring her brother, who is somewhat wary of the possibility. As a Hemingway parodist, Littless is hard to beat, as here when she thinks of emulating Jael in the Book of Judges, hammering spikes into the temples of the sleeping game wardens:

"What were you going to do?" he asked again. Littless leaned forward and spat toward the grill.

"How was that?"

"You missed the skillet anyway."

"Oh, it's pretty bad. I got it out of the Bible. I was going to take three spikes, one for each of them, and drive them into the temples of those two and that boy while they slept."

"What were you going to drive them in with?"

"A muffled hammer."

"How do you muffle a hammer?"

"I'd muffle it all right."

"That nail thing's pretty rough to try."

"Well, that girl did it in the Bible and since I've seen armed men drunk and asleep and circulated among them at night and stolen their whiskey why shouldn't I go the whole way, especially if I learned it in the Bible?"

"They didn't have a muffled hammer in the Bible."

"I guess I mixed it up with muffled oars."

"Maybe. And we don't want to kill anybody. That's why you came along."

"I know. But crime comes easy for you and me, Nickie. We're different from the others. Then I thought if I was ruined morally I might as well be useful."

You can yield to this and be delighted, but Littless is excessive even as parody. Essentially, this is Hemingway's version of a Shakespearean comedy routine, but it rings wrong in: "How do you muffle a hammer?" and "why shouldn't I go the whole way, especially if I learned it in the Bible?" We are listening to an incestuous love-song, rather than to an adventure story:

He loved his sister very much and she loved him too much. But, he thought, I guess these things straighten out. At least I hope so.

Perhaps "The Last Good Country" did not get finished because palpably Littless has no intention of letting things straighten out:

"Thank you for putting the Mackinaw on me. Wasn't it a lovely night, though?"

"Yes. Did you sleep all night?"

"I'm still asleep. Nickie, can we stay here always?"

"I don't think so. You'd grow up and have to get married."

"I'm going to get married to you anyway. I want to be your common-law wife. I read about it in the paper."

"That's where you read about the Unwritten Law."

"Sure. I'm going to be your common-law wife under the

Unwritten Law. Can't I, Nickie?"

"No."

"I will. I'll surprise you. All you have to do is live a certain time as man and wife. I'll get them to count this time now. It's just like homesteading."

"I won't let you file."

"You can't help yourself. That's the Unwritten Law. I've thought it out lots of times. I'll get cards printed Mrs. Nick Adams, Cross Village, Michigan—common-law wife. I'll hand these out to a few people openly each year until the time's up."

"I don't think it would work."

"I've got another scheme. We'll have a couple of children while I'm a minor. Then you have to marry me under the Unwritten law."

"That's not the Unwritten Law."

"I get mixed up on it."

"Anyway, nobody knows yet if it works."

Littless begins to seem more and more to have emerged from some wickedly delicious fairytale, but "The Last Good Country"'s authentic orgy is Heminway's prose exfoliating outrageously:

They went along down the creek. Nick was studying the banks. He had seen a mink's track and shown it to his sister and they had seen tiny ruby-crowned kinglets that were hunting insects and let the boy and girl come close as they moved sharply and delicately in the cedars. They had seen cedar waxwings so calm and gentle and distinguished moving in their lovely elegance with the magic wax touches on their wing coverts and their tails, and Littless had said, "They're the most beautiful, Nickie. There couldn't be more simply beautiful birds."

"They're built like your face," he said.

"No, Nickie. Don't make fun. Cedar waxwings make me so proud and happy that I cry."

"When they wheel and light and then move so proud and friendly and gently," Nick said.

This is very high rhetoric indeed, but not good training to go fifteen rounds with Count Leo Tolstoy. The influence of Hemingway upon Hemingway became overwhelming, and the work in the writer triumphed over the writer's work.

PHILIP YOUNG

Adventures of Nick Adams

Maria: "You were too young.... You were too young for such things."
Pilar: "Don't speak of such things. It is unhealthy."
FOR WHOM THE BELL TOLLS

On the Place Contrescarpe at the summit of the rue Cardinal Lemoine, Harry remembered, there was a room at the top of a tall hotel, and it was in this room that he had written "the start of all he was to do." Harry, dying of gangrene in a story called "The Snows of Kilimanjaro," can easily be connected with Ernest Hemingway, who wrote the story, and Hemingway had in mind some prose which finally went into his first significant book. This posed as a book of short stories, and was published in New York in 1925 with the title *In Our Time*. After Horace Liveright had bowdlerized one story (an amusing but rather nasty piece called "Mr. and Mrs. Elliot") and had cut out another completely ("Up in Michigan"), it consisted of thirteen short stories and several interchapter sketches. And it was as germinal a book for Hemingway as ever a book for a writer. It was truly the start of everything he was ever going to do.

The title *In Our Time* may simply have been meant to indicate, as is commonly thought, that the material was contemporary, and to some extent representative of early twentieth-century experience. But Hemingway

From *Ernest Hemingway: A Reconsideration*: 29–55. © 1966 by Philip Young.

delighted in irony and in titles that are quotations; it is almost certain that he intended here a sardonic allusion to that phrase from the Book of Common Prayer which Neville Chamberlain was later to make notorious: "Give peace in our time, O Lord," for the stories are mainly of violence or evil in one form or another. It is that there is no peace in them.

These stories alternate in the book with sixteen short "sketches," which are of contemporary scenes and for the most part are of sickening violence. These are arranged at least roughly according to the order in which their author experienced them. With one very notable exception, however, they have no other apparent relation to the stories. Moreover, half of the stories are unrelated to the main interest of the book, which is the spotty but careful development of an important but little-understood character named Nick Adams.

The stories about Nick are subtly, even obscurely, organized and presented. It is not always obvious that Nick is any more than an observer of the events they relate, and his age is never mentioned. But the book cannot really be understood at all without the clear perception that the stories are arranged in the chronological order of his boyhood and young manhood, and that the volume is in large part devoted to a scrupulously planned account of his character, and the reasons for it. The well-known "Big Two-Hearted River," for example, cannot possibly be read with comprehension unless one understands the earlier stories. One would think it no more than it pretends to be—a story about a man fishing—and it would be, as readers often used to complain, quite pointless. So the unrelated sketches and the stories not about Nick are to be more or less put aside for the moment in order that an obscure but meaningful pattern may emerge.

In Our Time opens with an "Introduction by the Author"—"Introduction" in the sense that it sets the tone for the whole collection; "by the Author" in that the events were particularly significant for him. This piece describes Turks and Greeks at a quai at Smyrna, where there are women who will not give up their dead babies, and soldiers who dispose of their baggage mules by breaking their legs and dumping them into the shallow water of the port to drown. And there is the harbor itself with "plenty of nice things floating around in it." "I got so I dreamed about things," says the "I" of the sketch in an apparently unimportant remark which actually looks very far ahead.

The first of the seven Nick stories, and a "typical" one, is "Indian Camp." A typical Nick Adams story is of an initiation, is the telling of an event which is violent or evil, or both, or at the very least is the description of an incident which brings the boy into contact with something that is perplexing and unpleasant. One of the reasons why these stories were once not generally understood is that it is not at first apparent that they are about Nick at all; they seem to be about other people, and it simply seems to happen that Nick is around. "Indian Camp," for example, tells about a doctor, Nick's father, who delivers an Indian woman of a baby by Caesarean section, with a jackknife and without anesthetic. The woman's invalid husband lies in a bunk above his screaming wife, Nick—a young boy—holds a basin for his father, and four men hold the mother down until the child is successfully born. When it is over the doctor looks in the bunk above and discovers that the husband, who has been through two days of screaming, had found the operation on his wife more than he could take, and had cut his head nearly off with a razor.

> "Take Nick out of the shanty, George," the doctor said.
> There was no need of that. Nick, standing in the door of the kitchen, had a good view of the upper bunk when his father, the lamp in one hand, tipped the Indian's head back.

This is Nick's initiation to pain, and to the violence of birth and death. The story ends (with Nick and his father rowing off from the camp) so "objectively," so completely without comment, that it is easy to understand why readers failed to see that Nick is the central character in a book of short stories that is nearly a novel about him, so closely related are the seven stories in which he appears. Here as elsewhere Nick is not recognized as protagonist unless one perceives that the last page of the five-page piece would be irrelevant if the story were about Indians or the doctor, and also unless one looks back later to see that Hemingway has begun with his first story a pattern of contacts with violence and evil for Nick that he develops in the rest of the stories until he has built what is actually a plot. Like the later and more famous "Killers," "Indian Camp" is Nick's story, with Indians and gangsters only devices for offering him some direct experience of peace in our time.

The next two stories of the collection are called "The Doctor and the Doctor's Wife" and "The End of Something," and they give the boy's first contacts with things that are not violent, but which complicate his young life considerably because they deeply perplex. They are prefaced with two very short examples of contemporary serenity. One is of a military evacuation with a girl holding a blanket over the head of an otherwise unattended woman who is having a baby; the other is about shooting Austrians to death, one after another. The two Nick stories which follow are somewhat more placid, but they are in the nature of early lessons which can be just as unsettling to a boy as violence. "The Doctor and the Doctor's Wife" teaches Nick something about the solidarity of the male sex; more precisely, it presents him with the conclusion that he is completely dissatisfied with his mother. A workman tries to pick a fight with Doctor Adams so that he can more easily avoid paying a large bill he owes for treatment of his wife. The doctor refuses to fight, and Nick's mother, who is a Christian Scientist and will not believe that a man would do what the workman has just done, quotes Scripture. When the doctor tells Nick that his mother wants him, and Nick wants to go hunting with his father instead, the doctor says, "All right. Come on, then," and they go squirrel hunting, leaving the doctor's wife to wonder where Nick is. Nick is still a small boy, apparently (he calls his father "Daddy"), but even so it is clear that he cannot stomach his mother's naïve refusal to face facts.*

"The End of Something" is the end of a sort of love affair that an adolescent Nick has had with a girl named Marjorie. For some reason, possibly because he feels he has an unpleasant task to perform, Nick is "out of sorts." He takes the girl trolling for trout, demonstrates some knowledge of fish and fishing, and finally gets the girl to leave, perhaps for good. These two stories make up the beginning of a somewhat peculiar attitude toward women which the Hemingway hero is going to have when he is grown—grown, for example, into Robert Jordan of *For Whom the Bell Tolls*. "The End of Something" is also one of the stories of which people complain that it has no "point." This is partly because what point it does have is subtle and slight. The "Old Lady" of *Death in the Afternoon* was not alone when she objected to Hemingway, after he told her another story that ended rather mysteriously:

> And is that all of the story? Is there not to be what we called in my youth a wow at the end?
> Ah, Madame, it is years since I added the wow to the end of a story.

When the old lady insists, however, on hearing the "point," and the author gives it to her, she complains:

> This seems to me a very feeble wow.
> Madame, the whole subject is feeble and too hearty a wow would overbalance it.

The end of "The End of Something," too, is rather less of a bang than a whimper: things can suddenly go all wrong with the pleasantest of love affairs. But the real difficulty in finding the meaning of this story of *In Our Time* is the same difficulty that has been encountered with "Indian Camp": the story is like a chapter of a novel (the book has Roman numeral chapter headings in addition to the usual story titles); it is like a chapter of a novel in that it by no means has all of its meaning when taken in isolation.

The next story, which follows a peaceful one-paragraph sketch describing more shooting of soldiers who are this time coming over a "simply priceless" barricade, is called "The Three-Day Blow," and relates among other things how "The End of Something" felt to Nick: the end of his affair with Marjorie felt like the autumnal three-day wind storm that is blowing: "All of a sudden everything was over.... Just like when the three-day blows come and rip all the leaves off the trees." The story extends the pattern of the previous ones and reveals the lesson Nick learned from the preceding episode. The lesson was not pleasant at the time, and it was also disturbing. Nick accomplished his purpose in "The End of Something," and got rid of the girl, but he was not at all happy about it. It is Nick's friend Bill who reveals the lesson, remarking that after all Nick might get back into the affair again. This thought is surprising to Nick: the end "had seemed so absolute.... He felt happy now. There was not anything that was irrevocable." And that is about all the "point" there is to this story; Nick is learning things. And now *we* learn—learn why it was that Nick forced that break with Marjorie: she was of the "wrong" class for a doctor's son. It is again Bill who brings this out. You just can't mix oil and water, he says; it's just like it was with Bill and "Ida that works for Strattons." Here is more perplexity for Nick, and the whole business makes him extremely uncomfortable. He did it, but he doesn't want to talk about it, as he says, and it is not until this point that we can really understand why he was "out of sorts" in "The End of Something."

"The Three-Day Blow"—a many-sided story—is also a kind of tour de force, a skillful representation of the conversation of adolescent boys. Nick and Bill discuss sports, drinking, women, and literature while with affected non-chalance they get drunk on Bill's father's whisky. Thus the story also effectively documents Nick's introduction to drunkenness, a condition which is to become important for the Hemingway protagonist and is therefore worth recording.

But these are not the primary issues of the book, and with the next one-paragraph sketch called Chapter V we are abruptly taken back from the experiences which perplex to the pattern of violence, pain and evil which began with the introduction to the book and the first story in it. This sketch describes the execution by firing squad of six cabinet ministers, and commences a crescendo which continues through the story that follows and then is climaxed by the next sketch to come, in which Nick is wounded in the war. After that event, the going is all down hill.

The center of attraction in the Chapter V sketch is a cabinet minister who is sick with typhoid. He presents a difficulty to his captors because he is too weak to support himself against the wall where he is to be executed. Finally he has to be shot separately, sitting in a puddle of water before the wall with his head on his knees.

This scene serves to introduce the story of Chapter V, called "The Battler." People who complain about the sordid nature of many of Hemingway's stories seldom if ever cite this one, perhaps because the unpleasantness is more in the undertones and in things not said than in the outer events which, though not happy, are not entirely extraordinary in our time. But if the subtleties are drawn out and examined, "The Battler" is as unpleasant as anything its author ever wrote.

It opens with an adolescent Nick who has left home and is out on his own for the first time. He has been "riding the rods" and has just been knocked off a moving freight by a brakeman. He is limping up the tracks, heading for the next town on foot, when in crossing a bridge he sees below him in the darkness a campfire with a man sitting beside it. Nick, in answer to the man's question, reveals that he got his black eye from the brakeman:

> "It must have made him feel good to bust you," the man said seriously.

In the firelight Nick makes out the stranger's face, which was queerly formed and mutilated. "It was like putty in color. Dead looking in the firelight." The man notices how the boy is staring and obligingly exhibits one cauliflower ear and a stump where the other ear should have been. This makes the boy "a little sick." The small man reveals then that he is Ad Francis, an ex-prizefighter Nick has heard of, and that he is "not quite right" in the head, is "crazy."** He also demonstrates that his heart thumps only forty times a minute. A Negro named Bugs then appears with some ham and eggs, which he fries in the fire. This is a very large Negro who is extremely soft-spoken and polite to his punch-drunk companion, and to Nick, whom he addresses with oppressive deference as "Mister Adams." He makes sandwiches:

> "Just close that sandwich, will you, please, and give it to Mister Francis."
> Ad took the sandwich and started eating.
> "Watch out how that egg runs," the negro warned. "This is for you, Mister Adams. The remainder for myself.... May I offer you a slice of bread dipped right in the hot ham fat?" Bugs said.

The men and the boy are eating when suddenly the situation, which has been growing somewhat uneasy, becomes extremely uncomfortable. Ad, who has been sitting in complete silence for some time, starts without provocation to pick a fight with Nick.

> "You're a hot sketch. Who the hell asked you to butt in here?"
> "Nobody."
> "You're damn right nobody did. Nobody asked you to stay either. You come in here and act snotty about my face and smoke my cigars and drink my liquor.... You're going to get your can knocked off. Do you get that?"

The battler approaches the boy and the situation all of a sudden is saved by the Negro, who creeps up behind Ad, sets himself, and taps him across the base of the skull with a cloth-wrapped blackjack. Bugs then tenderly treats the unconscious man with water until his eyes close; while he lies there still unconscious the boy and the Negro talk by the fire. This, Bugs explains smiling, is the way he has to "change" Ad from time to time—"he won't remember nothing of it." As they drink coffee the Negro sketches in Ad's past, the unpalatable decline of his career and intellect, and reveals that the two men met in jail, and have been together ever since, "seeing the country."

> "Right away I liked him and when I got out I looked him up. ... I like to be with him...."

After this conversation the story draws to a close. Bugs says that he should wake Ad now, and with a graceful apology he tells Nick that he'd better move along so that it won't be necessary to tap Ad again. He gives the boy directions and another sandwich to take along—"all this in a low, smooth, polite nigger voice." Nick walks out of the firelight and back to the tracks where he stops to listen:

> The low soft voice of the negro was talking. Nick could not hear the words. Then he heard the little man say, "I got an awful headache, Bugs."

> "You'll feel better, Mister Francis," the negro's voice soothed. "Just you drink a cup of this coffee."

The story ends with Nick starting away up the tracks. For the first time in the book we get an obvious word about what the *effect* of what he has seen, done and heard has had on him: Nick has been so stunned by this twosome that he walked quite a distance before he "found he had a ham sandwich in his hand and put it in his pocket."

Clearly, like "Indian Camp," this is a story of a boy coming in contact with violence and evil, and here for a moment the force of the impression has been registered. The story is also, however, among the most suggestive of Hemingway's; there is more that is sinister and unpleasant about this gentle, large, courteous and thoughtful blackjacking colored man than may at first meet the eye, and it can have only one very probable interpretation. The tender, motherly, male-nursing Bugs is too comfortable in the relationship with the little, demented ex-fighter. The companionship which started as a prison friendship and which is self-sufficient financially (the couple is sent money by Ad's ex-manager and wife) seems self-sufficient in other ways. Although Nick understands no more than that something is very wrong here, the reader may get the never-stated but potently suggested notion that it is not only Ad who is queer. This theme, which crops up in five other stories, in all but one of the novels, and violently, obsessively, in his posthumously published recollections of Paris, is normally used by Hemingway as it is used here—a kind of ultimate in evil. When this atmosphere is added to the violence of getting punched off a moving train at night, and nearly being beaten by an ex-champion, and meeting a highly polished Negro hobo who habitually blackjacks his companion in sweet good humor and then nurses him back to consciousness with a love that was present even in the blow, it is not difficult to see that here is another nice thing that the Author, as in his Introduction, may get to dream about.

The sketch, Chapter VI, which immediately follows "The Battler" is the only place in the book where the interchapter material meets with the stories, and this crossing unmistakably signals the climax of *In Our Time*: X marks the spot, as a short paragraph reveals that Nick is in the war, tells us that he has been hit in the spine, and that he has made a "separate peace" with the enemy, is no longer fighting the war for democracy. It would be quite impossible to exaggerate the importance of this short scene, which is to be duplicated by a new protagonist named Frederic Henry in *A Farewell to Arms*, and to serve as climax for all of Hemingway's heroes for at least the next twenty-five years.

This event, Nick's serious injuring, does two things for *In Our Time* and for the development of the character of the Hemingway hero. First the wound culminates, climaxes and epitomizes the wounds he has been getting as a growing boy. Life—as we have already partly seen—was really like this up in Michigan, where Nick was already well on the way to becoming a casualty. The effect of the wounds Nick Adams has been suffering (and will suffer more of when Hemingway later goes back, with more Nick stories, to fill in) is just beginning to be hinted at: this shell that has caught Nick in the spine is of a piece with the blows he took when he saw the jackknife

Caesarean, the nearly decapitated Indian, the battler and the blackjacking Negro, when he felt himself forced to repudiate his mother and his girl friend, when he hit the cinders after a blow in the face on a freight train. This wound, which is to be the same wound which "emasculates" Jake Barnes in *The Sun Also Rises* and is to hospitalize Lt. Henry in *A Farewell to Arms*, and whose scar Col. Cantwell bears more than thirty years later in *Across the River and Into the Trees*, is significant even beyond these facts.

From here on in the Hemingway hero is to be a wounded man, wounded not only physically but—as soon becomes clear—psychically as well. The pattern of Nick Adams' development, which exists so far only in sketchiest outline, is of a boy who, while with his father up in Michigan, and without him on his own as a hobo or with friends, has been learning some lessons about life. These lessons have more often than not proved to be the sort of experiences which could very well cripple an impressionable and sensitive boy. This is the kind of boy Nick is, as the author was shortly to make clear, and his experiences have indeed crippled him, as Hemingway was also to show, as surely as his initiation to shrapnel has done. This culminating blow in the spine is symbol and climax for a process that has been going on since we first met Nick; it is an outward and visible sign of an inward and spiritual dis-grace.

If there were no more to the event than this, it would be crucial for the development of the Hemingway protagonist, who will show the effects of his physical and psychical injuries right up to his most recent appearance. But in addition the injury has an immediate result that is nearly as important as the wound itself. Nick's first reaction, as he waits in the hot sun for a stretcher, is to turn to his friend Rinaldi who is also hit and say: "You and me we've made a separate peace.... Not patriots." Of course this could be taken to mean simply that for these two the war is over. But "not patriots" implies much more than that. When Lt. Henry in *A Farewell to Arms* (whose friend is also named Rinaldi) is wounded and has recovered, he is not patriotic to the point of deserting the army and society as a whole. This sketch sharply adumbrates the novel. A "good soldier" would still be fighting the war in spirit if no longer in body, but Nick has decided to hell with it: at this precise point begins the long break with society that is to take the Hemingway protagonist into his expatriation in *The Sun Also Rises*, is to be repeated in *A Farewell to Arms*, is to take Hemingway himself big game hunting in the *Green Hills of Africa* and to the bullfights in *Death in the Afternoon*, and is to help him make Harry Morgan in *To Have and Have Not* an outlaw up until the moment of his death, when he mends the break and decides that he was wrong. The wound itself the hero will never lose, either as an outward or an inward scar, as long as he lives.

All of this, of course, remained to be shown. It took Hemingway several books and many years to deal with the implications of this short paragraph, and—to make the pattern clearer—he had also to fill in many of the gaps in the sketchy outline we have of Nick. Even before he patched up Nick's biographical framework, however, he added one more important story dealing with Nick's adventures *In Our Time*, and before that a less significant and transitional one called "Cross Country Snow."

This latter story is prefaced with a paragraph, Chapter XII, which describes a fatally struck bull who is looking straight at his conqueror in the bullfight, "roaring blood ... and his legs caving." The story itself finds Nick recuperated from his injury, except that he cannot "telemark." The war is over, and Nick and a friend are skiing in Switzerland. Skiing (like fishing and hunting and bullfighting and drinking) is one of the things that become very important personal indulgences for the Hemingway protagonist now that he is outside society. The trouble here is that by now he is also married. What is more his wife Helen is pregnant, and they have to return to America. Nick doesn't particularly want to go, although he approves the idea of the baby. He says, somewhat hysterically, that if you can't ski, life "isn't worth while." However, he must go back, and the opposition between the fellowship and freedom of the slopes, and the mixed blessings of the United States and parenthood, is about all the meaning the story has.

But "Big Two-Hearted River" gets us back to the main show. This is a long, two-part tale which finds Nick back up in Michigan fishing. It is extraordinary for the often-remarked brilliance of the description of the fishing trip, which Nick takes alone, but there is a lot more to it than that. Yet of all the critics who struggled with it for twenty-five years only Malcolm Cowley discussed it perceptively, and no one really understood it. Cowley saw that some of Hemingway's stories are "nightmares at noon-day." "Big Two-Hearted River" is apparently a collection of sharp sensory details, he says, but if it is read closely one realizes that actually it is a kind of "waking dream." There are shadows in the story that one does not see at first; the thing goes on several levels. The fishing is an escape "from a nightmare or from realities that have become a nightmare"; it is for Nick a kind of rite, an incantation, "a spell to banish evil spirits."

Edmund Wilson, who is usually a perceptive critic too, and who wrote an introduction for an edition of *In Our Time*, refers to the Nick we see in this story as a "boy." This slip is only apparently trivial, for to fail to see that the boy Nick is by now a man is to fail to see the development that has been taking place in his character, and how the stories are related to each other; it is to miss seeing what *kind* of man he is, and therefore, of course, what made him that way, and thus it is to read the whole piece wrong. In order to read it right one must place it firmly in the evolution of the hero Hemingway has been tracing, and see how it is the unhappy result of the quiet and sketchy but meaningful pattern the author has been building up. The story is crucial for all of Hemingway because here and for the first time we get a sustained look at the remarkable effects of what has happened to the boy who innocently accompanied his father into the Indian camp so many years before.

At the outset of the story we are told that Nick has returned to country that had been burned out a year ago, though he hadn't known about it. He is excited over the trip because "it was a long time since Nick had looked into a stream and seen trout." Later he remembers that he and a friend of his, who is very wealthy and owns a yacht, were once going to cruise the northern shore of Lake Superior, but "that was a long time ago...." Obviously, Nick is a grown man now, who has been away. He has been abroad, as we have seen, and in a war.

The opening page of the fishing trip establishes the atmosphere of shadows and tensions Cowley is conscious of. When Nick first sees the river he is going to work he sees trout "keeping themselves steady in the current with wavering fins" and others "in deep, fast moving water, slightly distorted," and at the bottom of the pool he finally can make out the big ones. The whole trip is seen as these first fish are seen. Nick goes about his business exactly as if he were a trout keeping himself steady in the current, the whole affair is seen sharply but is slightly distorted, and there are now several deep pools in Nick's personality—where in the shadows lurk the "big ones." Nick is clearly in escape from something: as he walked along he "felt happy. He felt that he had left everything behind.... It was all back of him." He walks to where he is going to camp, pausing to catch grasshoppers for bait along the way, and then he finds a level piece of ground and pitches his tent. Each step of the process—smoothing the ground, arranging the blankets, cutting the tent pegs and raising the canvas—is related in a regular and monotonous sequence unrelieved by even a phrase of comment or a break in the rhythm. The action goes along against a backdrop of something only dimly seen; Nick goes through the motions now in a dead-pan, one-two-three-four routine which is rather new to him, and which suggests much less that he is the mindless primitive the Hemingway hero was so often thought to be than that he is desperately protecting his mind against whatever it is that he is escaping Finally he gets the tent up, and crawls in to test it:

> Nick was happy as he crawled inside the tent. He had not been unhappy all day. This was different though. Now things were done. There had been this to do. Now it was done.

Then why it is that he is happy becomes a little clearer:

He was settled. Nothing could touch him. It was a good place
to camp. He was there, in the good place.

Next Nick came out of the tent and, with the same deliberateness with which
he made camp, he cooked supper. He ate, and everything was going well
until suddenly "his mind was starting to work." This was all right, however,
for here was a night when he could stop it (later on there will be nights when
he cannot): "He knew he could choke it because he was tired enough." He
falls asleep at once, and Part I of the story ends.

Part II opens on the following morning and takes Nick through a day
of fishing. This fishing (and the breakfast he eats before it and the lunch he
puts up for himself) is again described in terms of chronologically ordered,
mechanical, deliberate movements which begin to wear on one's nervous
system. But here at least there can be, with proper understanding, no
objection to the pulsing monotony of the sentence-cadence: He did this. And
then he did that. And then he did that, and this—and so on, paragraphs
together. There can be no objection because the tense, exasperating effect of
this rhythm on the reader is extraordinarily appropriate to the state of Nick's
nerves, which is above all what Hemingway is trying to convey. A terrible
panic is just barely under control, and the style—this is the "Hemingway
style" at its most extreme—is the perfect expression of the content of the
story. Nick's mechanical movements—of cooking, casting, baiting his hook
and the rest—are the mindless movements of, say, a woman who all alone
busies herself with a thorough housecleaning on the morning after the
sudden death of her husband, or the movements of the hands of a badly shell-
shocked veteran who, while he can control himself, is performing simple jobs
over and over in a factory: this, and then that. And then that and this. When
the extreme excitement of a big strike from a trout intervenes the style
changes abruptly. The pressure is off the man, he is nowhere but right there
playing the fish, and then the sentences lengthen greatly and become
appropriately graceful:

> With the core of the reel showing, his heart feeling stopped
> with the excitement, leaning back against the current that mounted
> icily his thighs, Nick thumbed the reel hard with his left hand.

He loses this large one, and the excitement has been so great that he
feels sick and has to sit down. He does not dare "to rush his sensations any."
He tries to smoke, and when a baby trout strikes at the match he throws into
the current he laughs. This tells him that everything is all right; he can sit
there a while: "He would finish the cigarette."

Nick fishes all day, and in the course of following him around we see that he is very frightened by the something that is lurking in the back of his mind and that he is escaping. Also we get a picture of a man who has a great deal in the way of outdoor "know-how" and is superstitious as well. He knows precisely how to disengage and throw back a small trout so it will not suffer from the experience, and he spits on his bait for luck. Nothing much ever really happens. We learn that there is a place where "the river narrowed and went into a swamp," and that he doesn't want to go downstream into it today (this region has some connotation for him that is unpleasant but enigmatic, for the time being), and the story ends with him returning to his camp encouraged but thinking that he has gone as far with himself as is best for one day—"there were plenty of days coming when he could fish the swamp."

Clearly, "Big Two-Hearted River" presents a picture of a sick man, and of a man who is in escape from whatever it is that made him sick. And Nick obviously knows what is the matter and what he must do about it and must not do. He must keep physically occupied, keep his hands busy; he must not think or he will be unable to sleep, he must not get too excited or he will get sick, and he must not go into the swamp, which unlike the tent, "the good place," is the bad place. It is as though he were on a doctor's prescription, and indeed he is on the strictest sort of emotional diet but is his own nutritionist.

By now the cause of this condition should be equally clear. Fragmentary as the outline is so far it can already be seen that the causes of the difficulties which "Big Two- Hearted River" gives symptoms of are the experience, already partly related, of the man's past: the blows which he has suffered—physical, psychical, moral, spiritual and emotional—have damaged him. He has been complicated and wounded by what he has seen, done and been through. This is the whole "point" of an otherwise pointless story and with it Hemingway brought his book to a close. When one extracts from it as we have done the stories in which Nick appears one sees that actually Hemingway has plotted a story which covers perhaps as much as twenty years in the life of Nick Adams, first leading actor in a coherent drama to which he dedicated nearly four decades of his life.

To fill in some of the gaps in Nick's development Hemingway included two more stories about him in *Men without Women* (1927) and three more in *Winner Take Nothing* (1933). The first four of these are relevant here; the fifth fits in better later. The two stories which appeared in the 1927 volume, "Ten Indians" and "The Killers," take us first to Nick's early boyhood up in Michigan, and secondly to the trip, very likely, he was on in "The Battler."

In the Indian story we find "Nickie" a young boy who is being kidded about having an Indian girl friend named Prudence Mitchell. He is pleased about this until his father, who had walked that afternoon up to the Indian camp of the story of that name, tells the boy that he saw Prudie and Frank Washburn "threshing around" in the woods. When the father comes back we learn that Nick has been crying, and he tells himself "If I feel this way my heart must be broken." He goes to bed, and in the morning he is awake a long time before he remembers this tragic fact; he has learned another lesson.

"The Killers" is a more significant story. The scene is laid in a lunchroom where the boy—a guess would be that he is in his teens—watches and listens to two gangsters who are waiting for an ex-prizefighter, whom they are going to kill. Nick and a colored cook are bound and gagged in the kitchen, but when the victim does not appear the "killers" release them and leave. Nick knows where the fighter, Ole Andreson, lives, and he goes to warn him. He finds that the man is aware that he is going to be murdered and will do nothing to escape his fate. He is "an awfully nice man" who thanks Nick for his interest, and declines again to do anything to protect himself; Nick leaves. Back at the lunchroom we get the "point" of the story, which clearly consists of the boy's reaction to this somewhat sickening situation. Hemingway delineated three distinct responses: the cook (who, being colored and a short-order cook to boot, presumably has trouble enough of his own) wants nothing whatsoever to do with it—" 'I don't even listen to it,' he said and shut the door." George, the counterman in the diner, is more affected: "It's a hell of a thing." But it is of course the effect the incident has had on Nick that Hemingway was interested in:

> "I'm going to get out of this town," Nick said.... "I can't stand
> to think about him waiting in the room and knowing he's going
> to get it. It's too damned awful."

George then gives him the advice which Nick is later to give himself: "Well ... you better not think about it."

It is obvious here that Nick, far from being calloused, is an extremely sensitive, even an abnormally sensitive, human being. Of the three reactions here it is George's which is probably "average": Nick's is roughly as excessive as the cook's is deficient. Nick cannot "stand to think about him waiting in the room and knowing he's going to get it," and he has got to clear the town completely. If the Hemingway hero were the "bovine," "dull-witted," "wooden-headed," "heavy-footed," "village idiot" that Wyndham Lewis to much applause once made him out then such a story as this one would be unthinkable. The contact Nick has made here with impending violence and horrifying inertia has made its mark on him, and in "The Killers" the whole pattern of Hemingway's method of dealing with his boy is suggested in the space of a few sentences.

"The Light of the World" fills in more of this period "on the bum," and although the tale is not violent it does, like the two other incidents recording the trip Nick made, indicate that life up in Michigan might provide a boy with no better training for a proper middle-class existence in America than a war in Europe, especially if he got off on his own and saw some of it. Nick and an older friend called Tom, whom he is now traveling with, come into a small town in the evening, experience a little difficulty with a man in a bar who say that as "punks" they "stink," and go down to hang around the railroad station. The story is mainly taken up with the conversation in the waiting room, where there are five very fat prostitutes, six white men (of whom one is homosexual) and four silent Indians. This talk is fairly tough; two of the whores get into an argument ("you dried up old hot-water bottle," "you big mountain of pus"); the homosexual tries to pick up the boys; Nick is considering a woman of 350 pounds when the older Tom gets him to leave and the story ends. Nothing much has happened, except that Nick has been in close contact with things a young boy who had stayed at home would normally not meet—with things that the conventions governing the average boyhood do not define or present answers for, and that raise problems which the Scripture-quoting Mrs. Adams would not even admit let alone deal with. In the course of the piece the boy has been in on a discussion of adultery, fornication, homosexual and heterosexual "perversions," has conversed somewhat professionally with a grotesque prostitute and has been attracted to her, and has successfully escaped the advances of what one of the men calls a "sister." One gets the idea that this little vacation spent riding freights from town to town is bringing him into contact with more than may be "good for him."

That the experience of the war was not good for him is made patent by "A Way You'll Never Be" (in *Winner Take Nothing*, 1933). This can be placed, in time of action, between the Chapter VI sketch in which Nick was wounded in a visible way, and "Cross Country Snow," where he was about to return to the United States after the war. In this story one learns a good deal more about what made Nick the sick man he was when, back in America, he fished the Big Two-Hearted. One also finds that the Chapter VI paragraph telescoped the relation of the wounding to quitting the war and society somewhat: after Nick was hurt he did return for a time to a very peculiar kind of action before he finally walked out. This development also fits the experience of Lt. Henry in *A Farewell to Arms*.

"A Way You'll Never Be" (one depends on it) finds Nick in a simulated

American uniform making his way by bicycle through the Austrian dead to an Italian infantry battalion, where he seeks out a captain who was a friend of his before Nick got hit. It seems that it is his job (or at least he believes this is so) to be seen in this uniform, the hope being that it will help the Italian troops to feel that the Yanks are coming. Before Paravicini, the captain, discovers something is wrong with Nick they talk about various things, including drinking; Nick reveals that during attacks he used to get drunk on a mixture of Grappa and ether. Para says:

> "You're much braver in an attack than I am."
> "No," Nick said. "I know how I am and I prefer to get stinking...."

But Nick doesn't want to talk about this. Paravicini asks him if he is really all right and Nick says that he is, except that he cannot sleep without a light in the room. And then, suddenly:

> "What's the matter? I don't seem crazy to you, do I?"
> "You seem in top-hole shape."
> "It's a hell of a nuisance once they've had you certified as nutty," Nick said.

He finally agrees to lie down for a while, his trouble starts, and now we learn what it was that he was so closely guarding himself against on the fishing trip. Para has gone, and Nick pictures a night when he was in Para's outfit; a bombardment before an attack is taking place, and the captain has him lead a hysterical platoon two at a time out into the shelling to show them that it can be done. Nick has his chin strap bound tight across his mouth. Then, in a crazy way, he sees himself becoming a casualty, and then his mind goes completely:

> And there was Gaby Delys, oddly enough, with feathers on; you called me baby doll a year ago tadada you said that I was rather nice to know tadada with feathers on, with feathers off, the great Gaby ...

He comes out of this after a time, and is ashamed to see that various soldiers at the Command Post have been watching him. He begins to talk to them, explains that he is now "reformed out of the war" and is simply "demonstrating an American uniform" (see photograph opposite page 54, taken four months after Hemingway's own serious wounding). But then he begins to deliver a disquisition on grasshoppers and locusts, about which he is very erudite. An adjutant sends for the captain and Nick goes on with his speech. He jabbers along, a second runner goes to get Paravicini and finally the captain comes. Nick improves somewhat, though he complains of his helmet, the like of which he has seen "full of brains too many times," and then he must lie down again.

He sees in his mind a bad place—a house and a long stable, and a river, which imagery is customary for him during these spells, and so meaningful to him that almost twenty years later under the name of Dick Cantwell he will make a personal pilgrimage to this very place in reality. "Every night" he had this vision, in "A Way You'll Never Be," and "what frightened him so that he could not get rid of it was that long yellow house and the different width of the river." Nearly two decades were to elapse before Hemingway was to reveal, in *Across the River and Into the Trees*, that this scenery comes to Nick because this is the place where he was wounded. Furthermore, nearly one decade had already elapsed since he had described another bad place, an entrance to a swamp which Nick feared unaccountably on the Big Two-Hearted River. And now Hemingway gives a clue to that mystery. In the story of Nick's actual insanity, where in terror he relives the event of being badly shot up, it is something about "the different width of the river" which terrifies him. Later when he is fishing the Big Two-Hearted he dreads and is unable to go past the spot where "the river narrowed" and went into the swamp: the geography of the place where he was blown up is naturally, and deeply, associated in his mind with the blow itself; it was, as we suggested at the time, the re-experience of shrapnel that he avoided by fishing. A change in the width of the river was what made the swamp horrible: it is in such a way that Hemingway's work extends backward and forward, is enigmatic and then clearer, and is integrated, and bound tight about a core of shock.

"A Way You'll Never Be" is a discomforting as well as a revealing story. One never knows what is going on—why the half-crazy soldier is allowed to go about on the loose, or if he really is permitted to, or whether or not he is actually supposed to be demonstrating this bogus uniform, or what. But one thing is obvious: there are many things Nick Adams cannot stand to think about at all.

And this is the end, for the moment, of the stories about him. To assemble them chronologically and look at them very briefly makes the pattern Hemingway arranged for his protagonist clear; the nature of Nick's character can also be made out. Here is a boy, and after that a man, who both in his early environment and later out on his own has been coming in contact with "life" in our time. Each of these contacts has been in some way violent, evil, or unsettling in that no ready answers are available. The effect of these episodes is equally apparent. They have complicated and damaged the man who, when an exinfantryman, is a very unwell soldier. He cannot sleep at night; when he can sleep he has nightmares. He has seen a great deal of unpleasantness, not only in the war but earlier up in Michigan as well; and he has been wounded by these experiences in a physical way, and—since the spine blow is both fact and symbol—also in a psychical way. What has happened to Nick, in short, has made him sick.

This pattern is climaxed by rebellion, by two desertions which can already be dimly seen. One is of the respectable home Nick has left, and later—when the damage begun at Indian Camp is epitomized with a shell fragment—he deserts the whole of organized society.

Nick's character, too, has emerged. Here is a sensitive, humorless, honest, rather passive male. He is the outdoor man, who revels in the life of the senses, loves to hunt and fish and takes pride in his knowledge of how to do such things. He is virile even as an adolescent, and very conscious of his nerve; maturity has forced a reckoning with his nerves as well. Once grown he is a man who knows his way around but he is superstitious too, and is developing a complex ritual whereby thinking can be stopped, the evil spirits placated and warded off.

This pattern, this process and this figure, with whatever distortions seen, were going to be known half the world over, for the relationship of this Nick to what is called the "Hemingway hero" is intimate, to put it mildly: Nick is the Hemingway hero, the first one. The drawing of him is very sketchy as yet, but it is true and Hemingway never takes it back to cancel half a line: the experiences of childhood, adolescence and young manhood which shape Nick Adams shaped as well Lt. Henry, Jake Barnes, Col. Cantwell, and several other heroes. They all have had Nick's childhood, Nick's adolescence, Nick's young manhood. It is obvious that this man is not the simple primitive he was mistaken for, and it is equally clear that a good deal of what there is of the primitive in him is a defense, which trembles and cracks, against a terror which he cannot face head on. The "escapes" are escapes from horror; the Hemingway hero, the big, tough, outdoor man, is also the wounded man, and descriptions of certain scenes in the life of Nick Adams have explained how he got that way. The man will die a thousand times before his death, but from his wounds he would never recover so long as Hemingway lived and recorded his adventures.

NOTES

* Hemingway remarked once that this story was about the time he discovered his father was a coward. A writer's intention is not necessarily the same as his accomplishment.

** Hemingway surely had in mind Ad Wolgast, the "Michigan Wildcat," who became lightweight champion of the world in 1910 but lost most of his mind in the process, spent away a fortune and was declared legally incompetent in 1917. Blind but still shadow-boxing, he died in the psychopathic ward of the Stockton (California) State Hospital in 1955.

HORST H. KRUSE

Ernest Hemingway's "The End of Something": Its Independence as a Short Story and Its Place in the "Education of Nick Adams"

Interpretation of the seven Nick Adams stories of *In Our Time* and of the Nick Adams stories of Hemingway's later collections has always been drawn between two extremes. On the one hand they have been taken as individual works of art; on the other they have been found to constitute integral chapters in "a scrupulously planned account of [Nick Adams'] character,"[1] or rather in what has come to be called his "education." Interpretation of "The Killers" and the drawn-out debate over "whose story it is"[2] demonstrate the difficulty; and Hemingway's statement to Edmund Wilson that *In Our Time* "has a pretty good unity" does not resolve the dilemma, for at the same time that he thus asserts the essential unity of his first book, he also refers to it as consisting of fourteen *stories*. In explaining the arrangement of the stories and the so-called interchapters, he not only speaks of "the picture of the whole" but also of an examination of it "in detail."[3]

The dispute over whose story "The Killers" is and, by implication, whether it can be understood independently of the rest of the Nick Adams stories, would seem to be the result of the author's technique, of his decision to relegate Nick to the role of little more than a spectator of the action. In this respect "The Killers" is like several stories of Hemingway's first collection, "Indian Camp," "The Doctor and the Doctor's Wife," and, to some extent, like "The Battler." In "The End of Something," however,

From *Studies in Short Fiction* 4 (Winter 1967): 152–166. ©1966 by Newberry College.

Hemingway uses a different technique by making Nick the protagonist. Surely there can be no doubt that it is Nick's story. But this does not at all seem to imply that the story will yield its full meaning when interpreted as an individual work of art. Quite to the contrary, Philip Young asserts that

> the real difficulty in finding the meaning of this story of *In Our Time* is the same difficulty that has been encountered with "Indian Camp": the story is like a chapter of a novel (the book has Roman numeral chapter headings in addition to the usual story titles); it is like a chapter of a novel in that it by no means has all of its meaning when taken in isolation.[4]

Even so, Young explains, people are not justified in complaining that it has no "point." But taking the story in isolation, its point is "subtle and slight": "Things can suddenly go all wrong with the pleasantest of love affairs."[5] The real point of "The End of Something," Young maintains, is provided in "The Three-Day Blow," the next story of *In Our Time*. It is Bill who here interprets Nick's experiences for him and for the reader, and it is only now that the reader learns "why it was that Nick forced that break with Marjorie: she was of the 'wrong' class for a doctor's son." "It is not until this point," Young concludes, "that we can really understand why he was 'out of sorts' in 'The End of Something.'"[6]

I feel that Young's eagerness to prove his overall thesis has led him to misinterpret "The End of Something" and that the general validity of his thesis has apparently precluded an exhaustive evaluation of one of Hemingway's finest stories. The following suggestions for an interpretation aim mainly at establishing its independence as a short story and do not claim to be exhaustive. But it will soon become evident that to attempt to establish its independence also involves a reassessment of its place and its function in Hemingway's development of Nick Adams.

Formally, "The End of Something" shows a traditional three-part arrangement. A brief opening describes the history of the lumbering town of Hortons Bay, the setting of the subsequent action. The main scene opens when Nick and Marjorie appear, and it closes when Marjorie leaves after their final break. The conclusion introduces Bill, a new character. Nick's behavior, particularly his brief conversation with the friend, shows the impact of the action on the protagonist. Beginning, middle, and end are clearly marked, and their proportion (20-124-11 when expressed in the number of lines devoted to them) also meets traditional criteria. But formal arrangement alone is no more than a *conditio sine qua non* for an attempt to establish the independence of "The End of Something"; the *conditio per quam*, as Young's criticism would seem to suggest, involves meaning. Form, however, contributes significantly to the emergence of meaning in this story, and the formal arrangement deserves more than passing notice. Since it suggests Aristotle's criteria for the construction of epic poetry, it seems appropriate to ask whether the brief beginning, the extended middle, and the brief end do in fact make a whole. For the purposes of establishing that "The End of Something" is an independent story rather than a chapter in a larger work, the first crucial question we must ask is whether the beginning meets Aristotelian criteria in that it "does not itself come after anything else in a necessary sequence."

The question is an easy one to answer. In the twenty lines of its two paragraphs, the beginning provides more information than seems necessary for a delineation of the setting. Rather than start with the description of its concrete details, Hemingway combines its presentation with information about its history. The reader is taken back to the very beginning of Hortons Bay and follows the brief course of its development. Hortons Bay originated as a lumbering town. When "one year there were no more logs to make lumber," the two saws and other equipment were taken out of the mill and hoisted on board a schooner. It then "moved out of the bay toward the open lake, carrying with it everything that had made the mill a mill and Hortons Bay a town."[7] All that remained were empty buildings and "acres of sawdust."

Hemingway gives a description of the present condition of Hortons Bay, the actual setting of the story, only in the first sentence of the third paragraph: "Ten years later there was nothing of the mill left except the broken white limestone of its foundations showing through the swampy second growth as Nick and Marjorie rowed along the shore." While by definition the opening is a real beginning in that it presupposes nothing, it seems doubtful, however, that it is the beginning of Nick's story. The transitional sentence clearly raises the question of natural sequence. Nick's story, it appears, is deliberately cut off from the history of Hortons Bay. It begins ten years after the flush times of the town, and those flush times are not part of Nick's experience.[8] But some tenuous connection exists even in the transitional sentence: the limestone foundations of the mill are still there, and they have a very tangible function in the story. They serve as the first object to present the contrasting sentiments of Nick and Marjorie. Mention of the second-growth timber both in the transitional sentence and again twice afterwards in the story also serves as a link between the opening paragraphs and the main story. Its presence presupposes the history of Hortons Bay. A third connecting link points to a far more important function of the opening. When Marjorie asks, "Can you remember when it was a mill?" Nick answers, "I can just remember." Indirect as it is, this statement of Nick's age is essential to an understanding of the story. The point needs to be made that contrary to Philip Young's assertion that Nick's age is never mentioned in the stories devoted to him,[9] "The End of Something" comes close to giving a precise statement: Nick is shown to be between sixteen and eighteen years of age. The point also needs to be made that the reader need not turn to the next story, "The Three-Day Blow," to find that Nick is old enough to have thought about getting married.

While the indirect statement of Nick's age will be shown to be the most important of these three functions of the introductory paragraphs, none of them justifies the extent of the vignette of the history of Hortons Bay. Significant details in the sketch are not related to the subsequent story. Quite to the contrary, Hemingway gives the real beginning of the story of Nick and Marjorie, the exposition proper, analytically in the course of the story itself. Marjorie's reference to the dilapidated mill as "our old ruin" indicates that there indeed was a time when the plural of the possessive pronoun was justified. The assumption that Nick has been going with Marjorie for some time is corroborated in other ways; there is the statement that "she loved to fish with Nick," and at the climax of the story Nick says, "I've taught you everything.... What don't you know, anyway?" The final piece of expository information comes almost at the very end of the story; Bill's first question reveals that the break had been planned beforehand for that particular night. The presence of a distributed exposition leaves us to conclude that what formally poses as the beginning of the story is a beginning in a very limited sense only. Since its importance for the plot is but slight, though not altogether negligible, we must seek, and shall easily find, elsewhere its functional relation to the rest of the story.

The above synopsis of the opening paragraphs, inadequate as it must needs be for conveying all of the meaning of Hemingway's text, clearly indicates the author's attempt to present the history of Hortons Bay as having described a cyclical movement. One cannot fail to perceive that its cycle is meant to be an analogue for the subsequent plot, which also deals with the completion of a cycle, that of Nick's love for Marjorie. The introduction thus prefigures the story. It also elucidates and interprets the story, a necessary function, as the story itself does not detail the whole course of Nick's love affair. Rather than present its whole history in chronological order, Hemingway starts close to the climax and, by means of implication and revelation, eventually evokes the totality of the cycle while at the same time presenting its conclusion. The analogy provided in the introduction can be and must be carried beyond the mere exteriors of a cyclical movement. In that it is taken from nature it implies that the course which Nick's love for

Marjorie has taken is a natural one and as relentless as it is inevitable. The introduction, in fact, elucidates the lesson that the story has for the protagonist: all things run their natural course, and submission and acceptance are the only sensible responses.

An apparent inconsistency between introduction and main story, however, appears to be incompatible with the thesis that both are analogous. One can easily argue that while the cyclical course of the history of Hortons Bay is conditioned by natural events, the cyclical conclusion of the story of Nick and Marjorie is solely the result of Nick's decision to force a break and that it thus lacks the inevitability which characterized the rise and fall of the town. But to distinguish between exterior motivation of the introduction and interior motivation of Nick's story is to miss the essential point of the story. Hemingway demonstrates that the distinction is futile. When the supply of logs at Hortons Bay is exhausted, the mill workers accept the situation *and* they know how to cope with it; the machinery is taken out of the mill and hoisted on board the schooner "*by the men who had worked in the mill.*" Nature thus conditions man's decisions. Nick's case precisely parallels this. His decision to force a break with Marjorie is not at all momentary, and it is clearly not the result of an accidental quarrel. The concluding conversation with Bill reveals it to have been of some standing, and Hemingway's further use of analogues—as remains to be shown—reveals that it also proceeds from what must be called natural causes. It is this insight into the inevitability of the course of nature and its influence on the destinies of man that provides the real lesson of the story. It is the realization that a break should become necessary, rather than the fact that he has actually broken with Marjorie, that leaves Nick a wounded man at the end of the story. If the analogy between introduction and main story is at all inconsistent, then it is inconsistent only in so far as the mill workers unflinchingly accept the course of nature while Nick is still learning to do so. The workers provide the moral norm of the story from which the protagonist (as yet) deviates.

The conclusion demonstrates that the lesson is clearly a new one for Nick: it hits him with considerable impact. It is clear that the wound will be permanent, but it is also clear that he will survive it: he asks Bill to go away, then adds, "Go away *for a while.*" This reading is supported by many details in the introductory analogue. The spoliated landscape of Hortons Bay also has begun to recover. Nature has reclaimed the scene, covering swamp and sawdust with second-growth timber. A more significant prefiguration of Nick's eventual response to the lesson occurs in an image with Freudian overtones. While "the sails of the schooner filled and it moved out into the open lake," it contained the odds and ends "that had made the mill a mill and Hortons Bay a town." The open hold where these things are stored is *"covered with canvas and lashed tight."* This image, while it symbolizes Nick's future attitude, does not at all rely on subsequent stories to reveal its meaning, though one need not argue that the symbolic meaning may be extended to encompass his responses to the incidents described in later works, his experiences and his responses there being different in kind, not in character.

Obviously the analogy may be pursued still further. If the schooner symbolizes Nick, then the spoliated landscape and the deserted buildings stand for Marjorie. She, too, has learned a lesson. The focus of the story, however, is not on her responses. But in desisting from all argument, she seems to demonstrate passive acceptance and thus functions, as she does throughout the story, as a foil to Nick. Applying the analogy in this manner, the second growth is primarily a symbol of Marjorie's future. Such a reading would leave the machinery in the schooner's hold, the tools of destruction, a symbol for Nick's disruptive influence rather than for experiences repressed in his personality to the level of the unconscious. Different interpretations of the introduction are obviously possible; but far from confusing the meaning of the story, they give to the introductory analogue the complexity of a true symbol. Its meaning and its function, however, are somewhat narrowed by another kind of analogy which operates in the story itself. Though working on a different and totally unrelated level, it further elucidates the meaning of the action and similarly establishes the independence of the story.

Philip Young has summarized the action of "The End of Something" as follows: "[Nick] takes the girl trolling for trout, demonstrates some knowledge of fish and fishing, and finally gets the girl to leave, perhaps for good."[10] Inadequate as any summary must be in view of Hemingway's careful handling of materials, this statement of the contents of the story does not even attempt to find any significance below its perfectly credible, realistic surface. To accept the summary as rendering the action of the story is to accept the possibility of an absolute break between style and technique of the beginning and those of the middle. Such a possibility cannot be rejected altogether. The beginning, as has been shown, is not the actual beginning of Nick's story; and it is quite conceivable that in its function as an analogue it can be trusted to provide the terms in which we are to take the subsequent story and to point to a significance that the story itself is unable to convey.

But even if we are to ignore Hemingway's avowed principles of composition, this interpretation is hard to accept, since the introduction does not outspokenly proclaim its interpretative function: it is a part of the whole also in that it contributes necessary details to the surface reality of the story. To take this surface reality—the detailed account of trolling for trout and planting handlines, the abortive picnic, and mainly its conversation—as the end of Hemingway's description is either to approach the story very naïvely, or to approach it from its sequel, "The Three-Day Blow," where the surface, indeed the "skillful representation of the conversation of adolescent boys" that Young calls it,[11] does seem to be more of an end in itself.

Apart from the nature analogue of the opening scene, the first and most important key to an understanding of what really happens to Nick is provided in the oblique statement of his age. While it is not very precise, it is still precise enough to indicate that Nick is at the verge of maturity and that his affair with Marjorie is not "a puppylove affair with a 'nice' girl," as one critic asserts.[12] While the nature analogue of the opening scene merely suggests that Nick's love affair involves sexual relations, this implication is elaborated when Nick, having told Marjorie once that "It isn't fun any more," repeats the same words and then adds, "*Not any of it.*" Immediately before, another phrase that occurs in Nick's talk is repeated and amplified in a similar manner. Apparently trying to pick a quarrel, he tells Marjorie, "You know everything," then continues, "You do. You know everything. That's the trouble. You know you do." When Marjorie does not answer, Nick resumes once more, "I've taught you everything. You know you do. What don't you know, anyway?" The immediate cause of this outburst seems negligible (When Nick observes, "There's going to be a moon tonight," Marjorie answers happily, "I know it."), and quite obviously Marjorie's knowledge in this particular case merely triggers Nick's reproaches.

As his wording indicates, his concern is far more general. Marjorie knows too much of a number of things because he, Nick, has taught her too much. This may be construed to mean that Nick is dissatisfied with the state of things because his love for Marjorie has been, first and foremost, a mere satisfaction of his tutorial instinct.[13] What few indications the story contains of the nature of their relationship seem to support this. Nick instructs Marjorie in the proper preparation of bait, and Marjorie quite naturally assumes the role of pupil. Her obvious usefulness in fishing and the care which she takes in doing things in the right, that is in Nick's, manner indicate that the teacher-pupil relationship has existed for some time, probably for as long as both have been going with each other. What is thus demonstrated with regard to fishing and boating, both in the action of the story and in its dialogue, has led Austin McGiffert Wright to conclude that "Nick has tired of [Marjorie] because she has learned too well the boyish things he has taught her; she has become too much of a 'pal,' thus losing her romantic appeal."[14] Wright apparently failed to note that the same facts also demonstrate that Marjorie's insecurity is as yet quite pronounced, that she does need instruction and that she will continue to need it. It is quite clear that the progress she has made in learning the "boyish things" her tutor has taught her and its demonstration in action and dialogue, if taken as mere fact, must fail to yield a plausible motive for Nick's eventual outburst and his break with Marjorie.

To find the true reason for Nick's break it is necessary and, in fact, inevitable to take both action and dialogue as another explicative analogue, and it is also inevitable to observe the sexual implications of this commentary on the meaning of the story. Again the analogue functions as a portent. Rowing away from the old mill (to Marjorie "our old ruin" and "more like a castle," references to which Nick does not respond in kind), Marjorie "was intent on the rod all the time they trolled, even when she talked," and she "did not reel in until the boat touched the shore." She remarks that the fish are feeding and obviously expects that they will strike, but Nick emphatically asserts that they "aren't striking" and that they "won't strike."

Although the analogue is incomplete, there is a correspondence between this scene and the subsequent picnic in Nick's eating from Marjorie's basket of supper, but refusing to "strike" and instead breaking away from her "hook" for good. If it is not possible to establish an absolute analogy between conversation and actions in the boat and those on the shore, this does not mean that the analogue as such is not intended. It merely confirms that here, as elsewhere, Hemingway did not "violate realism for the sake of his metaphor."[15] Recurrence and accumulation, furthermore, sufficiently counterbalance the absence of allegorical equations. So far, however, the function of the analogue has been shown to be merely that of portent rather than explication. It foreshadows what will happen and in doing so it also elucidates the significance of the following events. It has failed, however, to provide a motivation for such events, unless the opening analogue and its affirmation of the operation of natural cycles be deemed sufficient as a motivation for Nick's break with Marjorie.

But man is not conscious of being a victim and a tool. Subject as he is to the laws of nature, he normally acts without insight into these laws. Rather than recognize the law and then act accordingly, Nick first responds accordingly and only afterwards is led to a recognition of the law he has followed in doing so. The plot of the story, therefore, must provide a specific cause for his break with Marjorie, a cause that leads to action and then to insight, which insight constitutes the lesson proper of the story. "The End of Something" provides the specific cause in an oblique statement made by Nick concerning the preparation of bait: "'You don't want to take the ventral fin out,' he said. 'It'll be all right for bait but it's better with the ventral fin in.'" When read as an analogue and interpreted as having physiological implications, the statement contains a perfectly satisfactory and plausible motivation for Nick's behavior. It exemplifies at the same time that it demands that the love affair between Nick and Marjorie has involved sexual relations and that Nick's teaching extended to initiating Marjorie into sex. Reproaching her for knowing too much implies that Nick reproaches her for having lost her virginity. Thus, the analogy implies, she has lost her attraction for her lover, and therefore Nick concludes, "It isn't fun any more. Not any of it." Having found the action and the dialogue to function as explicatory analogues of the sexual implications of Nick's and Marjorie's love, one can easily find supporting evidence within the story that suggests these implications even on the very surface of plot and dialogue. After all, Nick and Marjorie are out at nightfall and prepared to stay out well into the night, neither apparently having stolen away from home.

To pursue the problem of the unity and the independence of "The End of Something" in terms of Aristotle's definition of a whole in epic poetry, we still must find whether the end naturally proceeds from the events described in the middle and, more importantly, whether it has nothing else following it. Both questions seem easy to answer as long as the attention remains focused on the individual story. The end describes Nick's response to the break with Marjorie; it shows the impact of the action on the protagonist. But it also contains an important revelatory detail in a very subtle punch line assigned to Bill. His question "Did she go all right?" suddenly illuminates the preceding events in that it reveals Nick to have planned the break beforehand. This explains why Nick's reason for terminating the love affair, while truthfully stated in Marjorie's knowing too much, nevertheless proceeds somewhat indirectly from the dialogue. His first "You know everything" implies irony and even sarcasm, but gradually his remarks reach the level of subjective truth. But Bill's revelatory question poses still another problem. Since Nick's plan to force a break precedes the events as narrated in the story, are those portentous analogues as are provided in his statements, specifically his remarks that the fish "won't strike" and that perch is better bait "with the ventral fin in," to be taken as consciously ambiguous on the speaker's part? Despite Nick's youth, we cannot wholly exclude the possibility as long as we see the story only in its surface action. The ending, however, demonstrates that Nick himself has as yet but imperfectly understood the true nature and the importance of the lesson that this experience provides for him. His own fumbling attempt to explain to Marjorie the reasons for his break forms the beginning of such realization: "I feel as though everything was gone to hell inside of me. I don't know, Marge. I don't know what to say." It is here, when he first addresses Marjorie by name, that he actually exempts her from blame and also perceives himself to be subject to forces outside his own control. What these forces are, however, remains rather dimly recognized for Nick. For Hemingway it is sufficient to have shown Nick's progress toward such an understanding. What it will be is perfectly clear for the reader since the author has utilized both the nature analogue and Nick's own words to communicate the reason for the break as well as the nature and the meaning of the lesson. The end of the story thus is suggestive of future comprehension of the lesson by the protagonist; for the reader, however, it is a real end in so far as it "has nothing else following it" and leaves no questions unanswered.

To some readers the introduction of Bill in the concluding scene of the story has suggested that Nick is, at least latently, a homosexual.[16] The above interpretation, however, does not permit such a reading. Even to imply that Nick prefers male company to female does not coincide with the meaning of the main scene. Despite Hemingway's technique of implication and the density of symbolism and metaphor in this story, one feels no compulsion to postulate that Bill should have any function beyond that of providing another foil for Nick. Although the friends have discussed the possibility of Nick's break with Marjorie and although Bill attempts to show his sympathy, his main interest is to find out whether there was a scene. He selects a sandwich from the supper basket and goes to have a look at the fishing rods and in doing so clearly demonstrates that he fails to grasp what has actually happened to Nick.

A final test for both our interpretation and our thesis that "The End of Something" will indeed yield its full meaning when taken in isolation is to relate it to the other Nick Adams stories, particularly to "The Three-Day Blow." Not only must we find that the other stories do not contradict the details of our interpretation, but also is it important that they should not uncover additional levels of meaning. The sexual implications of "The End of Something" are not at all called in question by the following stories. "The Three-Day Blow" shows Nick to be indeed old enough seriously to have thought about marrying Marjorie; "Fathers and Sons," moreover, reveals him to have received his initiation into sex at a much earlier age by an Ojibway Indian girl named Trudy who "did first what no one has ever done better."[17] "The Three-Day Blow" also plainly excludes the possibility of homosexual relations between Nick and Bill. Homosexuals are first observed by Nick at a later time in "The Battler"; and homosexuality, as Philip Young asserts on the basis of the evidence of further stories, normally functions as "a kind of ultimate evil."[18] Finally, "The Three-Day Blow" shows that Nick has not yet fully accepted the lesson contained in the earlier story. Again, this does not contradict our interpretation of "The End of Something," since what Hemingway communicates to the reader concerning the true nature of the lesson is clearly shown to be but imperfectly perceived by Nick. To stress the significance for him of the lesson described in the earlier story, realism furthermore demands that in view of the short span of time that intervenes between the events described in the two stories (shorter than that between any other two Nick Adams stories) the break with Marjorie should occupy him on what probably is the very next day.

Corroboration of our interpretation by means of further details in "The Three-Day Blow" clearly runs counter to Philip Young's reading of the story. If the thesis that "The End of Something" reveals its full meaning when interpreted independently of the other Nick Adams stories is right, then Young's thesis that "[The Three-Day Blow'] reveals the lesson Nick learned from the preceding episode,"[19] must be wrong. Once we no longer see "The End of Something" and "The Three-Day Blow" as closely interrelated chapter, and once we interpret these two stories either as individual stories or in the order in which they are presented in *In Our Time*, we shall perceive that the supposed points of the second story have different meanings from those given by Young. Bill's suggestion that Nick has broken with Marjorie because "she was of the 'wrong' class for a doctor's son"[20] meets with no response on the part of his listener: "Nick said nothing." This is repeated several times in the course of Bill's discussion of his friend's love affair and occasionally varied with rather monosyllabic assent, clearly noncommittal. It seems highly improbable, therefore, that Bill's interpretation furnishes the true motive for Nick's behavior in "The End of Something." It is more likely that Hemingway is exploiting a favorite theme of his, that of failure of communication. The divergence between the views of the friends soon becomes overt when Nick falls to thinking: "Bill wasn't there. He wasn't sitting in front of the fire or going fishing tomorrow with Bill and his dad or anything. He wasn't drunk. It was all gone. All he knew was that he had once had Marjorie and that he had lost her...." Thematic exploitation of the contrast becomes still more obvious when Nick's imagination desperately clutches at Bill's advice—"You don't want to think about it. You might get back into it again."—and inadvertently reverses its intent:

> Nick hadn't thought about that. It had seemed so absolute. That was a thought. That made him feel better.—"Sure," he said. "There's always that danger."—He felt happy now. There was not anything that was irrevocable. He might go into town Saturday night. Today was Thursday.—"There's always a chance," he said.—"You'll have to watch yourself," Bill said.—"I'll watch myself," he said.—He felt happy. Nothing was finished. Nothing was ever lost. He would go into town on Saturday. He felt lighter, as he had felt before Bill started to talk about it. There was always a way out.

The divergence between his thoughts and his words establishes more than an amusing irony; it exemplifies the essential contrast between the friends and thus corroborates our interpretation of the role of Bill in the final scene of "The End of Something."

The second point of the story, according to Young, lies in Nick's coming to see that "there was not anything that was irrevocable." This interpretation fails to show that the story, though indeed as many-sided as Young finds it to be, still primarily deals with Nick's introduction to alcohol. Before Bill takes up the subject of Nick's break with Marjorie, the story meticulously records the quantity of whisky consumed and the responses it produces in Nick. Beyond all doubt, and notwithstanding the subjective statements that "He wasn't drunk" and that "He was still quite drunk but his head was clear," Hemingway establishes—again by means of direct communication with the reader through realistic detail in the story—that Nick is indeed quite drunk when he reaches the understanding that "there was always a way out." The author thus demonstrates the function of the "giant killer" on the physical as well as on the psychic level, but it is from the latter that the true lesson that the episode has for Nick actually proceeds: the "giant killer" produces illusions and renders the lessons of life more acceptable. Again, as in the preceding story, Hemingway only implies the impact of the lesson on the protagonist. Again, as in the preceding story, the author enters into direct communication with the reader and reveals to him the nature of the lesson as yet unperceived by the protagonist. The resulting dramatic irony is an important part of Hemingway's technique of implication; it obviates another story, one devoted to the dissolution of the illusion and a detailed explication of the lesson of "The Three-Day Blow."

When interpreted in this sense, "The Three-Day Blow" does not contradict our reading of "The End of Something." It is important to add, however, that this interpretation of the second story does not proceed from, nor depend on, our interpretation of the first story. The later story, too, will yield its full meaning when read in isolation. But while the two stories are not interrelated, the interpretation of each can still be used to control that of the other; and details in each, though not essential to an understanding of the meaning of the other, still tend to emphasize certain of its points. Hemingway obviously devoted as much care to establishing the independence of the individual story as he did to relating it to the larger context of the education of Nick Adams. It is not necessary, therefore, to approach "The End of Something" from its supposed "points" in the subsequent story. To do so, in fact, not only robs the earlier, but also the later, story of what we find to be their independently developed and independently stated "true points."

In attempting to establish the independence of "The End of Something," we have discovered what we find to be its true point and its true lesson, and we have thus indicated a necessary reassessment of the function of the story in the biography of Nick Adams. But we have also shown the story to possess a far greater complexity and power than it has previously been credited with. Even if considered alongside those of the Nick Adams stories whose frequent presence in anthologies proclaims their independence as short stories, "The End of Something" would occupy a prominent place, for to isolate it does not require us to postulate the existence of two unrelated levels; the very point which makes it an independent story also relates it meaningfully and significantly to the education of Nick Adams.

NOTES

1. Philip Young, *Ernest Hemingway* (London, 1952), p. 2.

2. *Cf.* esp. Cleanth Brooks and Robert Penn Warren, *Understanding Fiction*, 2nd ed. (New York, 1959), pp. 303–312, and Oliver Evans, "The Protagonist of Hemingway's 'The Killers,'" *MLN*, LXXIII (December 1958), 589–591.

3. EH to EW, Paris, October 18, 1924; quoted in Edmund Wilson, *The Shores of Light* (New York, 1952), p. 123.

4. *Ernest Hemingway*, p. 6. I am not sure Young is right in taking the Roman numerals as "chapter headings"; they seem to refer to the interchapters only. Young also does not mention here that not all of the stories of *In Our Time* deal with the experiences of Nick Adams.

5. *Ibid.*

6. *Ibid.*, p. 7.

7. These and the following quotations from "The End of Something" and "The Three-Day Blow" are taken from *The Short Stories of Ernest Hemingway* (New York, 1955). Page references have not been included since the stories are short and quotations can easily be located. Italics that occur in the passages quoted from these two stories are mine.

8. I disagree with Austin McGiffert Wright, who, apparently also faced with the problem of unity, assumes that "the old mill and the old days [of Hortons Bay] are clearly on Nick's mind as he rows, although it is Marjorie who makes the connection explicit: "There's our old ruin, Nick.'" (*The American Short Story in the Twenties* [Chicago, 1961], p. 318.) The fact that Nick can only "just remember" the mill seems to preclude the possibility that Nick is thinking about the old days of the town. Marjorie's reference to "our old ruin" most likely evokes no associations other than those of the far more recent "love among the ruins" episode of their common history. Another critic, George Hemphill, has similarly been worried by the question of unity. He finds that the story "fails because no necessary connection (other than biographical, perhaps) between the end of the boy-and-girl affair between Nick and Marjorie and the end of the old lumbering days in Michigan is suggested." ("Hemingway and James," *Ernest Hemingway: The Man and His Work*, John K. M. McCaffery, ed. (Cleveland and New York, 1950], p. 333.)

9. *Ernest Hemingway*, p. 2.

10. *Ernest Hemingway*, p. 5.

11. *Ibid.*, p. 7.

12. Earl Rovit, *Ernest Hemingway* (New York, 1963), p. 57.

13. *Cf.* Alice Parker, "Hemingway's 'The End of Something,'" *The Explicator*, x (1951/52), Item 36.

14. *The American Short Story in the Twenties*, p. 94.

15. E. M. Halliday, "Hemingway's Ambiguity: Symbolism and Irony," *American Literature*, xxviii (March 1956), 14.

16. See Joseph Whitt, "Hemingway's 'The End of Something,'" *The Explicator*, ix (1950/51), Item 58.

17. *The Short Stories of Ernest Hemingway*, p. 497.

18. *Ernest Hemingway*, p. 11.

19. *Ibid.*, p. 7.

20. *Ibid.*

JOSEPH M. FLORA

Soldier Home: *"Big Two-Hearted River"*

W hen Hemingway came to arrange the stories of *In Our Time*, there was probably no question about which would come last. Four stories to appear in the book would be new; three of them were about Nick, insuring that readers would find him the most important character of the book. Although the final story would not be one of the new ones, it would be about Nick—the Nick story that showed best what the group as a whole meant. That story is, of course, "Big Two-Hearted River." It is unquestionably the most brilliant of the collection. It is also the story that had cost Hemingway the most labor, but it provided unmistakable proof that its young author had mastered his craft.

"Big Two-Hearted River" in the final placement also has the advantage of balancing Nick's trauma in the opening "Indian Camp" with the resolution to his trauma in war. It should not be forgotten that Hemingway had published "Indian Camp" under the Joycean title "Work in Progress." Throughout his career Hemingway gave high praise to Joyce, whom he considered a true master. *Dubliners* was partly a model as he arranged *In Our Time*. He knew from it, as well as from *Winesburg, Ohio*, that a book of stories could be more than a collection; so he vigorously protested well-meaning efforts of his publisher to alter the unity, as he saw it, of *In Our Time*. His book, because of its incorporation of *in our time* into the structure, would be

---

From *Hemingway's Nick Adams*: 145–175. © 1982 by Louisiana State University Press.

unlike either Anderson's book or Joyce's, but it would owe as much to *Dubliners* structurally as it owed to *Winesburg*. *Dubliners* begins with three stories, arranged chronologically, about a boy. The boy disappears thereafter, but the reader may well remember the boy's peculiar disposition when he reaches the final story of the book, "The Dead." The intervening stories are arranged into groups illustrating various aspects of Dublin life, many of them heavily satirical. *In Our Time*, similarly, moves from the early Nick stories to a grouping about three young men who come to crucial experience in war and revolution. It is followed by a grouping of stories about young married couples (all set in Europe). The two groupings have a good bit of satire in them. "My Old Man" stands somewhat alone. It is set in Europe, too, but it recalls much of the youth and innocence of the boyhood stories at the beginning of the book—and plays also on the theme of the shattering of innocence. More than any other story Hemingway wrote, it shows the influence of Sherwood Anderson. But "My Old Man" (one of the stories of *Three Stories and Ten Poems*) would not have served as satisfactory coda. We need to come back to Nick. Joyce had originally ended *Dubliners* with "Grace," but he was not satisfied with the total effect of the book. There were aspects of Dublin life he had not shown, and the book seemed too disparaging about Dublin, in some sense not true to what Joyce knew about Dublin and life. He countered with "The Dead," the longest story by far in the collection and a masterpiece. Hemingway would also end his book with a major story—something uniquely his. It would not remind readers of anyone but Hemingway.

Hemingway stressed the importance of "Big Two-Hearted River" to *In Our Time* by dividing it into two parts and listing each part in the table of contents. He further insisted on the division by having an interchapter between the two parts. Together the parts are the longest Nick story we have. It is unique in being almost totally descriptive and in having only one human character present—Nick. While he was working on the story, Hemingway explained to Gertrude Stein that he was "trying to do the country like Cézanne."[1] He was trying to do in fiction what had not been done before, and he knew he was succeeding. In "Big Two-Hearted River" his hero was also dealing, more meaningfully than he had ever done before, with the issues of life and death—as was Joyce's Gabriel Conroy in "The Dead." Finally, Hemingway was giving us the most affirmative note of *In Our Time* in that concluding Nick story, as his title "Big Two-Hearted River" emphasizes—the more so since it was doubly given.

Late in his career, reviewing his Paris years for what came to be *A Moveable Feast*, Hemingway described the effect he was trying to achieve in "Big Two-Hearted River":

What did I know best that I had not written about the lost? What did I know about truly and care for the most? There was no choice at all. There was only the choice of streets to take you back fastest to where you worked....

I sat in a corner with the afternoon light coming in over my shoulder and wrote in the notebook. The waiter brought me a *café crème* and I drank half of it when it cooled and left it on the table while I wrote. When I stopped writing I did not want to leave the river where I could see the trout in the pool, its surface pushing and swelling smooth against the resistance of the log-driven piles of the bridge. The story was about coming back from the war but there was no mention of the war in it.

But in the morning the river would be there and I must make it and the country and all that would happen.[2]

At least one of the things "Big Two-Hearted River" is about is the trauma of war, although the story never mentions the war. The reader of *In Our Time* has a large frame of reference against which he should evaluate "Big Two-Hearted River"—the war experience for Nick and others being major in that background. Probably no other Nick story illustrates how greatly Hemingway was concerned with Nick's career as a whole, as an on-going thing, as "work in progress." "Big Two-Hearted River" cannot stand alone in the way "The Dead" can stand alone. *In Our Time*, from the first interchapter on, and after 1930 from "On the Quai at Smyrna" on, had insisted that war and revolution are the central fact of our time. As we have seen, one interchapter specifically places Nick as a part of the great conflict of his time.

In *Death in the Afternoon* Hemingway eloquently explained a central component to his theory of writing, a theory that had been basic to his method from the start: "If a writer of prose knows enough about what he is writing about he may omit things that he knows and the reader, if the writer is writing truly enough, will have a feeling of those things as strongly as though the writer had stated them. The dignity of movement of an ice-berg is due to only one-eighth of it being above water."[3] The theory is helpful for describing no story more than "Big Two-Hearted River"; however, when we apply the theory to the story we may be reminded that the reader, like the writer, sometimes has to know some things not mentioned in a particular story. Understandably, "Big Two-Hearted River" has been anthologized frequently, for anthologizers like to include the best of a writer if they can get it. But if the reader does not already know Nick, he will miss much of the story's impact—even though he would probably enjoy reading it. He could get a great deal from the story by itself—and still not think of World War I.

"Big Two-Hearted River" gains immeasurably from the context that Hemingway meant us to have.

The opening of Part I recalls "The Battler"—where Nick also had been traveling alone by train. There Nick's destination was vague, but here it is precise, and his purpose is precise. He intends to go fishing alone on the Big Two- Hearted River. Previously Nick had been hoboing; this time he has paid his fare, and he does not need to pick himself up from the ground. Indeed, the action here is quite the reverse. The baggage man pitches his baggage to him from the baggage car. But almost immediately Nick sits down—and from shock. The opening anticipates the course he will take in Part II when he is actually fishing. The narrator does not tell us that Nick is shocked, but we know that he is. We experience the shock with him. Sheridan Baker puts it effectively: "It is almost as if the Nick of this story, not Ernest Hemingway, had written 'The Big Two-Hearted River.'"[4] And if we have read "A Way You'll Never Be" the shock also takes us backward in time, for it is like the shock at the start of that story where we see what Nick Adams saw at Fossalta. The first sentence of the story leaves Nick alone surrounded by destruction: "The train went up the track out of sight, around one of the hills of burnt timber" (*IOT*, 177; *NAS*, 177). Sitting on the bundle, Nick, almost like some Waste Land fisher king, surveys the wreckage around him. Seney, Michigan, has been burned to the ground. Only the foundation of the Mansion House hotel shows above the ground. "Even the surface had been burned off the ground." This destruction perforce reminds Nick of the earlier destruction he has seen. His journey has begun ominously, for he has not found what he expected, but what he sought to forget. He is immediately tested.

The river of the title, never mentioned in the story, counteracts the image of the destruction of the opening paragraph. The river is there and the railroad bridge. The fire has not, after all, destroyed everything man-made. Nick reaffirms the conviction that started him on this journey; he has to build his life on what is there, not on what is not. The quest is to find what is there, what he can be certain of. In this frame, the simplest sentence can take on the profoundest meaning. "The river was there" (*IOT*, 177; *NAS*, 177). More, it is alive, moving. It swirls against the log spiles of the bridge. Having returned to the States from Europe (which his training had presented as possessing the greatest traditions of civilization), Nick turns to nature to see if he can find there a sustaining force.

For a long time Nick is a man at the bridge. He looks down at the trout he means to fish, and they become more than objects of sport—they are, in the terms of Santiago of *The Old Man and the Sea*, brothers. Nick would like to be like them. They are beautiful as they keep themselves "steady in the current with wavering fins." Although not called so, the river running through Seney immediately becomes a big two-hearted river.

As Henry David Thoreau put it in *Walden*, "Time is but the stream I go a-fishing in." Rivers inevitably—and certainly here—make us think of time. Man lives his day in time, and some men even survive for many days— like the big trout at the bottom of the pool. Hemingway establishes that the theme of time will be an important one in the story: "It was a long time since Nick had looked into a stream and seen trout" (*IOT*, 178; *NAS*, 178). Time moves on, but man is the only creature who can stand on a bridge and get a perspective on his unique place in the stream of time. Thus, while "Big Two-Hearted River" takes place on a particular day in fully realized country, a part of the experience of the story, paradoxically, is moving out of time. Like Nick, we cannot be rushed, or we will miss what we should find. Nick did not at first see the big trout. The kind of experience Nick has in "Big Two-Hearted River" is similar to that Robert Frost presents in "Directive." Both works are concerned with quest. Nick's experience is like that which Frost describes as the necessary starting point in the quest for wholeness:

Back out of all this now too much for us,
Back in a time made simple by the loss
Of detail, burned, dissolved, and broken off
Like graveyard marble sculpture in the weather....

Nick's search becomes more significant as we sense what he leaves behind. Even though he journeys to an unnamed destination, he could hardly seem to be acting more precisely by directive. There is no grail image for what he seeks, but his quest is nonetheless religious. The other Nick stories—continually suggestive in their titles and imagery and motifs of the problem of good and evil and the possibility of faith—should help to prepare us for consideration of "Big Two-Hearted River" in terms of religious quest. Even the very act of fishing has established symbolic value for Western civilization, especially the challenge of Jesus to become fishers. The fish is an established icon for Jesus.

The reader of "Big Two-Hearted River" may at first be puzzled about where Nick is. Seney will be found in only the most specialized of gazetteers. Once notorious in its region, the town is now most famous because of Hemingway's story. Because the first paragraph mentions Seney's thirteen saloons, the reader of *In Our Time*, having just finished several expatriate stories, would take the American usage *saloon* as indication that Nick was back in his beloved north woods, and this belief would soon be confirmed. The reader can also gradually place Seney, somewhat but only gradually. We discover that Nick is in Lake Superior country—hence it must surely be Michigan's upper peninsula. Only when Nick prepares his meal near the end of the day do we discover the route he has traveled to arrive at Seney. He came by way of St. Ignace. It is worth pausing over this geographical lesson.

"Big Two-Hearted River" is the only Nick Adams story—indeed the only story by Hemingway—set in the upper peninsula. Nick knows the Big Two-Hearted River, but it is not in his country. The Adams-Hemingway country is the area around Little Traverse Bay—Walloon Lake, Lake Charlevoix, Horton Bay (called Hortons Bay in the stories), Petoskey. Nick has not gone to Seney from Chicago, but from his northern country—an area filled with the ghosts of many summers. He needs a further remove. In Nick's time, to get from the Little Traverse Bay area to Seney was no easy task—you had to want to get there. "Big Two-Hearted River" begins with a great deal of travel already behind Nick, and certainly travel more primitive than that to which modern readers are accustomed. Nick had to travel to Mackinaw City and then await a ferry to cross the four miles of the Straits of Mackinac to St. Ignace. (Even after World War II and the construction of a great bridge the trip could not be recommended for those in a hurry.) The upper peninsula remained remote and sparsely settled country. It was too far for Michigan's downstaters to go for weekend respite. Nick is the only human we actually see in "Big Two-Hearted River"; the baggage man has already tossed down his baggage, and the train is going out of sight as the story begins. Such isolation is just what Nick has been seeking. He has traveled far, and he will travel farther—this time by foot.

The kind of experience that Nick is having might appropriately be called primitivistic, and many literary historians have noted the importance of the doctrine of primitivism in American literature. *Huckleberry Finn*, the work Hemingway found basic in American literature, is the classic representation. In nature, away from civilization, Huck finds what is truly his own view, what *he* feels rather than what society has told him he ought to feel. Nature is good; civilization is corrupt. In twentieth-century literature this faith is not unique to Hemingway. Faulkner at least saw the appeal of such a view, and Nick's experience in the upper peninsula can be compared profitably with Isaac McCaslin's in *Go Down, Moses*, especially in "The Bear" and "Delta Autumn" stories of that novel. There, the hunters feel a yearly need to tap elemental roots, to reaffirm somehow their connection to the forest and its life. The task becomes more difficult as the years pass and the wilderness vanishes. In "The Bear," Ike, as a young boy, must divest himself of the implements of modern civilization before he can see Old Ben, the bear who symbolizes the wilderness. And he must meet Ben alone. In "Big Two-

Hearted River" Nick does not need to use his map after he leaves Seney. And he needs no compass. He can tell where he is from the position of the river.

Nick here is older than the Ike of "The Bear," and "Big Two-Hearted River" is not an initiation story. Nick's needs are not the same as Ike's. Nick is seeking himself by losing himself—as Frost's poem and the biblical admonition have it. It may be helpful to see Nick's experience in terms of that of René Descartes, the first of the modern philosophers. Descartes' method was philosophical and abstract. Nick's approach is to suspect the abstract, to deal with the concrete. (Because the reader experiences Nick's progress so vividly, he will hesitate using a label like primitivism which seems to lessen the experience.) Nevertheless, Nick and Descartes are not far apart.

In seeking to prove God's existence, Descartes started by doubting everything that could be doubted. He decided that he could not even trust his senses, for they gave him conflicting information about a single piece of data. Finally, Descartes was left with only himself. He could not doubt his own existence. "I think," he declared, "therefore, I am." Having reduced everything to an undeniable assertion, Descartes felt that he could then move forward. At least to his own satisfaction, he was subsequently able to verify God's existence.

Nick is not interested in syllogisms. Thinking is what he wishes to avoid. But he is modern man in the sense that faith in the Old World and in himself has been taken from him. Hence he has tried to reduce life as much as he can, to get away from people, memories, his personal needs: "He felt he had left everything behind, the need to think, the need to write, other needs. It was all back of him" (*IOT*, 179; *NAS*, 179). Nick will rely on his senses, on what he feels. He will start where Descartes started, with what he could absolutely trust. Then—like Descartes—he can move forward, to find—perhaps—what he cannot lose, maybe even God.

Despite the setback at Seney, all the evidence mounts to indicate to us that Nick's program of reduction before advancement is working. As the trout moves, Nick feels "all the old feeling" (*IOT*, 178; *NAS*, 178). There are things he has not lost, despite the trial by fire. Nick bears a heavy burden, even "too heavy" a burden the staccato rhythms insist, as he begins the walk "up-hill" (*IOT*, 179; *NAS*, 179), leaving the burned country. Paradoxically, the burden becomes easy, even a joy. Twice we are told that Nick feels happy.

There is a complex poetry here, and the repetitions are an important part of it. They function to make us share in shouldering Nick's burden in his climbing and in the joys of his success. Repetition also connects this day with the day recounted in "A Way You'll Never Be." Nick is at least one year from his time at the front, probably more—it has been "a long time since Nick has looked into a stream and seen trout" (*IOT*, 178; *NAS*, 178). We

know that Nick refers to more than calendar time, for other Nick stories
have stressed that psychological time is different from calendar time.
Hemingway emphasizes the heat of the day during the action of "A Way
You'll Never Be." Nick is reminded of that heat, but he will not let himself
deliberately think on it. Seney is associated with Fossalta: we are told that
Nick is "leaving the burned town behind in the heat" (*IOT*, 179; *NAS*, 179).
Hemingway the symbolist is obviously at work. In terms of naturalistic
probability, Nick would not inevitably find the kind of hot day in the upper
peninsula that he does find. As likely as not, a bright summer's day will be
invigoratingly chilly. On any day of the summer, a swim in Lake Superior will
be very brief.

Hemingway is doing more than creating country in the story; he is
showing us man in country. As Nick commences his climb, the description is
at once precise and suggestive: "He hiked along the road, sweating in the
sun, climbing to cross the range of hills that separated the railway from the
pine plains" (*IOT*, 180; *NAS*, 179). He is a man against the sky, although
more immediately rendered than any character in Robinson's philosophical
poem. He is Bunyan's Christian, although the allegorical is replaced with a
naturalism and we see Nick clearly as a creature of our time. The
descriptions of Nick's climb can also remind us of another famous climb up
a hill—even as we sense echoes of promises of easy burdens. Hemingway's
handling of scene in "Big Two-Hearted River" is unmistakably assured, and
the scenes are never mere photographic realism. From the top of the hill
Nick's view reveals the joy of accepted challenge. From the height, Nick can
put Seney (and Fossalta) in perspective. He is like Descartes, now ready to
move forward: "Seney was burned, the country was burned over and
changed, but it did not matter. It could not all be burned. He knew that"
(*IOT*, 180; *NAS*, 179). Nick has completed an important piece of thinking.

Having made such judgment, Nick is ready for advancement, and he
proceeds, like the road, "always climbing." The pictorial aspect of the story
shifts. We have been aware of Nick as a character in the scenes. The country
is made to be majestic and to call for the hand of a painter. Now we look with
Nick, who already has a part of his reward: "Ahead of him, as far as he could
see, was the pine plain. The burned country stopped off at the left with the
range of hills. On ahead islands of dark pine trees rose out of the plain. Far
off to the left was the line of the river. Nick followed it with his eye and
caught glints of the water in the sun" (*IOT*, 180; *NAS*, 179). Nick can see
nothing but the pine plain until far in the distance arise the "far blue hills" of
the Lake Superior height of land. Because of the heat-light, the vista reminds
us even more of a painting—perhaps of a Cézanne. If Nick looks too steadily,
the blue hills are gone, but if he only half-looks, they are there, "the far off

hills of the height of land." Furthermore, Hemingway's description echoes a famous poem of A. E. Housman's *A Shropshire Lad*, "Into My Heart an Air That Kills," and Nick's postwar frame of mind resembles the disillusionment of Housman's narrator.

> Into my heart an air that kills
> From yon far country blows:
> What are those blue remembered hills,
> What spires, what farms are those?
> That is the land of lost content,
> I see it shining plain,
> The happy highways where I went
> And cannot come again.

It may be, however, that Nick will find more contentment than did the Shropshire lad. Hemingway makes the importance of Nick's view of this wilderness country unmistakable. Nick sits down, as he had earlier upon arriving at Seney. The destruction he witnessed there is perforce recalled to our minds. Nick will take in this scene, too. In his epigraphs to *The Sun Also Rises* Hemingway would later play off Gertrude Stein's famous "lost generation" indictment against the affirmation of the statement from Ecclesiastes, "but the earth abideth forever." Here, for similar effect, we contrast the two scenes Nick views.

The second scene looks forward as well as backward. Nick now sits leaning against a charred stump, and his legs are stretched out in front of him. Both details recall the description of war in interchapter VI where Nick sat against the wall. Here he notices a grasshopper and then many other grasshoppers—to discover that they have been made black by the burned-out country side. (Sheridan Baker reports that in realistic terms this is an improbability: the detail is not likely to disturb the reader since it is so symbolically right.[5]) Nick, wondering how long they would stay that way, may make us think not only of his state but that of other soldiers. The grasshoppers also bring to mind Nick's lecture on them in "A Way You'll Never Be." Since his attention is here on a particular grasshopper, we are also reminded of Nick's experience with a particular salamander in "Now I Lay Me" when he engaged in his ritualistic night fishings. The salamander seemed too human as he "tried to hold on to the hook" with his tiny feet. "Now I Lay Me" also echoes because Nick smokes a cigarette as he sits. His smoking reinforces our idea of the tautness of his nerves.

Smoking also anticipates other events of the story. Nick will smoke whenever he wishes to slow down his responses. The vista Nick surveys is given a special punctuation by his stopping to smoke. Hemingway's "war" story that does not mention war creates country; it creates country as antidote to the horrors of destruction.

Nick shows compassion to the grasshopper he has so carefully examined—as in "Now I Lay Me" he had decided not to use the crickets for bait because of the way they were about the hook. Nick is hypersensitive to the simplest forms of life after his encounter with mass destruction. That hypersensitivity is emphasized when Nick speaks to the grasshopper, for there is almost no use of speech in this longest of the Nick stories. When used, speech must then receive more than ordinary attention. "Go on, hopper ... Fly away somewhere" (*IOT*, 181; *NAS*, 180). Nick tosses the hopper into the air and watches him sail away. He has seen himself in that hopper. As soon as Nick sees the hopper land, he arises and again commences to travel. Provocatively, Hemingway repeats the opening sentence of "The Battler": "Nick stood up."

There is something at work other than Nick's earlier war memories. We know there has been no speech in the story before the episode with the grasshopper, and Hemingway calls that lack of speech to our attention, stating that Nick was "speaking out loud for the first time." He is, in part, telling us to pay heed to later speaking, but he is not giving us new information. More important, he is emphasizing the verbal atmosphere of the whole story. "Big Two-Hearted River" is Hemingway's account of Genesis. That "for the first time" is haunting. The biblical and religious overtones of the story are insistent.

Nick will need no map as he goes into the country he has just viewed. Like Adam, he will keep his direction by the sun. He starts walking again, and soon the road and the fire line are behind him. Nick makes judgments on his experience that have a pristine quality: "Underfoot the ground was good walking" (*IOT*, 182; *NAS*, 180). The word *good* comes in for frequent play in Part I. *Good* in Genesis is God's verdict on the world He has created. Nick's senses will likewise continuously assert that life is good: "Then it was sweet fern, growing ankle high, to walk through, and clumps of jack pines; a long undulating country with frequent rises and descents, sandy underfoot and the country alive again" (*IOT*, 182; *NAS*, 181).

Few stories attempt to call all of the reader's senses into play as fully and as continuously as does "Big Two-Hearted River." Usually a story seems to be underway when the dialogue starts, when what characters say engages us intellectually. Even Hemingway stories sometimes work that way. Not here. We feel the heat of the day, the weight of Nick's pack, and we come with Nick to look with primordial wonder at the world. We rediscover our senses. The fern smells sweet, and Nick makes that good count. He breaks off some sprigs and puts them under his straps so that he can relish the smell as he walks. Only the sense of sound is underplayed: there is little attention to forest or river sound in "Big Two-Hearted River." Consequently, as we have seen, the breaking of the silence by the human voice has a powerful effect, partly Adamic but also useful for reminding us of Nick's past. Ultimately, the muted sounds of "Big Two-Hearted River" are a powerful means of reminding us of the clamor of war, of the sounds that Nick means to forget or minimize on this trip. The silences of "Big Two-Hearted River" contrast with the sounds of the Nick war stories discussed in the previous chapter, stories that often build on the sounds of war and depend on dialogue to carry large sections of the narrative.

As Nick makes his journey through the forest, it is evident that he wants to get tired, since he wants to go "as far upstream as he could go in one day's walking" (*IOT*, 183; *NAS*, 181). But there is much to discover as he goes, and there are places that have special meaning and accent the healing silences Nick has sought. The fishing is not everything; the getting to the place of the fishing is as worthy of our attention as is the fishing action of Part II.

In describing one place with special meaning for Nick, Hemingway evokes one of the most memorable scenes of *The Red Badge of Courage*, the scene in which Henry Fleming after his flight from battle finds temporary solace in nature. Under the boughs of great pines Henry is reminded of a chapel, but the religious feeling the setting has aroused is dissipated when he finds a corpse ugly in its state of decay; Henry, appalled, is soon in flight. In Hemingway's story, Nick deliberately seeks an island of pine, and he, too, finds a chapel-like place. There is, however, nothing to appall him in it, nothing to make him flee. After Nick has passed through his chapel he pauses as if to mark the quality of the experience. He lies on his back and looks into the pine trees: "The earth felt good against his back" (*IOT*, 183–84; *NAS*, 182). The creature is at one with the creation. Sleep comes blessedly to Nick—Nick for whom sleep in war was something he often wished to avoid.

When he awakens, stiff and cramped, the sun is nearly down, but he feels no panic. He takes up his heavy pack again, comes to a meadow, and then the river. Nick was "glad" to get to the river. It has been his point of reference—he knew he could always get to it. He has journeyed by faith.

The joy at anticipation of the fishing reasserts itself. Again, the story pauses. Before going down to the river, Nick stops on the spot of high ground near the end of the meadow where he will make camp. He looks down at the river in the light of early evening. The insects from the swamp across the stream have come to the river. The river is silent, but is fast and smooth and full of significant life. The trout jump high out of the water for the insects.

The meaning of the trout at the opening of the story is again to the fore—for Nick and the reader. The pictorial view—and again the long view—serves to vindicate the faith behind Nick's journey: "As far down the long stretch as he could see, the trout were rising, making circles all down the surface of the water, as though it were starting to rain" (*IOT*, 185; *NAS*, 182).

Thus assured, Nick is ready to set up camp. We are told exactly how he does so and why he does it as he does. Hemingway's prose in its steady detail mirrors the values that Nick is seeking in his life—order, neatness, purpose. Nick makes camp before he cooks, exemplifying the kind of discipline that he believes should mark the good life. Much later, in *A Moveable Feast*, Hemingway will say that hunger is good discipline. So it is here. Work never seemed more purposeful or more rewarding than when Nick sets up camp. The process takes on the aura of ritual. Although he does not think of it in these terms, Nick is thoroughly Pauline. In I Corinthians 14:40 Saint Paul admonishes: "Let all things be done decently and in order." Such values have been passed on to Nick by his father. Work carries its own reward, as we feel when we go inside the tent with Nick:

> Inside the tent the light came through the brown canvas. It smelled pleasantly of canvas. Already there was something mysterious and homelike. Nick was happy as he crawled inside the tent. He had not been unhappy all day. This was different though. Now things were done. It had been a hard trip. He was very tired. That was done. He had made his camp. He was settled. Nothing could touch him. It was a good place to camp. He was there, in the good place. He was in his home where he had made it. Now he was hungry. (*IOT*, 186; *NAS*, 183–84)

The crawl inside the tent builds on the essential rhythm of Part I, with its stop-go quality. There has been movement, then pausing to survey, for varying lengths of time, what is there. After such pauses Nick can make a sound judgment, as he does here—pronouncing the place good. Nick has arrived someplace; twice Hemingway uses the word *home*. Home is paradoxically the traditional goal of every pilgrim who ever shouldered a heavy load. And Hemingway is at pains to suggest these religious connotations: "Already there was something mysterious and homelike." *Mysterious* with *homelike* is powerfully evocative. In its way, the tent prefigures Hemingway's later "A Clean, Well-Lighted Place," although this one is more reassuring. How blessed it is to have arrived where Nick is: "Nothing could touch him." And the whole tent scene is couched in the symbolic shadows of evening: "It was quite dark outside. It was lighter in the tent." The Nick stories have repeatedly used light-dark imagery. Hence, the lines are even more forceful.

Again, the story moves from contemplation to action. Now Nick will eat. "He did not believe he had ever been hungrier" (*IOT*, 187; *NAS*, 184). In the context, that is an immensely positive statement. Eating has been an important literary motif in most of the Nick stories. In "The Light of the World" the story beings with the denial of food, except for pay. In "The Killers" Al and Max mock "the big dinner" and eat with their gloves on. Marge and Nick have a joyless night meal together in "The End of Something." The vibrations are more positive in "Ten Indians" when Nick's father serves him dinner—but ambiguity shrouds that less than satisfactory ending to an otherwise happy Fourth of July. Nick and Bill do not eat together in "The Three Day Blow"—they only drink, and this suggests that Nick's opting for male camaraderie is only temporary. There is the breaking of bread together in "The Battler," and tasty it is. Nick takes from that campfire a sandwich—reenforcing the positive qualities of the light he had found in the clearing of Bugs and Ad.

The eating in "Big Two-Hearted River" is even more memorable—in both Parts I and II. Eating is another good for Nick. The reader, too, is likely to become hungry and relish the cooking and the eating, for the cooking is as important as the eating. The fare is quite simple, but it is something to be remembered for a long time afterwards.

When Nick takes from his pack a can of pork and beans and a can of spaghetti, he speaks for the second time in the story: "I've got a right to eat this kind of stuff, if I'm willing to carry it" (*IOT*, 187; *NAS*, 184). He finds his voice strange in the darkening woods and so does not speak again. The strangeness comes because the verbal expression somehow violates the sense of mystery and blessedness that the erection of the tent in the good place has produced. At the same time Nick's words, comic on one level, reenforce the primitivism that the cans seem to violate.

With Nick, we experience the food through sight, smell, and, finally, taste. Nick stirs the beans and spaghetti together over the fire: "They began to bubble, making little bubbles that rose with difficulty to the surface. There was a good smell" (*IOT*, 187–88; *NAS*, 184). Hemingway makes the most of the taste experience. After Nick spreads the beans and spaghetti on his plate, he sets it aside so that the food can cool: he knows the food is too hot. Fire becomes potentially an enemy—almost hobgoblin. Nick looks from the fire to the tent (the symbol of order and home): "he was not going to spoil it all by burning his tongue." There are rumblings from the past: "For years he had never enjoyed fried bananas because he had never been able to wait for them to cool" (*IOT*, 188; *NAS*, 185).

Hemingway does not falsify the world as it is, even as he insists that there is a place for Nick to build from. Another ominous image appears—taking us back to "The Battler" as well as anticipating the rest of the story: "Across the river in the swamp, in the almost dark, he saw a mist rising" (*IOT*, 188; *NAS*, 185). Turning from the swamp and mist, Nick looks at the tent once more, and he cannot doubt that he has found what will fortify. He speaks for the third and final time—not to be denied. (There is no speaking in Part II.) "Chrise," he says, "Geezus Chrise," and Hemingway adds the adverb *happily*. Nick's words are not in isolation—he has taken his first mouthful; hence the expression is appropriate to the action of tasting the hot food and to the faith that he feels as regards the future. He again judges what has happened as a "good."

Coffee time follows the meal. It is a more leisured time traditionally. After the diners have satisfied initial hunger, the pace of most meals slackens. Nick also seeks to end his meal on the relaxed key of coffee and dessert. The activity sets the tone for the ending of Part I—extremely different from the earlier portions when Nick was expending so much energy. Nick must go down to the river to get water before he can make the coffee. The challenge of the river and its complex associations are reasserted. Nick finds the other bank in "white mist." As he kneels on the near bank the grass is "wet and cold." When he puts his bucket in the water, we are reminded of the strength of the current, for the bucket bellies and pulls hard. The water is ice cold. The contrasts with the heat of the day and the long walking are stark. "Up away from the stream" Nick finds it "not so cold" (*IOT*, 189; *NAS*, 185).

As Nick begins making the coffee, the point bores deeper that he has not been camping for a long time. The story had begun on such a note. Now Nick tries to recall the procedure for coffee making. Other people, by design not included in the excursion, enter Nick's consciousness. In a very deliberate and qualified way, "Big Two-Hearted River" becomes a remembrance of things past. The making of coffee had once been an issue between Nick and his friend Hopkins. Nick and Hopkins had once argued about everything. Argumentation would not, however, be desirable on this outing: as we have observed, Nick is seeking something more elemental. And in Nick's thinking, now, Hopkins is no threat; hence Nick makes the coffee in Hopkins' way. While he waits for the water to boil, he has his dessert—apricots. He again trusts what his own experience (and memory) reveals: the canned apricots are better than fresh apricots.

When Nick takes the coffee from the grill, he judges it a triumph for Hopkins. Nick's stream of memory touches on Hopkins, and his melancholy side becomes evident as he recalls the good times he, Hopkins, and Bill had had in earlier years on other Michigan fishing trips. Hopkins is one of the things he has lost. After Hopkins inherited money, they never saw him again. But since Nick decidedly feels that was a long time ago, the memory is not now stinging. We again get suggestions of the lost camaraderie and of Nick's sense of humor in the remembered use of nicknames. Hopkins was "The Hop Head" and his girl "The Blonde Venus"—the latter reference the only one to women in the story. Nick will choke off his thinking before it gets to the complications of women and love. (In "Now I Lay Me" Nick reports that thinking of girls turned out unsatisfactorily, so he "gave up thinking about them almost altogether.") Nick's mind seems to work with Hemingway's to insist on the religious qualities of the day's happenings. Nick thinks of the coffee as "straight Hopkins": it was coffee made "according to Hopkins." These are playful references to the four gospels—and Nick can take his own jokes, for the coffee (too soon judged a triumph) proves to be bitter. He laughs—viewing the ending with ironic amusement, seeing it as part of a story and himself as writer: "It made a good ending to the story" (*IOT*, 191; *NAS*, 187). The bitter coffee has not ruined the evening.

Nick has handled the memories of other Michigan fishing days very well. But his mind is clearly starting to work, and it is time to choke it off; Nick lights another cigarette. He will not rush his memories. It is time for sleep. From the tent, Nick watches the glow of the fire. It bodes well for the night's sleeping that the swamp is "perfectly quiet." Only a mosquito in the tent threatens to disturb Nick's rest, but with a match he gets rid of the mosquito. It makes "a satisfactory hiss in the flame" (*IOT*, 191–92; *NAS*, 187). There will be no humming in his head this night—no listening to mosquitoes or to silkworms. Nick lies down to blessed sleep. "And the evening and the morning were the first day" (Genesis 1:5).

By dividing his story into two parts, and so labeling it, Hemingway emphasizes the two-heartedness of the river, and he also re-enforces the rhythm of Genesis. The story will give us one day exactly. Nick is like Adam at creation, for sleep has—the structure indicates—brought no disturbing dreams. A part of the two-heartedness of the river comes from the abundant sense of renewal that Hemingway's story conveys. The imagery at the opening of Part II suggest birth: "Nick crawled out under the mosquito netting stretched across the mouth of the tent, to look at the morning. The grass was wet on his hands as he came out." He is like Adam gazing out on creation, and we have another broad perspective, since we look with Nick: "The sun was just up over the hill. There was the meadow, the river and the swamp. There were birch trees in the green of the swamp on the other side of the river" (*IOT*, 195; *NAS*, 187). The swamp has been rendered considerably less ominous than it seemed as the shadows lengthened in Part I. The greenness associates the swamp with the forces of life. And the greenness comes from the leaves of the white birch. No cause for alarm here—especially when Nick observes a mink cross the river on the three logs that cross the river into the swamp.

Nick's awakening conveys to us the exhilaration of the aubade—joy in the morning. Even though Hemingway tells us he could never read Thoreau, it is difficult for those who have done so not to think of him when they read "Big Two-Hearted River." In *Walden* Thoreau declares that there are parts of us that are alive in the morning that slumber the rest of the day. In any event, Nick is full of expectancy as he considers the possibilities of the day: "He was excited. He was excited by the early morning and the river" (*IOT*, 195; *NAS*, 188).

Nick has to check his enthusiasms: he has to remind himself to be practical (practicality being an aspect of his character that received comic treatment in "The Three Day Blow"). He knows that he needs a good breakfast before he goes about the day's business—fishing. Nick will be thoroughly practical about that, too. He makes his fire and puts on the coffeepot. While he waits for the water to boil, he goes searching for the grasshoppers he needs for bait before the sun dries the grass. Time (but not clock time) has been of the essence from the beginning of the story and will continue to be so. Without the dew Nick knows it would take him all day to get a bottleful of good grasshoppers—and he would have to be "messy" in doing that, having "to crush many of them, slamming at them with his hat" (*IOT*, 196; *NAS*, 188). Such destruction Nick would avoid; he intends to be a good fisherman. He soon has his hoppers, and the reader may get here—as elsewhere in the story—practical suggestions for fishing. Nick puts a pine stick in the bottle as a cork: "It plugged the mouth of the bottle enough, so the hoppers could not get out and left plenty of air passage" (*IOT*, 196; *NAS*, 188).[6] But more than getting practical suggestions, the reader should be aware that with these hoppers Nick will be testing his fragile nerves and his reluctance to use bait like salamander or crickets "because of the way they acted about the hook" ("Now I Lay Me," *MWW*, 220; *NAS*, 145).

Having gathered the hoppers with dispatch, Nick turns his attention to preparation of his breakfast. On a hasty judgment, "Big Two-Hearted River" is sometimes described as a story in which nothing happens. Actually, a great deal happens, as attention to such details as bait reveals. "Big Two-Hearted River" might more precisely be termed a story of significant action. Therein lies its true distinction. We have seen deliberateness in the gathering of the hoppers—and now we see it in Nick's preparation of his breakfast. Since Nick knows that he should eat breakfast, he does so with heart. Although the narrator does not tell us so, except through the detailed presentation of what Nick does, we know that Nick has all the old feeling as he makes his buckwheat pancakes. The reader sees it all—so that when the cakes begin "to firm, then brown, then crisp" (*IOT*, 197; *NAS*, 189), he is ready to enjoy the fare with Nick. We are reminded, too, of the deliberation of Nick's actions in Part I—of his program of measuring and evaluating circumstances through the validity of the experience, the sensuous experience. Again, it is measured action. Nick plans for a future time. He prepares a third cake for later eating, along with the onion sandwiches that he next prepares. Nick is ready to confirm yesterday's evaluation: "It was a nice little camp" (*IOT*, 198; *NAS*, 189).

Nick next inspects and readies his fishing gear. The reader is given a precise accounting of this process too, and Hemingway uses many sense words to make the experience also physically real. Nick uses a "heavy double tapered fly line," one "made heavy to lift back in the air and come forward flat and heavy and straight to make it possible to cast a fly which has no weight" (*IOT*, 198; *NAS*, 189–90). Nick removes the coilers from the damp-flannel pads, dampened so that the leaders will be soft. The hook is "springy." Nick pulls the line "taut" to test the knot and the spring of the rod. He is "careful not to let the hook bite into his finger." Nick is ready for the stream: "It was a good feeling" (*IOT*, 199; *NAS*, 190). Without a doubt, feeling is foremost in "Big Two-Hearted River."

Nick appears as the man fully prepared. He is "professionally" happy, ready for the adventure of fishing. But action is always different from the anticipation of action, and Hemingway's simplicity in describing the moment of Nick's entry into the stream is powerfully suggestive: "He stepped into the stream. It was a shock. His trousers clung tight to his legs. His shoes felt the gravel. The water was a rising cold shock" (*IOT*, 199; *NAS*, 190). The big trout who kept themselves steady in the current challenged Nick's imagination at the bridge in Seney. Now Nick is in the destructive element with the fish. He cannot control events in the way he could on the journey to the good camp; he has to wade "with the current." How destructive the element can be, Nick at once *sees* as a grasshopper jumps out of the bottle to be sucked under in a whirl. The hopper surfaces, then floats "rapidly, kicking" until he disappears when a trout takes him. A part of Nick is feeling with the hopper.

The second hopper goes on Nick's hook. What might have been merely a precise detail is surely more than that to the reader who knows "Now I Lay Me": "The grasshopper took hold of the hook with his front feet, spitting tobacco juice on it" (*IOT*, 200; *NAS*, 191). Even though "Now I Lay Me" was written after "Big Two-Hearted River," it is clear that by establishing Nick's faith in the sacred in nature, by showing similarities between Nick and the hoppers, Hemingway meant us to see Nick's action with the second hopper as affirmative, an important gain. Nick not only feels professionally, he now can act professionally. Although he is killing the hopper, he respects the hopper's life. Nick has a sense of communion with the creatures different only in degrees, not kind, from what Santiago will later demonstrate in *The Old Man and the Sea* when he kills the marlin. Nick in looking at the first hopper has seen the rhythm of the Big Two-Hearted River—the rhythm of life and death. War is a violation of this sacred rhythm. Here Nick reaches below the conscious levels of his mind and touches the sacredness of the intended order. By dropping his line into the river, Nick finds that order good.

Hemingway does not let us miss the religious aspects of Nick's fishing, for his first strike is more than an ecological lesson. The first trout is small, but he is the essence of life. Nick sees "the trout in the water jerking with his head and body against the shifting tangent of the line in the stream" (*IOT*, 201; *NAS*, 191). He brings him to the surface, and the trout appears a thing of beauty: "His back was mottled the clear, water-over-gravel color, his side flashing in the sun" (*IOT*, 201; *NAS*, 191). Nick is careful to wet his hand before he lets the trout—too small to keep—off the hook; thereby Hemingway gives the reader a practical lesson in fishing. If the hand is not wet, a fungus will attack the part where the delicate mucus has been disturbed. To instruct in the art of fishing is not the purpose, however. Nick's consciousness reaches back to previous time when he found many dead trout in the river because of careless fishermen. Moreover, the passage—the only one to make direct reference to other human beings in Part II—is an image of life in our time when the sacredness of life has been wantonly violated. Nick recalls that "again and again" he had come upon dead trout. By keeping the memory general, Hemingway increases the symbolic value of the reference. We may indeed be reminded of World War I and the horrors Nick has witnessed. For Nick, and precisely because of what he has seen in war, life is sacred. He not only sees the beauty of the small trout, he *feels* it, and then his conscious mind works: "As Nick's fingers touched him, touched his smooth, cool, underwater feeling he was gone, gone in a shadow across the bottom of the stream. He's all right, Nick thought. He was only tired" (*IOT*, 201; *NAS*, 192).

There is no disappointment that the trout is too small. Rather, Nick has already proved something to himself: "He was certain he could catch small trout in the shallows, but he did not want them" (*IOT*, 202; *NAS*, 192). He wants the big trout, and he knows that they will not be in the shallows at this time of day. They will be ahead in the "fast, dark water." Like Santiago, Nick prepares, as it were, to launch out into the deep. He must accept the greater challenge. Hemingway marks the decision by presenting another still shot, locating Nick for us in psychological time: "Now the water deepened up his thighs sharply and coldly. Ahead was the smooth dammed-back flood of water above the logs. The water was smooth and dark; on the left, the lower edge of the meadow; on the right the swamp" (*IOT*, 202; *NAS*, 192).

Almost immediately thereafter Nick is caught in intense struggle with the largest trout he has ever seen. The contrast with Nick's fishing in the shallows could hardly be greater. The rod becomes "alive and dangerous." Nick, the rod and line, and the trout seem one thing, as the trout maintains "a heavy, dangerous, steady pull" (*IOT*, 203; *NAS*, 193). Nick lets the line go when he feels "the moment" when the pressure is at its maximum before the leader would break. This marks the peak of the action in "Big Two-Hearted River": "The reel ratcheted into a mechanical shriek as the line went out in a rush. Too fast. Nick could not check it, the line rushing out, the reel note rising as the line ran out" (*IOT*, 203; *NAS*, 193).

From the beginning of the story Nick has carefully tested his emotions, keeping a delicate balance between heart and head knowledge. In the action of the dangerous fishing, all that he has achieved he might suddenly lose. His heart feels "stopped with the excitement." The leader breaks, and Nick's mouth is "dry, his heart down" as he reels in. We are carried back to Nick's initial testing when he saw the ruins of Seney. Nick reels in slowly: "The thrill had been too much" (*IOT*, 204; *NAS*, 193). Feeling vaguely "a little sick" he decides it would be better to sit down, as he had in Seney.

It is significant, however, that even as Nick prepares to depart from the stream, he is feeling with the trout as earlier he felt with the hopper and the little trout. He thinks of the trout "somewhere on the bottom, holding himself steady over the gravel, far down below the light, under the logs, with the hook in his jaw ... He'd bet the trout was angry. Anything that size would be angry. That was a trout" (*IOT*, 204; *NAS*, 193–94). Nature is filled with determined survivors.

As Nick climbs out into the meadow, he is no longer feeling like Adam experiencing the dew of his first morning. Rather, the water images suggest baptism into experience; Nick stands "water running down his trousers and out of his shoes, his shoes squlchy." He will need to let this baptism come into some kind of focus—and on an emotional rather than an intellectual level. Nick, wisely, does "not want to rush his sensations any" (*IOT*, 204; *NAS*, 194).

Sitting on the log, Nick lights a cigarette—as he has done previously when there has been a lot to take in. Almost immediately we sense the wisdom of Nick's leaving the stream in order to sort things out. A tiny trout rises at the match swimming in the fast current. A big trout would know better, Nick thinks and laughs—taking us back to the moment in Part I when he laughed upon finding the coffee made according to Hopkins' formula bitter. Nick could put his memories of early fishing in an adult perspective— and he will be able to put the incident of the big trout into perspective, too. The scene Nick contemplates as he finishes his cigarette is reassuring. The river never seemed more "two-hearted." Nick's sensuous being takes in the affirmation he needs: "He sat on the logs, smoking, drying in the sun, the sun warm on his back, the river shallow ahead entering the woods, curving into the woods, shallows, light glittering, big water-smooth rocks, cedars along the bank and white birches, the logs warm in the sun, smooth to sit on, without bark, gray to the touch" (IOT, 205; NAS, 194). The feeling of disappointment leaves Nick. His mind can conceptualize what his senses have confirmed. He thinks, "It was all right now." Recovery and return—that is the pattern of the story, but not return to mere sameness.

The symbols carry darker meaning after the climactic action of the big trout. More seems to be required of Nick after this recovery. As he reenters the river, he does so at a particular spot that reveals more fully than at any previous moment the nature of the river. Nick does not return to the fishing with any unfounded optimism. On the left, where the meadow ends and the woods begin, Nick notices a great elm uprooted. The white birches are true, but so is the elm, "its roots clotted with dirt, grass growing in them, rising a solid bank beside the stream" (IOT, 205; NAS, 194–95). The elm had gone over in a storm, and there is no escaping the implications of this bank sinister. The river cuts to the edge of the uprooted tree. The currents cut deep channels. Woods, meadow, and stream come together. Nick accepts the condition of the world—and resumes fishing.

The fishing results in another surge of great energy. This time Nick lands a big trout. What is most impressive about the description of Nick's landing of this trout is the emphasis Hemingway places on Nick's new knowledge or acceptance of the river in its relationship to the tree as the key to his success: "Holding the rod far out toward the uprooted tree and sloshing backward in the current, Nick worked the trout, plunging, the rod bending alive, out of the danger of the weeds into the open river" (IOT, 206; NAS, 195).

Once Nick has the big trout, the pace of the story changes noticeably. The theme of not wanting to rush his sensations becomes even more insistent. Nick has, now, achieved what he set out to achieve on *this* trip. He does "not care about getting many trout" (IOT, 197; NAS, 195–96). However, his success with the big trout puts his mind on the future—future catches, future challenges—in a noticeable way. Heretofore, the fiber of the story has been decidedly on present action. Memories of the past have been kept in check.

The change in mood is signaled by reference to the sun—in a sentence that is also a paragraph: "It was getting hot, the sun hot on the back of his neck" (*IOT*, 207; *NAS*, 195). The exhilaration of the aubade gives way completely to sober awareness. Even though it is not yet afternoon, Nick is thinking of afternoon and evening. In thinking of future catches and about where the trout would be (always in shadow) Nick thinks of another stream, the one he had fished with Hopkins and others, but he does not think of them. That river was the Black. In Part I, the name seemed only a name. Now it becomes charged with the emotional overtones of the serious awareness that is Nick's after he catches the first big trout:

> The very biggest ones would lie up close to the bank. You could always pick them up there on the Black. When the sun was down they all moved out into the current. Just when the sun made the water blinding in the glare before it went down, you were liable to strike a big trout anywhere in the current. It was almost impossible to fish then, the surface of the water was blinding as a mirror in the sun. Of course, you could fish upstream, but in a stream like the Black or this, you had to wallow against the current and in a deep place, the water piled up on you. It was no fun to fish upstream with this much current. (*IOT*, 207–208; *NAS*, 196)

Nick continues fishing, but he does so with new caution. He is aware of deep places and deep holes and deepening water. Branches hang down over the water, adding to the somberness. He proves that he can navigate the more treacherous waters of the Big Two-Hearted River. He eventually lands another trout. When he sees the second trout in the sack with the first, he realizes that he has had enough of fishing for one day. It is time to leave the river.

Nick wades through "the deepening water" to a gray log where he can sit in the cool of the shade, with the simple and profound aim of sitting and watching—much as he had done on other occasions in the story. He sits "smoking and watching the river," ready to take another long view; the picture he sees picks up on the suggestions of the evening and coming night that the first successful trout catch aroused: "Ahead the river narrowed and went into a swamp. The river became smooth and deep and the swamp looked solid with cedar trees, their trunks close together, their branches solid. It would not be possible to walk through a swamp like that. The branches grew so low. You would have to keep almost level with the ground to move at all. You could not crash through the branches. That must be why the animals that lived in swamps were built the way they were, Nick thought" (*IOT*, 210–11; *NAS*, 198).

The Big Two-Hearted river is the river of life and death, and each implies the other. In terms of the image of the very first day that Hemingway has built upon, it is the river of both morning and evening. The joy of morning implies the journey to the darker shadows.

There is something enticing about the swamp scene Nick is watching. It seems to call to him even as he pulls away from it. It is like the woods in Frost's "Stopping By Woods on a Snowy Evening." They are lovely, dark and deep. But the time has not yet come for the speaker of the poem to enter them. He has promises to keep. Youth, especially, pulls back from the entry, but it too can feel the pull. Nick tries to check thoughts of the swamp. He wishes, for the first time, that he had brought something to read. A book could challenge him to another view of experience. But he has no book, and his thoughts revert to the swamp. Nick's conscious mind has to check the pull the thrice-stated decision that he does not want to go into the swamp partly belies: "in the fast deep water, in the half light, the fishing would be tragic. In the swamp fishing was a tragic adventure. Nick did not want it. He did not want to go down the stream any further today" (*IOT*, 211; *NAS*, 198).

The way to check the call of the deep woods or the dark swamp is to resort to action. Frost's persona must put his horse back into motion towards the fulfillment of his obligations. Nick will tend to the fish he has caught. He "whacks" the necks of the trout, cleans them, tossing the offal ashore "for the mink to find." He completes the proper care of his trout, a deed of pleasure that surely confirms the accomplishment of this day.

The ending of the story is sober, but convincingly affirmative. Nick gives the "yes" to life that means he will write truly of war and life. The final paragraph reverses the first paragraph of the story. There "Nick sat down." Now "Nick stood up" (*IOT*, 212; *NAS*, 199). He becomes man in motion as he climbs the bank and cuts into the woods. He is going back to camp—the good place, to fortify himself for the challenge of fishing in future days. He looks back: "The river just showed through the trees." Nick knows about that river and accepts its two-heartedness. The final sentence is not whistling in the dark: "There were plenty of days coming when he could fish the swamp." This is the affirmation that the artist needs, a belief that the future matters, a belief that he will have the chance to create work that will have a life beyond life. All of that is implied in the ending of "Big Two-Hearted River." What is most immediately before us is the large sense of miracle, or recovery of the wounded Nick. On that level the title of the story affirms the religious tone that has marked the whole. The river is two-hearted because it creates for Nick the second chance, the miracle of beginning—as it were—all over again.

Notes

1. Charles Fenton, *The Apprenticeship of Ernest Hemingway* (New York: Viking Press, 1958), 157.

2. Ernest Hemingway, *A Moveable Feast* (New York: Charles Scribner's Sons, 1964), 76.

3. Ernest Hemingway, *Death in the Afternoon* (New York: Charles Scribner's Sons, 1932), 192.

4. Sheridan Baker, "Hemingway's Two-Hearted River," in Jackson J. Benson (ed.), *The Short Stories of Ernest Hemingway: Critical Essays* (Durham: Duke University Press, 1975), 157.

5. *Ibid.*

6. Nick's search for hoppers may meaningfully be set against an event that Frederic Henry tells us about late in *A Farewell to Arms* as Catherine is dying. Henry says: "Once in camp I put a log on top of the fire and it was full of ants. As it commenced to burn, the ants swarmed out and went first toward the center where the fire was; then turned back and ran toward the end. When there were enough on the end they fell off into the fire. Some got out, their bodies burnt and flattened, and went off not knowing where they were going. But most of them went toward the fire and then back toward the end and swarmed on the cool ends and finally fell off into the fire. I remember thinking at the time that it was the end of the world and a splendid chance to be a messiah and lift the log off the fire and throw it out where the ants could get off onto the ground. But I did not do anything but throw a tin cup of water on the log, so that I would have the cup empty to put whisky in before I added water to it. I think the cup of water on the burning log only steamed the ants" (New York: Charles Scribner's Sons, 1929), 327–28. The religious overtones are vastly different in "Big Two-Hearted River" when Nick turns over a log and discovers there a grasshoppers' lodging house. Nick carefully selects fifty, leaving the others unharmed. He rolls the log back, knowing he can get hoppers there every morning. The difference between the log of *A Farewell to Arms* and this is on one level the difference between a fallen and unfallen world. The novel is clearly after the fall, whereas the story creates the edenic world. In "Big Two-Hearted River" the creatures of the world are placed under man's dominion and are to be used (not misused, obviously) for his good. A part of the glory of "Big Two-Hearted River" is that Nick—who has been in Frederic Henry's war and at his front—could touch so much of that unblemished world. Henry's verdict on God and creation tells us more about Henry's state of mind as he tries to adjust to his loss than it does about the world. Powerful as the passage is, we cannot take it as the novel's meaning.

NICHOLAS GEROGIANNIS

Nick Adams on the Road:
"The Battler" as Hemingway's Man on the Hill

A young fellow needs to know how to handle himself if he elects to carry
on in the tramp life.

—Jack London[1]

... I traveled on, scarce knowing which Way I went, and making it my
chief Care to avoid all public Roads, and all Towns, nay, even the most
homely Houses; for I imagined every human Creature whom I saw,
desirous of betraying me.

—Henry Fielding[2]

"The Battler" was the last story that Ernest Hemingway included in the
first American edition of *In Our Time*.[3] While vacationing in Schruns,
Austria, he began to write the story in approximately December 1924 and
finished it on 13 February 1925. A few days before, Horace Liveright had
cabled his formal acceptance of *In Our Time*; however, in an accompanying
letter, Liveright rejected "Up in Michigan" from the collection and stated his
objections to a passage in "Mr. and Mrs. Elliot." When Hemingway mailed
his signed contract to Liveright on 31 March, he included a typescript of
"The Battler" to replace the "censorable" "Up in Michigan." In his letter, he
instructed Liveright on where the new story was to be placed in the
collection; he wanted it to follow "The Three Day Blow." "The new story

From *Critical Essays on Ernest Hemingway's* In Our Time, edited by Michael S. Reynolds:
176–188. © 1983 by Michael S. Reynolds.

makes the book a good deal better," Hemingway wrote. "It's about the best I've ever written and gives additional unity to the book as a whole."[4] The first and last parts of this statement are true; however, Hemingway's claims for this story could be excused as the outpouring of the author's pride in his most recent work. But "The Battler" is a far more important chapter in the life of Nick Adams than has been generally perceived.

Remarkably, what is probably the first draft of this story[5] is very similar to the published version. That draft is entitled "The Great Man"; in the enclosures inventory at the end of his letter to Liveright, Hemingway listed the story as "The Great Little Fighting Machine," crossed that out and typed in "The Battler" (*Letters*, p. 155). The final title focuses on Ad Francis' tragic flaw: he battles society.

Although the story has a youthful protagonist, it is about complex emotions, and it is written with a technical mastery—selection, timing, and compression—which places it firmly in the succession of the outstanding stories it follows in composition. Hemingway wrote "The Battler" shortly after realizing his now well-known "iceberg theory."[6] What Hemingway omits from this story—the mass beneath the surface—is the importance of the encounter to Nick.

Dramatically, "The Battler" is at the end of the beginning of *In Our Time*; the story serves as a gateway. Nick Adams is on the road, beyond the events and the setting of the four previous stories which deal with his family and the close circle of acquaintances at his home in northern Michigan. In "The Battler" the craziness of the outside world has penetrated the deep woods, the last good country. Nick encounters deceit, violence, insanity, and incest. On the one hand, the experience proves that Nick is not safe or exempt from the fates of the greater world. On the other hand, by keeping Nick passive and his background ambiguous, Hemingway manages to make distinctions between real violence and threatened violence, between craziness and toughness, and between physical and emotional injuries. In the process he defines the difference between Ad Francis and Nick Adams.

Nick's encounter with the two hobos in the woods near Mancelona, Michigan, moves him into a larger, darker world of relationships. Because this is a chance encounter with unusual characters, the events in "The Battler" are generally not considered to be as important as the more central events of the earlier stories. But Nick's encounter with Ad Francis, the battler, and with Bugs, the caretaker, presents him with a frame of reference, a perspective on his past and an insight into his possible future. Ad Francis is a possible projection of the belligerent side of young Nick. The battler's head is the scarred outward form of his stunted personality. Ad's craziness is an example to Nick against which he can silently gauge his own life.

In the life of Nick Adams, Nick's encounter with Ad Francis is as important as Tom's encounter is with the Man on the Hill in Henry Fielding's *Tom Jones*. After Tom has been banished from his home for apparent sins, he meets the Man on the Hill and hears his story. Superficially, the events of the Man's life sound prophetically similar to the problems in Tom's life. The reader is left to imagine Tom's discomfort upon recognizing the similarities. But Tom realizes toward the end of the Man's tale that the old sinner is afflicted with a central flaw: throughout his life he has lacked a discriminating sensibility. The old Man on the Hill is a stunted man, limited by his lack of perception. When he traveled in the world he avoided contact with the particular elements of the regions he visited and supported his opinions by noticing only the squalor of the threatening general scene. Tom, on the other hand, is a sensualist in love with the particular, and he rejects the Man's misanthropy. Likewise, Nick's meeting with the battler gives him a new awareness of the consequences of the tough kid role he has adopted, and a new insight into his own transgressions.

Whether Hemingway consciously intended "The Battler" to serve a similar purpose in *In Our Time*, as Fielding's Man on the Hill chapters did in *Tom Jones*, is beside the point. He certainly could have. Hemingway was quite familiar with *Tom Jones*; shortly after writing "The Battler," he used Fielding's novel as a framework for his parody *The Torrents of Spring*. Later he planned a picaresque novel set in America, and after *The Sun Also Rises* was published, he wrote 45,000 words of yet another novel he projected as a modern *Tom Jones*. Perhaps he abandoned that project because the novel would not take form. Fielding's world was homogeneous; Hemingway's was fragmented. His Tom Jones was Nick Adams, in part, and he was already writing that story in a manner that reflected the time: fragmented and non-sequential.

The structural and some of the thematic qualities of Fielding's work obviously appealed to Hemingway generally. But for particular literary qualities—subject, setting, and character—Hemingway's American fiction ascends from the literary tradition of Jack London. This is difficult to consider objectively because of the muddled critical view of London's work, but if we look at London's *The Road*,[7] we can discover the world of Hemingway's youthful imagination. Many of Hemingway's assumptions as a young man derive directly from the legend of London's life on the road. The "road" in London's parlance is the railroad; to go "on the road" is to be a tramp, to "ride the rails." *The Road* is a collection of related autobiographical articles about London's life as a tramp which were serialized in *Cosmopolitan* magazine under the muckraking title *My Life in the Underworld*. The subject of runaway boys was common to many stories and essays that appeared in family periodicals and in boys' magazines during the time that Hemingway was growing up in Oak Park, Illinois, and in northern Michigan. The undisputed model for the tramp-hero was Jack London. Whether he wrote about himself or was written about by others, until his death by suicide in 1916, London's life was a popular subject for American magazines. It seems that Hemingway was attracted to the popular legends of London the tramp in a world of rootless boys. Indeed, young Hemingway often adopted the role of a tramp. In the summer of 1915, he and some friends hiked from Oak Park to the Hemingways' summer cottage at Walloon Lake, Michigan. Again in 1916, Hemingway and a friend explored in upper Michigan. Traveling by train and hiking, they journeyed over the same territory from Walton Junction to Kalkaska to Mancelona that Nick Adams covers in "The Battler." A photograph probably taken on one of these trips shows Hemingway posed on the ladder of a boxcar, looking like one of London's road-kids.[8] But there is something about Hemingway in that photograph that suggests an essential difference between him and London the tramp at about the same age: Hemingway is grinning a wide, toothy, naive, Illinois schoolboy's grin, there is no trace of London's roughness in Hemingway's smile.

Nevertheless, there is much in Hemingway's Nick Adams stories, and particularly in "The Battler," that is strikingly similar to the world presented in *The Road*. Before going on the road, young London had been Prince of the Oyster Pirates on San Francisco Bay. Similarly, Nick Adams is a poacher (as is Tom Jones). London first went on the road with his mate Nickey out of Oakland. At times Nick Adams travels with a friend. A scene of "Hoboes That Pass in the Night," the last chapter of London's book, quite possibly served as the inspiration for the opening to Hemingway's "The Light of the World"; London and a friend have a run-in in a saloon with a punk-hating bartender who snatches their beers away from them. Throughout *The Road* London matches wits with the wily "bulls." Nick Adams may be on the road in the London tradition in "The Battler," but he does not possess London's cynicism or craftiness; otherwise, he would not have been tricked by the brakeman.

At the beginning of "The Battler" Nick Adams has just been ditched. We learn later that Nick caught the train in Walton Junction, which is about thirty miles south of Mancelona; when he gets sucked in by the brakeman (a "bull"), who sends him tumbling off the train, he is still a few miles south of Mancelona. Nick's destination is probably the Petosky region, which is about thirty miles beyond Mancelona. So Nick is headed north, toward home, when his adventure begins.

One of the qualities of "The Battler" is its economic style; had London written this story it probably would have been twice as long. Hemingway dispenses with Nick's run-in with the brakeman, giving the reader the needed material through implications and Nick's thoughts. In this way we discover what happened at the same time that we learn what effect the incident has had on Nick. His reaction is juvenile: "That lousy crut of a brakeman" (p. 65). In "The Great Man" manuscript (*Catalog*, Item 269) the reading is "son of a bitch"; but Hemingway changes the initial expletive to the naive sounding "crut" in the untitled typescript (*Catalog*, Item 270). In later references to the brakeman, "son of a bitch" (and its derivatives) are kept in this typescript; so we must assume that there were changes made later in the publishing process, perhaps by someone other than Hemingway. In his thoughts Nick does two things: first he admonishes himself for falling for the brakeman's call to him, "a lousy kid thing to have done" (p. 65); then he generalizes by vowing "They" would never do anything like this to him again. His anger is not specific. He repeats the scene of his ditching in his mind. In the tough talk of the retelling, we detect the style of an adventure yarn; we sense the beginning of a self-conscious reputation.

Walking along the tracks toward Mancelona, Nick is at ease in the dark woods. But when he sees a fire below the railway embankment he circles toward it like a candlemoth. Hemingway's economy works very well in the introduction of Ad Francis to the story (p. 67). Strangely, Ad does not move when Nick walks up to him, and he responds to Nick's greeting by asking, "Where did you get that shiner?" (p. 67). Hemingway thus compresses the scene by skipping the stock chit-chat and opening with a professional insight; also, he introduces an element of strangeness into the story. Ad's understanding of and apparent sympathy for what happened to Nick underscores their potential sameness. Nick echoes Ad's word to describe the brakeman—"The bastard!" (p. 68). But Ad is speaking "seriously" when he talks about Nick's encounter with the brakeman; he is used to dealing with all matters of violence earnestly and absolutely. Nick's responses are juvenile—a general vengeful "I'll get him" (p. 68). Ad's advice for revenge is objective and specific: "Get him with a rock sometime when he's going through" (p. 68). Perhaps put off by this direct and dishonorable suggestion, Nick replies by saying merely that he'll get the brakeman. Ad recognizes something in Nick. "You're a tough one, aren't you?" he asks Nick (p. 68). Then as they bandy the word "tough" back and forth it loses its power. Ad is not tough; this is a quality only the young can affect. Ad is "misshapen"; his face is "Dead looking in the firelight" (p. 68). He has an ear on one side of his head and a "stump" on the other (p. 69). These are all outward signs of a man who once thought of himself as being tough. These are also the marks of a fighter. He is a man who pitted his head against other men's hands. Nick is uncomfortable around this man and at first declines Ad's invitation to sit and eat. But the man's friendliness draws Nick nearer, just as the brakeman's apparent harmlessness did on the train.

The dialogue takes on the rhythm of a sparring match. Emotionally, Nick seems to be bobbing, at times feeling safe, the next moment jarred into discomfort. "I'm not quite right," Ad announces; "I'm crazy" (p. 69). The statements taken together define the far side of tough. Nick is put off balance; because he is young, he feels like laughing. He does not understand yet what Ad means, but he plays along. Nick has never been crazy so he asks Ad, "How does it get to you?" (p. 69). Ad responds that he does not know; no one knows when he's crazy. You are not conscious of being crazy so it is impossible to deal with and overcome. It's frightening. The only thing to do is to learn how it happens so you can avoid it. The round is over, but not without some intended deception: for the moment Nick (and probably the reader) must associate Ad's craziness with his mauled appearance.

In the next passage Ad reveals his identity, and Nick is comfortable again because he recognizes the professional boxer. (Hemingway wrote to Carlos Baker that he modeled his fictional boxer after Bat Nelson and Ad Wolgast, and the fictional Bugs was modeled after Wolgast's trainer.[9]) Nick's recognition of Ad Francis seems to define their roles and adds to the economy of the story. Nick would now be the neophyte while Ad would be the master. Hemingway sets up a parody of a fighting tactic; Ad used the fighting method of taking punishment in order to wear down his opponents, thus letting the other's strength beat itself. The method and Ad's way of explaining it remind Nick (and the reader) of his battered mind. Ad's explanation of how he beat his opponents begins to resemble an absurd vaudeville routine as he attempts to prove that his stamina is a result of an unusually slow heartbeat. Nick is made to hold Ad's wrist and count his pulse; he plays along again by telling Ad what he expects to hear.

The next round of the story is a short affair. Bugs, Ad's "negro" companion suddenly enters camp. Nick seems to be apprehensive at this moment because he does not even turn to look at the intruder. Bugs is silent, distant, indifferent, and polite. In "The Great Man" draft (*Catalog*, Item 269) Bugs is servile; by changing his speech, Hemingway created an imposing and enigmatic character. Bugs could be dangerous. Nick probably isn't feeling very safe when Ad introduces his friend and adds, "He's crazy, too" (p. 71). Nick does not speak. Bugs asks him where he's from, and Nick replies, "Chicago," the tough town; Nick does not give his provincial home in northern Michigan. And Hemingway does not handicap his hero by giving him the genteel Oak Park for a hometown. The passage ends in a prophecy for Nick:

"He says he's never been crazy, Bugs," Ad said.

"He's got a lot coming to him," the negro said. (p. 71)

As this is being spoken Hemingway is setting the stage for what will lead to the conflict which is the climax of the story. The next scene's power is built around elemental feelings and primitive reactions. Bugs is frying ham and eggs for sandwiches. He seems submissive to Ad. Hemingway builds a delicious and tense sensuality around the preparation of the sandwiches. Nick is hungry. He tries to help by using his knife to cut the bread. Ad asks for the knife. Suddenly, in a turnabout, Bugs orders Nick to hang onto his knife (p. 72). Bugs is thus revealed as a dominant character. All the while, Bugs maintains control through his deliberate manners. The "prizefighter" (a menacing word suddenly introduced) withdraws into a dangerous silence. Hemingway reduces the action to matters of the senses. Bugs seems to enjoy his deliberate preparation of the three sandwiches. His cool manners float over the hot tension. He asks Nick to hand a sandwich to "Mister Francis" (p. 73). The three men begin to eat the "wonderful" tasting sandwiches. Bugs makes apparent small talk about Nick being "right hungry" (p. 73); he is trying to distract Ad. Hemingway counters this with an explicitly menacing reference to Ad's potential power when he notes that Nick is aware that "the former champion was silent" (p. 73). Furthermore, Ad is staring at Nick. Bugs's formal calls cannot distract him. The tension is strung between silence and softness; the threat to Nick is great. Ad's eyes are hidden in the darkness under the bill of his cap. An athlete usually cannot determine his opponent's intentions unless he is able to see his eyes.

The attack comes quickly. It is primitive and vicious: an attack on a guest over offered food (p. 74). Ad accuses Nick of eating his food and then getting "snotty" about the knife. Nick is stung. But Ad is obviously confused, which makes the threat to Nick even greater since his attacker is both dangerous and illogical; Ad seems to be living in some memory when he accuses Nick of smoking his cigars and drinking his liquor. Nick is stepping backward; Ad is stalking him using a boxer's shuffle. Like a schoolyard bully, he invites Nick to hit him, making it clear that whether Nick wants to fight or not, he is "going to take a beating" (p. 75). Boxers who fight like raging bulls lower their heads as they advance and gauge their opponent's actions by watching their feet. When Ad makes his move by looking down at Nick's feet, Bugs steps up behind him and knocks him out with a blackjack.[10]

The physical threat to Nick is over, but the story has not yet made its point. It is in Bugs's epilogue that the importance of this encounter takes shape. When Nick asks him what made Ad Francis crazy, Bugs responds that there were many causes. The many beatings that Ad took "just made him sort of simple" (p. 76). What made him *crazy* was the affair with his "sister" (p. 77). Ad and his female manager were promoted as being brother and sister; they looked enough alike to be twins. (Before the beatings Ad had been handsome.) But when they were married, to the public it was incest. There was a lot of trouble. Ad's wife left him. It was then that he went crazy. Ad began "busting people all the time" (p. 77) and was put in jail, where he met Bugs. Presumably, it was this angry period that Ad was recalling when he began his confused attack on Nick. Nick is only another piece of the world that Ad is fighing; this is what makes him a battler. After Ad's fall his wife became his benefactress, which supports the conclusion that Bugs seems to draw that she left Ad because of social pressure rather than because of a change of heart. On the money that she sends them, Ad and Bugs travel around the country, keeping away from people (p. 78). Bugs apologizes to Nick for not warning him about Ad, adding that he thought things seemed to be all right because Ad seemed to like Nick (pp. 78–79).[11] Bugs's long speech hustles Nick out of camp. Hemingway omits Nick's responses and all stage directions; movements are implied through Bugs's monologue. Bugs is in control, handing Nick his sandwich, pointing the boy toward Mancelona, and all the while preparing to wake Ad.

Nick is dazed and helpless, like Ad. He is more shaken by Bugs's story about Ad and his "sister" than he was by the threat from Ad. Moments after it seemed that Ad was going to beat him, Nick was collected enough to notice Bugs's blackjack and to tell Bugs he was "all right" (p. 75). But Nick is not all right when he walks out of camp. He does not focus until he is walking along the tracks. He looks back at the firelight in the clearing. What that fire in the dark woods represents is quite real; the story of Ad Francis cannot be dismissed.

The story that Bugs tells at the end of "The Battler" finally answers Nick's original question about being crazy—"How does it get to you?" (p. 69); all that has happened in the story to that point has merely given Nick a glimpse at what crazy looks like. Nick Adams, like Tom Jones, has faced a man whose life acts as a warning to him.

Fielding's Man on the Hill becomes a recluse because he is disgusted with mankind. But, in fact, he is a victim of his own poor judgment. The Man has a caretaker, an old woman who tends to his needs at the hilltop retreat. The caretaker is a go-between; she worries over the old Man, but she still has contacts with the social world below. It is through her that Tom first becomes interested in the Man. But after hearing the Man's tale and his thoughts on mankind, Tom realizes that there is a profound difference between himself and the Man: although he has erred as the Man did, he acted out of youthful zest; Tom has been promiscuous but he has never committed a sin of the heart. Tom has a goodness of soul, not a goodness of strict behavior. Fielding dramatizes the difference between Tom and the Man. At the beginning of their night together, Tom saved the Man from ruffians. After their night of talk they go walking on the Man's hill and come upon a man attacking a woman. Tom slides down into the ravine immediately to rescue the woman, thus beginning the next adventure of his journey. The Man, Tom notices after the scuffle, remained detached on his hilltop perch and never moved to help his fellow creature. Interestingly, Tom sets out with the half-naked woman and quickly becomes amorously involved with her; of course, to the world (and soon to the reader) she is Jenny Jones, Tom's long-banished mother. So the Man on the Hill interlude is followed by a mock-incestuous involvement.

Ad Francis's case is also one of mock-incest. Ad has not committed incest in the literal sense. But it does not seem that it would have mattered to him anyway. What he cannot understand nor accept is the loss of his wife; he becomes a battler outside the ring. Finally he withdraws (or is withdrawn) from the world of men and women. And Bugs is his caretaker, going into town and bringing food back to Ad in the woods. He watches over Ad like an old woman watching over a pot of boiling soup, treating him gently, sensitively controlling and timing the things that stimulate him, and when he boils over relieving his pressure with the blackjack.

Nick is like Ad in superficial ways just as Tom is similar to the Man on the Hill. Before the beginning of the story, Nick was hit (probably with a club of some sort); Ad is hit at the end. Nick knows enough about Ad's profession to known about the former boxing champion. And, more importantly, even considering "The Battler" alone, Nick seems to be an outsider, waging a little war with the world. Both Ad and Nick escape society by going into the woods.

But Hemingway omits the true similarity between Ad Francis and Nick Adams from "The Battler." The groundwork for our understanding was established by Hemingway who selected the case of possible incest and its consequences with which to confront Nick Adams. Hemingway never meant for the boundaries of his fiction to be the boundaries of the subject as well. For the "iceberg theory" to work, understanding must come beyond the fiction, but within the framework of experiences presented in the fiction. To understand the mass beneath the surface of this story we should consider briefly other material.

Nick Adams too is running the risk of being accused of incest. With the publication of "The Last Good Country"[12] and the placing of Hemingway's papers in the John F. Kennedy Library, the material that we have needed to help us to fully understand "The Battler" is finally available. The published version of "The Last Good Country" deals centrally with Nick Adams's incest-like relationship with his sister Littless and with the couple's escape into the wilderness, away from society; material omitted from the published version reinforces the meaning of the incest theme to this story and to Nick's life.

First of all, let us review the incest-related material that is in the published version of "The Last Good Country." The relationship between Nick and Littless is tinged with innocent sensuality, at least on the girl's part. Nick, however, is a sexually experienced young man and must foresee the possibilities of their tender loving. Danger often arouses sensuality. As the two approach the Adams' house where two wardens are waiting to arrest Nick for poaching, Nick says to Littless, "Let me kiss you just for an emergency" (*Nick Adams*, p. 79). They kiss a great deal throughout the story; the regularity and the situations of their kissing seem to be the only outward manifestations of their feelings. Kissing is the only physical thrill they engage in (hardly a sin). The "whore's assistant" yarn that Littless spins is told while she is sitting on Nick's lap (*Nick Adams*, pp. 113–14). This humorous tale, along with some of Littless's other comments, indicates that she is innocent but certainly not ignorant. Littless wants to be Nick's companion; she wants to care for him and to be like him. In order to achieve psychological tension and sexual satisfaction in his fiction, Hemingway often obscures sexual definitions. Littless cuts off her hair in order to look like Nick. (Remember that in "The Battler" Nick hears several times the refrain that Ad and his wife looked enough alike to be twins.) To ensure that they stay together, Littless admits that she plans to trap Nick into marriage by becoming his common-law wife (she read about it in the newspapers). She is going to have cards printed: "Mrs. Nick Adams, Cross Village, Michigan—common-law wife" (*Nick Adams*, p. 122). Part of her scheme, she tells Nick, is to have a couple of children by him while she is still a minor. Littless is single-minded in her pursuit.

Some interesting passages (approximately 550 words) were omitted from the published version of "The Last Good Country" which are central to this story and important to recognizing Hemingway's development of the incest theme.[13] Littless says at one point that they have done something wrong; Nick reacts strongly by saying that they have never done anything wrong together (*Catalog*, Item 542, p. 3). His sister says that she did not mean something wrong like what Nick does with Trudy. Trudy in this story plays a similar (but offstage) role as Prudie does in "Ten Indians" and Marjorie in "The End of Something." But all references to Trudy are omitted from the published version of "The Last Good Country"; interestingly, in these passages Hemingway has inferred much about the spiritually incestuous relationship between Nick and Littless. The longest omitted passage (*Catalog*, Item 542, pp. 11–13)[14] follows Nick's request for a kiss quoted above. Littless asks who will kiss him if he goes away by himself. Nick says that he may try to find Trudy. Littless asks jealously whether he isn't through with Trudy. Littless is concerned that Nick will go back to Trudy and make her pregnant again. (This is the only mention of Trudy's having been pregnant; it is ambiguous whether it was by Nick. This material is reminiscent of Tom Jones's relationship with the luscious Molly.) Littless reveals that she could not stand the hurt and humiliation of having to listen to the family discuss Nick and Trudy. Nick and Littless have banded together in opposition to the other members of the family. Littless does not want to fight like the others; she wants to be with Nick and for them to take care of each other. In another omitted passage Nick admits he needs Trudy to help him not be lonesome. Littless asks whether he would ever be lonesome with her; he answers no (*Catalog*, Item 543, p. 11). She asks him if it is dirty for a brother and sister to love each other. He responds by asking who told her it was. She answers that it was a member of the family. He says he can guess who it was. She tells him not to.

Certainly there is a great deal of irony in this material (published and unpublished); the characters' own senses of irony are evident from their speeches, and Hemingway exhibits a broader ironic sensibility as author. However, Nick's relative quietness is a sign that there is great seriousness beneath this pubescent experiment in country living. The reader of "The Last Good Country" must begin to feel that unless Nick and Littless go home soon, all of the playfulness and petting could turn into the real thing. Emotionally, it is already real enough. But the brother and sister do not go back; at the end of the story they make plans to hike to a place where they can find berries, and Nick is about to read to Littless from *Wuthering Heights*, a story unsurpassed in emotional withdrawal and passionate romance. We leave them in their garden and remember that even Adam and Eve were brother and sister.

All of this is part of the Nick Adams history. Hemingway wrote the words, but we must remember that of all of this material he published only "The Battler." "The Last Good Country" was not written until 1952—27 years after "The Battler"—and it was published posthumously. All that we can say with certainty is that he continued to be interested in Nick Adams and that he continued to be interested in the incest theme. A story fragment probably written from four to six years before "The Battler" experiments with a brother/sister love affair.[15] In this fragment the sister goes snake hunting in the wilderness with her brother. The girl walks behind her brother like an Indian woman, but she does not want to be like a squaw; there is an important distinction made: she does not want to be subservient; she is merely breaking away from mores and constraints. Her love for her brother becomes obvious to others; he drops her and goes hunting with boys. Initially, the girl is identified as "my sister" in the manuscript; later this changes to "his sister." Nick Adams is not mentioned. But the existence of the fragments proves that Hemingway was experimenting with the incest theme even before he wrote "The Battler."

That Hemingway did not connect the incest theme to Nick explicitly in "The Battler" is not surprising. First of all, as mentioned earlier, it was contrary to his style to do so. Then, as a new author he would have run a great risk (even if Liveright had accepted a story that suggested an incestuous relationship between teenagers); the theme would have stigmatized Hemingway. But there is no reason to leap from Hemingway's employment of the incest theme (and the many echoes of it throughout his works) to his personal life. Incest is good stuff for fiction and he had favorite literary sources to refer to as testaments to its potency.[16] And by his own admission much of his writing was inspired by other literary works.

Whether Nick's experiences of "The Last Good Country" come before or after the events in "The Battler" is not important. The relationship between Nick and Littless is certainly older than the events of "The Last Good Country." Anyway, an unchallengeable order of the Nick Adams material is neither desirable nor possible. Hemingway, like London, obscured chronology in creating his myths.

Nick's relationship with his sister is certainly concealed in his heart while he is listening to Bugs tell him about Ad. But Nick Adams and Tom Jones are superior to the false doubles they meet. They have youth for one thing, and thus the possibility for change. They have insight; they are not obsessed with the problems of their lives. In "The Last Good Country" Littless has apparently accepted Nick's tough talk at face value; but when he hears his sister echo his threats, Nick is aware of the serious difference between tough talk and really killing somebody. In the same way he is not willing to commit himself to the definite revenge upon the brakeman suggested by Ad Francis. Despite his affectations as a road-kid, Nick Adams foregoes the tough reaction; the character who is stalked by the battler is a sensitive boy.

Toward the end of "The Last Good Country" Hemingway writes of Nick: "He loved his sister very much and she loved him too much. But, he thought, I guess those things straighten out. At least I hope so" (*Nick Adams*, p. 119). It is not a conclusive statement. The lesson of Ad Francis must weigh heavily on Nick Adams' mind as he walks in the dark along the tracks toward Mancelona.

NOTES

1. Quoted from Nat Fleischer, *50 Years at Ringside* (1940; rpt. New York: Greenwood, 1969), p. 259.

2. Henry Fielding, *Tom Jones*, ed. Sheridan Baker (New York: Norton, 1973), p. 365. The Man on the Hill episodes comprise Book VIII, Chapters 10–15; and Book IX, Chapter 2.

3. Ernest Hemingway, *In Our Time* (New York: Boni and Liveright, 1925). Scribner's published the revised edition of *In Our Time* (New York: Scribner's, 1930), the uniform edition (1955), and the paperback edition (1962); the pagination is uniform in these three Scribner's editions, and all subsequent references to "The Battler" will be to these uniform editions.

4. Carlos Baker, ed., *Ernest Hemingway: Selected Letters, 1917–1961* (New York: Scribner's, 1981), p. 155. All subsequent references to Hemingway's letters will be to this edition.

5. "The Great Man" (The Ernest Hemingway Collection, Item 269, John F. Kennedy Library, Boston); pages 1–3 are typed; pages 4 and 6–20 are handwritten; page 5 is missing. A second copy of this story is Item 270, an untitled typescript, pages 1–14. The list of the Hemingway material at the archive is now generally available in *Ernest Hemingway: Catalog of the Manuscripts, Correspondence and Other Material in the John F. Kennedy Library* (Boston: G. K. Hall, 1981). All subsequent references to Hemingway's manuscripts and typescripts will be made by Item number and will conform to the published catalog; page numbers will refer to the manuscripts and typescripts.

6. Ernest Hemingway, *A Moveable Feast* (New York: Scribner's, 1964), p. 75.

7. Jack London, *The Road* (New York: Macmillan, 1907). The articles were serialized in *Cosmopolitan* between May 1907 and March 1908; London wrote other related articles before and after the publication of *The Road*. See Jack London, "The Road," in *Jack London Reports*, ed. King Hendricks and Irving Shepard (New York: Doubleday, 1970), pp. 311–21. About this tramping article Hendricks and Shepard write: "Among the letters written to London is a vitriolic attack upon him for publishing such articles for the American boy to read which the writer said destroyed the image of the boys' ideal of Jack London" (p. 311). It is this ideal image that has obscured London's place in American letters. London's tramping articles are important reading for anyone interested in the road tradition in American literature.

8. For an account of these hiking trips see Carlos Baker, *Ernest Hemingway: A Life Story* (New York: Scribner's, 1969), pp. 20, 24–25. For the photograph see Peter Buckley, *Ernest* (New York: Dial, 1978), p. 179; or Ernest Hemingway, *88 Poems*, ed. Nicholas Gerogiannis (New York: Harcourt Brace Jovanovich/Bruccoli Clark, 1979), p. 2.

9. Oscar Battling Nelson ("The Durable Dane") and Ad Wolgast ("The Michigan Wildcat") were in their heyday as lightweight champions intermittently from 1905–1913, although both of their careers stretched over a longer period of time. In those days many fights were scheduled for 45 rounds. In 1906, Nelson went 42 rounds before losing to the great Joe Gans. Nelson and Wolgast fought a series of great fights; Wolgast knocked out Nelson in the 40th round of their 1910 championship fight. Jack London, who was a great fight fan and a highly respected fight reporter, claimed to have sparred with Bat Nelson (Fleischer, pp. 258–59); London coined his famous fighting phrase "the abysmal brute" after watching Nelson defeat Jimmy Britt in 1905 (London, *Jack London Reports*, pp. 253–58). Ad Francis' stamina is modeled after Nelson's almost inhuman capacity for taking punishment. Ad's simple mindedness and confused memory are modeled after Wolgast's mental problems; Wolgast, who fought with his face, was institutionalized after having been cared for privately by Jack Doyle, who owned a boxing arena in Vernon, California.

Doyle was white and he was not Wolgast's trainer; Hemingway was mistaken on this point in his background notes to "The Battler" (see Baker, *Life Story*, pp. 141, 587). But, most importantly, neither Nelson nor Wolgast was ever managed by his sister (or any woman) and neither ever married his sister, or was ever involved in a scandal that resembles what happened to Ad Francis. On this essential point, Hemingway was not reporting or recasting for fiction—he was creating, which emphasizes the importance of this material to "The Battler."

10. Nick's observations on Bugs's blackjack lying on the grass, and the subsequent dialogue concerning the blackjack are not in "The Great Man" (Item 269); the material is in the untitled typescript (Item 270). This addition suggests that Hemingway had a specific purpose for including the blackjack material.

11. The sentence "I'd have warned you ... going to be all right" is not in "The Great Man" (Item 269); the line is in the untitled typescript (Item 270).

12. Ernest Hemingway. *The Nick Adams Stories* (New York: Scribner's, 1972), pp. 70–132. All subsequent references to "The Last Good Country" will be to this edition.

13. There are three copies of "The Last Good Country" in the Hemingway archives: untitled manuscript and typescript (Item 542); untitled typescript (Item 543); and untitled typescript (Item 545).

14. In the published version Nick is quoted as saying, "Just for in an emergency. Let's go down and watch them drinking" (*Nick Adams*, p. 79). However, in Hemingway's manuscript (Item 542) these sentences are two pages apart.

15. Untitled manuscript (Item 514).

16. Fielding employed incest (false) for ribald humor in *Tom Jones*. Much closer to the point, in Gabrielle d'Annunzio's *The Flame* (1900) the hero's great secret is finally revealed late in the novel: he bears an unfulfilled incestuous love for his sister. This keeps him from returning to his beloved home. Hemingway was quite fond of *The Flame*; see my analysis of the literary relationship between Hemingway and d'Annunzio in "Hemingway's Poetry: Angry Notes of an Ambivalent Overman," *College Literature*, 7 (Fall 1980), 248–62; rpt. ed., *Ernest Hemingway: The Papers of a Writer*, ed. Bernard Oldsey (New York: Garland, 1981), pp. 73–87.

KENNETH G. JOHNSTON

"A Way You'll Never Be": *A Mission of Morale*

"Listen, Jack, I'll tell you a funny thing. Who hasn't been crazy hasn't been nowhere."

—Ernest Hemingway*

In 1922 Hemingway made a pilgrimage to the village of Fossalta along the lower Piave River in northeast Italy to revisit the scene of his wounding four years earlier during the war. He was strangely disappointed by what he saw— and by what he failed to see. "'All the shattered tragic dignity of the wrecked town was gone,' he wrote. 'In its place was a new, smug, hideous collection of plaster houses.'"[1] He was struck by the discrepancy between his vivid memory of the shattered and shattering past and the peaceful scene before him:

> [There was] nothing to remind you of the war except the scars in the trees which are growing over and healing. Not a sign of the old trenches. All the wrecked houses rebuilt.... I found where I'd been wounded, it was a smooth green slope down to the river bank.... The Piave was clean and *blue*, there'd been no rain, and they were towing a big cement barge up it with horses working along where the parapet had been.[2]

From *Studies in Short Fiction* 23, no. 4 (Fall 1986): 429–436. © 1987 by Newberry College.

"'Chasing yesterdays,' said he, 'is a bum show, and if you have to prove it, go back to your old front.'"[3]

Hemingway used his old front as the locale for his short story "A Way You'll Never Be." In the story the Hemingway hero, Nicholas Adams, is also chasing yesterdays, but his is not a sentimental journey. In fact, as Sheldon Grebstein points out, "two journeys are being made concurrently: one toward the geographic setting, the actual scene of the fighting that caused Nick's wound; the other an inward journey toward a confrontation with the crippled psychic self produced by the physical wound."[4] The time is late spring or early summer, 1918. The decomposing bodies of the dead lie in the fields of grass and grain on the outskirts of Fossalta, deserted and broken by the shelling. Despite the recent fighting, the battle zone "was all very lush and over-green since he had seen it last."[5] Nick's failure to recover his full health is in sharp contrast to the renewal of nature.

Nick's ostensible mission is to boost the morale of the Italian troops by touring the lines in an American uniform to create the impression that more American troops will soon be coming; and to hand out cigarettes, chocolate, and postcards.[6] But his American uniform is "'not quite correct'" (410), and he was unable to obtain any tobacco, candy, or postcards. Furthermore, Nick's mental health is fragile, at best; twice during his brief stay at the front, he suffers a mental relapse, an attack of hysteria. In his present state, Nick's presence at the front is a demoralizing factor, as Captain Paravicini is quick to realize. "'I'm sure your appearance will be very heartening to the troops,'" Paravicini says to Nick with obvious irony (406). Later he raises a military objection to Nick's visit: "'If you move around, even with something worth giving away, the men will group and that invites shelling'" (413). In short, the official reason for Nick's daylight visit to the front lines simply does not hold up under inspection.

"'I know it's silly,' Nick said. 'It wasn't my idea'" (413). Then whose idea was it? Nick had earlier referred to a vague "they," as the ones who had told him "to circulate around anyway" (406), even without the gifts for the soldiers. Very likely the idea had originated with the doctors assigned to Nick's case. The real reason for Nick's visit, then, is therapeutic: that is, to boost Nick's morale and restore his confidence. He has been given a seemingly useful military assignment that, by sending him back into the battle zone, may exorcise some of his fear and self-doubt. As Nick admits, "'It's a hell of a nuisance once they've had you certified as nutty.... No one ever has any confidence in you again'" (407). And "no one," of course, includes Nick himself.

The motif of identification dominates the opening stages of "A Way You'll Never Be." For Nick, who has only a tenuous grip on his sanity, the question of "Who am I?" is of paramount importance. This explains his keen interest in the papers which litter the ground around the dead, whose pockets are invariably emptied in an attempt to identify the men and their units. The letters, the photographs of village girls, the mass prayer books, the occasional pictures of children, the "group postcards showing the machine-gun unit standing in ranked and ruddy cheerfulness as in a football picture for a college annual"—these give a truer answer to "Who were they?" than the "humped and swollen" bodies swarming with flies (402). At first Nick walks unchallenged among the Italian positions where the battalion is dug in along the river bank, but then as he comes around a turn in the mud bank his identity is demanded at gunpoint by a young second lieutenant:

> "Who are you?"
> Nick told him.
> "How do I know this?"
> Nick showed him the tessera with photograph and identification and the seal of the third army. He took hold of it.
> "I will keep this."
> "You will not," Nick said. "Give me back the card and put your gun away. There. In the holster."
> "How am I to know who you are?"
> "The tessera tells you."
> "And if the tessera is false? Give me that card."
> "Don't be a fool," Nick said cheerfully. "Take me to your company commander." (404)

The exchange is very revealing. Nick is determined not to give up his identification card, for this piece of paper provides him visible assurance of who he is, an assurance which he desperately needs, given his mental state. And if the tessera is false? What if Nick is no longer the same person whose photograph is shown? Captain Paravicini's greeting at battalion headquarters is not reassuring: "'Hello,' he said. 'I didn't know you'" (405). The remark is prompted, at least in part, by the strange uniform that Nick is wearing; nevertheless, it casually touches on a concern of utmost importance to Nick.

Nick's thoughts during his spells are seemingly a jumble of events, people, and places touching on his life in Paris and at the front. Presented in a stream-of-consciousness manner, the memories center on his doubts, anxieties, insecurities, and fears.[7] He recalls wearing his chin strap tight across his mouth to keep his lips from trembling before an attack; his girl going off with someone else; his fear of hailing the same taxi twice, the one they had earlier slipped out of as it was going slowly up a steep hill in Paris.

The memories are not entirely unrelated: his girl cheated on him; they cheated the taxi driver out of his fare; and Nick cheated death. In fact, there is a certain internal logic which explains the association of ideas throughout the entire sequence of recall. For example, charging up and then retreating down the slope in a military attack leads into a memory of Gaby Delys, a sensational entertainer who starred at the Folies-Bergère in Montmartre, a section of Paris situated on a hill dominated by the white domes of Sacré Coeur. This allusion to the church of the Sacred Heart naturally lends itself to the ideas of purity and betrayal (Christ's) and fuses with memories of his girl, whose unfaithfulness raises questions about Nick's manhood. And the girl who wounded his pride gives way to memories of the place where he was blown up at the front.

Nick reveals that he is most frightened by his dreams of a yellow house by a wide, still river outside Fossalta. "Now he was back here at the river, he had gone through that same town, and there was no house. Nor was the river that way" (409). In his dreams, it is quite clear, Nick revisits the scene of his wounding.[8] But now that he has actually returned to the very place, he finds that the scene has changed, for the yellow house has been destroyed in an attack and the width and current of the lower Piave River varies with the season. Now that Nick is aware of how fragile his hold on life and sanity is, neither the river nor, for that matter, anything else will ever appear quite the same again.

When Nick dreams about a yellow house by a river, he awakens, "soaking wet, more frightened than he had ever been in a bombardment" (409). Sigmund Freud remarked on this form of "illness made so common by the war":

> The traumatic neuroses demonstrate very clearly that a fixation to the moment of the traumatic occurrence lies at their root. These patients regularly produce the traumatic situation in their dreams; in cases showing attacks of an hysterical type in which analysis is possible, it appears that the attack constitutes a complete reproduction of this situation. It is as though these persons had not yet been able to deal adequately with the situation, as if this task were still actually before them unaccomplished.[9]

Nick's recurring nightmares and his inability to sleep without a light give clear evidence that he has not yet been able to deal adequately with his traumatic situation.

Nick's rambling lecture on grasshoppers, which so alarms the adjutant that he sends runners to summon the Captain, provides another revealing symptom of his mental state. Nick is desperately trying to prevent a slide into mental chaos by fastening his thoughts on a safe and sane topic from another time, another place. The grasshopper is associated in Nick's mind with the trout fishing of his youth. (see "Now I Lay Me" and "Big Two-Hearted River") The grasshopper monologue is Nick's frantic attempt to block out disturbing thoughts and to reclaim some of the serenity, confidence, and peace of mind of that earlier, simpler time. He concludes it by quoting Sir Henry Wilson:[10] "'Gentlemen, either you must govern or you must be governed'" (412). The implications are clear. Either Nick must govern his thoughts and actions, or someone else will have to control his activities.

When Captain Paravicini returns, he immediately realizes that he has underestimated the seriousness of Nick's condition. Gently but firmly, he imposes discipline and control on Nick. He all but orders Nick to go back to Fornaci. "'I won't have you circulating around to no purpose,'" he tells him (413). But when Nick's replies become irrational, the Captain tries to delay his friend's departure. Nick is especially upset by the unburied dead: "'Why don't they bury the dead? I've seen them now. I don't care about seeing them again. They can bury them any time as far as I'm concerned and it would be much better for you. You'll all get bloody sick'" (413). At the beginning of the story Nick appeared not to have been shaken by his inspection of the corpses. They were simply part of "the débris" of the battle. Like a disciplined, dispassionate soldier, he observed in detail the carnage and noted that the positions of the dead showed "the manner and the skill of the attack" (403). But now we learn how disturbing to Nick that sight had been—a vivid reminder of his own mortality, his own condition. For Nick, too, in his present state, is part of the débris of war. And the unburied dead, like his own unburied past, pose a threat to his mental health.

At Paravicini's urging, Nick once again lies down to rest a while, but his thoughts immediately center on "a long, yellow house with a low stable and the river much wider than it was and stiller" (414). The mention of the stable evokes an ironic allusion to the Christ child: "On earth peace, good will toward men" (Luke 2:14). But neither Nick's world nor his mind is at peace, and he abruptly interrupts his flow of memories. "'Christ,' he said, 'I might as well go.'" Paravicini offers to send along a runner, but Nick declines: "'I'd rather you didn't. I know the way.'" When the Captain starts to repeat the offer, Nick interrupts him: "'No,' said Nick. 'As a mark of confidence'" (414).

It is very important to Nick and his self-confidence that he retrieve something from this abortive mission of morale. To accept the escort would amount to a public admission of dependence and mental illness. However, as the story ends, Nick is privately worried: "'I'd better get to that damned bicycle,' Nick said to himself. 'I don't want to lose the way to Fornaci'" (414). Little wonder, for already twice that day, psychologically speaking, he has lost his way.

The autobiographical element is very strong in "A Way You'll Never Be," but Nick's head wound and severe mental condition are fictional inventions. As Hemingway once wrote, "For one thing that I had seen or that had happened to me I knew many hundreds of things that had happened to other people who had been in the war in all of its phases. My own small experiences gave me a touchstone by which I could tell whether stories were true or false and being wounded was a password."[11] But it is true, as Hemingway's brother reveals, that "not all of Ernest's wounds were physical. Like hundreds of thousands of other soldiers before and since, he had received some psychic shock. He was plagued by insomnia and couldn't sleep unless he had a light in his room."[12] Some thirty years later while on safari in Africa, Hemingway himself would recall the troubled nights of his early years in Paris after the war: "I had bad dreams then as a residue, or inheritance, from a badly organized war, and sleep, or his brother death, were all that interested me at night."[13]

Hemingway had especial difficulty in writing "A Way You'll Never Be." "'I had tried to write it back in the Twenties, but had failed several times. I had given up on it but one day here, fifteen years after those things happened to me in a trench dugout outside Fornaci, it suddenly came out focused and complete. Here in Key West, of all places. Old as I am, I continue to be amazed at the sudden emergence of daffodils and stories.'"[14] But still the opening to the story did not come easily. The manuscript and typescript fragments at the Kennedy Library show five false starts, one of which reads:

> July was a bad month for him. He was born in July and wounded
> on the eighth of July and he lay in the grass outside the edge of
> the town.[15]

Today this discarded opening could well serve as a synopsis of Hemingway's own life and death: Hemingway was born on July 21, 1899; wounded on July 8, 1918; and laid to rest "in the grass outside the edge of the town" (Ketchum, Idaho) on July 6, 1961. Using a double-barreled shotgun, Hemingway killed himself on July 2 in the oak-paneled foyer of his Ketchum home two days after his return from Mayo Clinic, where he had undergone a series of shock treatments for mental illness.

NOTES

* "The Art of the Short Story," manuscript 251 b, Kennedy Library. Quoted with permission of Mary Hemingway.

1. Hemingway, quoted in Carlos Baker, *Ernest Hemingway: A Life Story* (New York: Scribner's, 1969), p. 94.

2. *Ernest Hemingway: Selected Letters, 1917–1961*, ed. Carlos Baker (New York: Scribner's, 1981), p. 86.

3. Hemingway, quoted in Carlos Baker, *Ernest Hemingway: A Life Story*, p. 94.

4. Sheldon Norman Grebstein, *Hemingway's Craft* (Carbondale and Edwardsville: Southern Illinois University Press 1973) p. 18.

5. Ernest Hemingway, "A Way You'll Never Be," in *The Short Stories of Ernest Hemingway* (New York: Scribner's, 1953), p. 404. All further references to the story will be cited parenthetically in the text. "A Way You'll Never Be" first appeared in *Winner Take Nothing* (New York: Scribner's, 1933).

6. Nick's mission of morale had some basis in fact. Hemingway, who had volunteered for duty at the Red Cross canteen at the village of Fossalta, did bicycle to the front everyday "'laden down ... with chocolate, cigars, cigarets, and postcards'" (Charles A. Fenton, *The Apprenticeship of Ernest Hemingway: The Early Years* [New York: Farrar, Straus & Young, 1954], p. 64). And an American regiment was sent to Italy "to stimulate the Italian morale." "Mr. Orlando, the Italian Prime Minister, wanted them sent direct from the States in order that they might go through Italy by rail to show the people that Americans were actually there" (John J. Pershing, *My Experiences in the World War* [New York: Stokes, 1931], II, 37, 94). The American regiment arrived in Italy in late July 1918, several weeks after Hemingway was wounded. It made a propaganda tour of the country and saw action only in the last few days of the war.

7. "Some day when the psycho-an are forgotten," F. Scott Fitzgerald believed, "E.H. will be read for his great studies into fear" (*The Notebooks of F. Scott Fitzgerald*, ed. Matthew J. Bruccoli [New York: Harcourt Brace Jovanovich/Bruccoli Clark 1978] p. 385).

8. Years later, another Hemingway hero (Colonel Cantwell) revisits this same scene: "A few weeks ago he had gone through Fossalta and had gone out along the sunken road to find the place where he had been hit, out on the river bank. It was easy to find because of the bend of the river, and where the heavy machine gun post had been, the crater was smoothly grassed. It had been cropped, by sheep or goats, until it looked like a designed depression in a golf course. The river was slow and muddy blue here, with reeds along the edges, and the Colonel, no one being in sight, squatted low, and looking across the river from the bank where you could never show your head in daylight, relieved himself in the exact place where he had determined, by triangulation, that he had been badly wounded thirty years before.... Then he looked across the river to the rebuilt white house that had once been rubble, and he spat in the river" (Hemingway, *Across the River and into the Trees* [New York: Scribner's, 1950], pp. 17–19). Hemingway himself had revisited the scene again in the fall of 1948.

9. Sigmund Freud, "Fixation upon Traumas: The Unconscious," in *A General Introduction to Psycho-Analysis*, trans. Joan Riviere (1922: Clarion Book rpt., New York: Simon & Schuster, 1969). p. 243.

10. Sir Henry Hughes Wilson (1864–1922), British soldier, became Chief of the Imperial Staff in 1918. After the crushing Italian defeat at Caporetto, he traveled to Italy

to confer with General Porro, the Italian Chief of Staff, and to tour the newly established Italian front on the Piave River.

11. Hemingway, "On Writing in First Person," unpublished section of manuscript, 178, Kennedy Library. Quoted with permision of Mary Hemingway.

12. Leicester Hemingway, *My Brother, Ernest Hemingway* (Cleveland: World, 1962), p. 56. Like his brother and his father, Leicester Hemingway committed suicide. Depressed because of problems with diabetes, he shot himself to death on September 13, 1982.

13. Hemingway, "An African Journal, Part 3: Imperiled Flanks," *Sports Illustrated*, Jan. 10, 1972, p. 49. Several times in his journal of the 1953 safari, Hemingway writes of his troubled sleep. On one sleepless night, he tries to recall F. Scott Fitzgerald's haunting line from *The Crack-Up*; "In a real dark night of the soul it is always three o'clock in the morning, day after day." On another "bad night," a rainy night, he awakens twice "sweating with nightmares," and drinks some gin ("the old Giant Killer") to make himself "brave against the nightmare" ("An African Journal, Part 1: Miss Mary's Lion," *Sports Illustrated*, Dec. 29, 1971, pp. 60-61).

14. Hemingway, quoted in A. E. Hotchner, *Papa Hemingway: A Personal Memoir* (New York: Random House, 1966), pp. 162-163.

15. EH typescript fragments, 814, Kennedy Library. Quoted with permission of Mary Hemingway.
The other false starts for "A Way You'll Never Be" are as follows:

1) "As I came into the town walking the bicycle along the street to avoid the shell holes"—

2) "The line ran along the"—

3) "We had come up to the river a week before just at dusk and ever since we had been living"—

4) "It is all over now and has been for a long time and we would do better not to mention it but once we lay in the tall grass outside the edge of the town." (manuscript fragment, 813; EH typescript fragments, 814, Kennedy Library. Quoted with permission of Mary Hemingway.)

LAWRENCE BROER

Hemingway's "On Writing":
A Portrait of the Artist as Nick Adams

A fragment omitted from Hemingway's summer 1924 masterpiece, "Big Two-Hearted River," "On Writing" remained unpublished until 1972, when Philip Young included it in the posthumous anthology The Nick Adams Stories. *"On Writing" contains Nick's reflections about the literary life as he fishes for trout, reflections undisguisedly Hemingway's own as Nick muses about what he has learned from James Joyce, Ezra Pound, Gertrude Stein, Theodore Dreiser, Sherwood Anderson, Ring Lardner, Donald Stewart, Nathan Asch, e.e. cummings, Archibald MacLeish, bullfighting, and Cézanne landscapes. Critics have probably neglected the "story" for the same reason that Hemingway wisely omitted it from "Big Two-Hearted River"—"On Writing" commits the identical sin of which it accuses James Joyce: "That was the weakness of Joyce. Daedalus in Ulysses was Joyce himself, so he was terrible. Joyce was so damned romantic and intellectual about him." Yet in Lawrence Broer's opinion, "the weakness of Joyce" is the strength of "On Writing." Because Hemingway uses Nick in "On Writing" as Joyce used Daedalus in* Portrait of the Artist as a Young Man, *the "story" becomes an illumination of the generic artist's formative process and an intriguing comment not only on "Big Two-Hearted River" but on other Nick Adams stories as well.*

Critics have praised Hemingway's "objectivity" as if the author's precise presentation of concrete detail were his major accomplishment. In landmark

---

From *Hemingway's Neglected Short Fiction*, edited by Susan F. Beegel: 131–140. © 1989 by Susan Field Beegel.

discussions of Hemingway's craft, Mark Schorer cities "insistence on the objective and unreflective, on the directness and the brevity of syntactical constructions"[1] as the style that made Hemingway famous, and E. M. Halliday argues that the clarity and sharpness of Hemingway's objective projection of reality are two of Hemingway's most "celebrated virtues."[2] Unlike Joyce, Halliday says, Hemingway leaves no confusion as to where the subjective (the labyrinth of the hero's mind) ceases, and the objective (the material world) begins.[3] Harry Levin notes that in Hemingway's quest for "immediacy," the writing seems so intent upon the "actual" that his readers become "beholders."[4] Finally, John Graham observes that "the testimony of the participant's senses can be accepted as objective, if limited, fact."[5] Graham recognizes that Hemingway's typical narrator is no mere receiving instrument, but reflects that the relationship between subject and object may be so direct and simple that no challenge is offered to the reader demanding extended mental activity, subtle or otherwise.[6]

Few writers have been as successful as Hemingway at projecting felt experience—what *feels* or *seems* actual—with such vitality and immediacy. The view of Hemingway as a literalist or objectivist was of course encouraged by Hemingway's axiom that a writer should only write about what he has personally experienced, by correspondences between Hemingway and his protagonists, and by the author's frequent use of aesthetic absolutes to describe his artistic goals, his quest for the "true," the "pure," and the ideal." In a famous passage in *Green Hills of Africa* (1935), he said that "A writer's problem does not change.... It is always how to write truly and having found what is true, to project it in such a way that it becomes part of the experience of the person who reads it."[7] Oft quoted is Hemingway's declaration in *Death in the Afternoon* (1932) to write— "knowing *truly* what you really felt, rather than what you were supposed to feel," and to put down "what *really* happened in action ... the *real* thing, the sequence of motion and fact which made the emotion...."[8] In a letter to his father, Hemingway declared that he could achieve a third or even a fourth dimension in prose—"the feeling of actual life"—so that "when you have read something by me you actually experience the thing."[9] Hemingway's forte was to evoke poignantly the good things life offers—the earth's sensual rhythms and tactile delights—but praise of verisimilitude in Hemingway's work has too often steered critical interest to the character of Hemingway rather than to the nature and quality of his art. The view of Hemingway's action as therapeutic process—Cowley's or Young's readings of the work as exorcism or ritualistic expiation[10]—suggests even a kind of creative helplessness in which the author was not in control of his art. Hemingway, Cowley said is a novelist who wrote not as he should or would but as he must, subject to personal demons.[11] Or the author comes across as a kind of master recorder—a writer capable of the most lucid modern prose—but somehow more artistically simple-minded and straightforward than his more praised contemporaries, Joyce and Faulkner.

In *The Garden of Eden* (1986) and the posthumous Nick Adams story called "On Writing,"[12] Hemingway shows that his use of personal experience, his approach to "truth," was far from simple or direct. Rather his relationship to his material was intricate, complex, and profoundly subjective.[13] "Above all else," the aspiring writer declares in "On Writing," "you had to do it from inside yourself" (239). "Nick in the stories was never himself," he explains, rather you had to "create your own people" (238), to reconstitute reality in the crucible of imagination.

Hemingway had said it before—prose was architecture, not interior decoration.[14] In *A Moveable Feast*, he wrote, "I was learning something from the painting of Cézanne that made writing simple true sentences far from enough to make the stories have the dimensions that I was trying to put in them...."[15] The "real thing," that which produced beauty and great emotion, was not the simple reproduction of people and events, the "objective data of experience,"[16] but that which the artist makes in rearranging conventional ways of seeing the world. This is exactly what David Bourne does in *The Garden of Eden*. The novel's numerous references to "invention" and to things "made up" indicate Hemingway's interest in the postmodern theme of subjective reality—reality as artifice—which he employs here in an ambitious and ingenious way. Through David's preoccupation with "imperfect memory,"[17] and through the interweaving of the fictions David writes with the one he is in, Hemingway portrays fiction and reality as indistinguishable—suggesting that it is not literal truth that matters, which is always shifting and elusive, but the symbolic or personal truths that we ourselves create through "imperfect remembering" and subjective coloration. David Bourne's creations are humanistic and vital; Catherine's are perverse and self-destructive. With the blocking of life-directed, creative energies, Catherine's tormented mind turns to dangerous, exotic forms of invention which intensify to disaster by the story's close.

As with David Bourne, writing is the chief passion in life for the protagonist of "On Writing." When discussed at all, "On Writing" is viewed as a fragment of or alternative ending to "Big Two-Hearted River."[18] As we shall see, the similarity of setting and character does make for informative intertextual study. Nick in "On Writing" is still exorcising some nameless anxiety typical of the shell-shocked hero of "Big Two-Hearted River"— anxiety related to the mutilations of war, the end of human relationships, the death of love. Nick remembers experiences we know from "The End of

Something," "The Three Day Blow," "Cross-Country Snow," "My Old Man," "Indian Camp," and "Big Two-Hearted River." But "On Writing" is no mere appendage or missing portion of the iceberg of the more famous story. Like *The Garden of Eden*, "On Writing" is intriguing metafiction that comments not only upon other Nick Adams stories but upon the entire corpus of Hemingway's fiction. Its exuberant tone and fluid imagery project a far more hopeful and healthy character, one aware of the power of art to shape human destiny and less afraid of complexity.

Hemingway uses Nick in "On Writing" precisely as Joyce uses Stephen Daedalus in *Portrait of the Artist as a Young Man*—to illuminate the formative process of the generic artist while using art to exorcise personal demons to reshape a world of failed traditional values. Like Stephen, Nick exults in creativity as his greatest pleasure and raison d'être. Nick "felt almost holy about it" (239). But Nick chides Joyce for working too close to life, for using Stephen Daedalus as a too-literal representation of himself in *Ulysses*. Nick's joy of invention comes from personal discipline and from learning to transform discontent into creative energy. He always worked best, Nick reflects, when Helen was unwell: "Just that much discontent and friction" (238). But most of all his pleasure comes from learning to reconstruct rather than copy reality, which makes writing "more fun than anything" (238). As with Cézanne, Nick's major artistic inspiration, his fidelity is not to external experience but to the reality inside himself. He remembers that at one point, his "whole inner life had been bullfights" (236). Writing about "anything actual" was in fact a mistake. "The *only* writing that was any good was what you made up, what you imagined. That *made* everything come true" (237). Everything he had done well "he'd made up," like "My Old Man": he'd never seen a jockey killed and the next week Georges Parfrement was killed at that very jump and that was the way it looked…. None of it had ever happened" (237). Nick says his family could not understand that. They assumed it was all personal experience. He had, for instance, "never seen an Indian woman having a baby. *That* was what made it good" (238). Later he reflects, "If it sounded good they took your word for it" (240).

We would today call the subject of this story postmodern—exploring the connections between audience and art, and the interrelatedness of life and art as fictional constructs. As with Stephen Daedalus and David Bourne, Nick's salvation lies in learning to approach life as an open-ended text in which he can write his own life story. Far from being an orthodox tale about the problems of Nick's war trauma and postwar emotional readjustment, "On Writing" transforms itself into a provocative story about ways of perceiving reality, about the impossibility of determining truth in absolute terms, about the way perception arises from the relative roles we play, and about the way the nature of the perceiver determines what is perceived. It is the text's nonclosure, its plurality of meaning, its presentation of character multiple perspectives, and its rejuvenated system of language (the use of new "signifieds" for old "signifiers") that hold center stage.[19]

Nick consciously disputes surface objectivity, blurring the distinction between art and the actual by describing himself walking across the stream in a Cézanne painting. When Nick writes that he steps into water that was "cold and actual" (240), it is simultaneously Cézanne's conception as well as the real stream that Nick wades. As with David Bourne, the narrator lives half in the world of invention and imperfect memory and half in the present. Fantasy and reality merge as Nick reconstructs bullfights, fishing trips, and complex relationship with old friends: "sometimes he had it that way in dreams" (236).

Central to Nick's fluid epistemology is that nothing stands still. Events are recounted as a kaleidoscopic blur of shifting, elusive emotional associations, "storms on the lake ... climbing up, sliding down, the wave following behind ... the mail and the Chicago paper under a tarpaulin ... the wind in the hemlocks ..." (236). Truth is always situational, determined by mood, a weather change, for instance, variables of time or place, others' perceptions, or entrenched prejudice. Subjects such as fishing or bullfighting, love or poetry were tragic or comical, fake or real, because people "thought" they were so; people treated you this way or that because you were Spanish or French, English or American (234). Nick's imperfect remembering consists of surmise, hearsay, images from movies, phrases from newspapers, so that he can only "guess" why he has lost certain girls, why he first liked bullfights, or who the great writers are. Your values come from "this fake ideal planted in you" and "you lived your life to it" (235). Struggling to understand his love of bullfighting, he reflects, "That must have been Maera" (237). What Nick remembers about his "horror" of people getting married "*probably* [my italics] resulted from his association with older ... non-marrying people" (235). He knows that whether fishing was more important than marrying was something "he had built ... up" (234). Evaluating writers, he muses that "Young Asch had something but *you couldn't tell*" [my italics] (239). So did Ring Lardner—"maybe" (239). Ironically, only the greatest impressionist of them all, Gertrude Stein, would know if he, Nick, ever got things right (239).

Nick dislocates fixed perceptions by introducing a simultaneity of conflicting points of view in the manner of a Picasso collage, what Patricia Waugh calls an "interpretation of frames."[20] As those impenetrable, problematical currents and shadows and blinding glare pile up on Nick to complicate his musing about the "truths" of fishing, hunting, bullfighting, art, and love, he, along with the reader, must sort out contradictory explanations of "the way it was" from multiple perspectives provided by Helen, Bill, Bill's dentist, Kate, Odgar, and others whose realities are as personal and ambiguous as his own. Helen is remembered a certain way because Nick's friends did not like her, which also distorts her feelings about them (235). Nick, Don, Chink differ on bullfighting because they view it with varying degrees of *aficion* (237). Perceptions of reality, of value, are as self-reflexive as the river's "mirror" that symbolizes the swirling currents and shadowy depths of Nick's own mind (233).

Nick's awareness of reality as an open, dynamic text informs his efforts to construct a more durable, authentic self. His playful use of language foregrounds his narrative as artifice, connecting linguistic systems to the formation of the "actual" or "real." "Once Bill meant Bill Smith," he muses. Now it means Bill Bird. Bill Bird lives in Paris now" (234). Nick knows that sentimental language and the duplicitous moral abstractions of movies or romantic novels make the world "unreal" (233, 237) and that short of avoiding language altogether, he must challenge the traditional signification of words that have turned into clichés by inventing new language conventions. Nick resists the outworn language and traditional wisdom of all the books" (233) and seeks more inventive or "true" systems of signification that will overturn the "fake" language, fake ideals, of his cultural inheritance.

The aesthetic perspective of "On Writing" shows that Hemingway's quest for "the real thing" was a matter of simulation rather than recalling and simply reproducing what he had seen or felt. Such a view obligates us to examine Hemingway's characters as complex, independent creations rather than simple projections of Hemingway. It challenges the view of the code hero as a static or inflexible individual closed to new ideas. Finally the story's postmodern formulations remind us that Hemingway is a writer for all times whose resources of imagination and invention are too seldom emphasized. It illustrates the problematical richness of fiction whose meanings vary and which possesses multiple dimensions—physical, psychological, literary, social, and metaphysical. In *Critical Practice*, Catherine Belsey explains why a story such as "On Writing" excites our interpretive imagination and why its reader must be an active participant in the creation of meaning rather than a "beholder" of direct or simple truths: "Composed of contradictions, the text is no longer restricted to a simple, harmonious and authoritative reading. Instead it becomes plural, open to rereading, no longer an object for passive consumption but an object of work by the reader to produce meaning."[21]

We can only guess what it is that Nick holds "in his head" at the end his narrative (241), as Nick can only guess what has happened to the dazed rabbit he helps on the trail. He no doubt identifies with its hurt as he picks the animal up, pulls ticks from its head, and places it under a sweet fern bush beside the trail. Just moments before, Nick had freed trout from his sack back into the stream, rationalizing that they were too big to eat. These life-,affirming actions conclude a portrait of a young artist who was gentle, compassionate, and vulnerable, and for whom self-discipline and artistic ingenuity made life worthwhile.

In their treatments of "Big Two-Hearted River," to which "On Writing" was originally appended, Philip Young and Sheridan Baker appear impressed more with the usual correspondences between Nick and Hemingway than with the aesthetic implications of "On Writing" for the larger story. Young stresses the interchangeableness of author and protagonist; for example "the river narrowed" may be a direct reference to the river at Fossalta.[22] Baker highlights events Hemingway recorded directly rather than those he made up. What Hemingway counts as fiction, Baker says, contains a "high saturation of actuality."[23]

To foreground the story's verisimilitude rather than its artifice again compromises the author's remarkable inventive skill and obscures the story's epistemology. Like the streams Nick makes up in "Now I Lay Me" ("Some nights I made up streams ... it was like being awake and dreaming"), it is the symbolic stream Nick fishes, his psychic experience, that matters in this tale. Baker himself notes Hemingway's breach with journalistic accuracy. The river is not the Two-Hearted River, it is the Fox. Its color comes from swampy vegetation, not, as Hemingway seemingly reports, from pebbles on the bottom. Projecting figurative rather than literal meanings, Hemingway changes the time of the burning of the town of Seney, increases its devastation, and defies fact by blackening his grasshoppers. He puts the flat site of Seney on a hillside to make Nick's climb an allegorical one and to foreground impressionistic effects.[24]

The therapeutic aspect of Nick's fishing trip has been much discussed.[25] Just as the trout hold themselves "steady in the current,"[26] Nick seeks to distance himself from the painful memories of war and to calm his nerves by occupying himself with the simple, elemental challenge of making a good camp. Nick can manage tasks that are direct and physical, but allowing his mind to work will invite feelings of vulnerability and helplessness associated with the war. The only memory Nick allows himself ("his mind was starting to work" [218]) is of a friendship with Hopkins, the loss of which troubles Nick. The physical therapy is effective; he welcomes the earth against his back, the smell of canvas and sweet fern, the taste of hot beans and coffee; the ailing Fisher King is on the mend, his "now living rod" (224) resurrected amid the primitive rhythms of wood and stream. Nick feels stable as long as he avoids philosophical abstractions or moral complexity, those parabolic shadows and swampy tangles that prevent him from fishing the stream's darker, faster water until a later time. Suggesting psychic exploration for which Nick is not yet prepared, such fishing would be "a tragic adventure" (231), facing hidden depths and unpredictable currents where the water suddenly piled up on you (229), and vision was obscured by "the half light" (231) and overhanging trees.

Ironically, Nick feels he has left such thinking behind, with the concomitant need to write (210), whereas it is only when he fords the deeper stream, the stream of consciousness as well as the stream of life itself, bringing repressed experience to consciousness, that he will complete his return to health. Herein lies the essential difference between the wounded exsoldier in "Big Two-Hearted River," who can let out his mental line only so far before the strain becomes unbearable and he becomes sick and shaky (226), and the aspiring writer in "On Writing," who has acquired the courage to confront traumatic past experience and the necessary knowledge of self and craft to transmute such experience into art and thus create a more stable and durable identity. In short, the Nick of "Big Two-Hearted River" is not sufficiently ready to practice what Nick in "On Writing" has learned from Cézanne—that people and events restructured in the imagination will produce greater satisfaction than anything he has ever known. Conversely, as Philip Young observes, "On Writing" recalls the "very moment when the mature career began." Nick is "off to start the story that Hemingway writes in 'Big Two-Hearted River.'"27

In "Big Two-Hearted River," then, Hemingway has superbly mastered the artistic and epistemological intricacies with which his protagonist must come to grips. While Nick resists the exertions of mind, Hemingway's mind and artistic conscience operate brilliantly, exemplified by the creation of an imperfect and morally uncertain, parabolic world whose meanings defy closure and in which truth is personal and self-created. Nick's best efforts to steady or fix or simplify life are contradicted by a world of flux, perpetual motion, and moral uncertainty. Nick's vision during his climb through the fire-burned countryside is blurred by aching muscles, by the dark, fragmentary pine trees (211) which he "could hardly see" in the heat-light ("If he looked too steadily they were gone. But if he only half-looked they were there ..." [211]), by the unsettled dust, frequent rises and descents (212), rising mist (216), and dark vegetation (229). Later, his efforts to hold himself steady in the stream are met by uncooperative currents, varying shallows and deep pools, and tortuous bends. The elusive trout change "their positions by quick angles" (209); the glassy convex surface of the pool distorts their shapes, and the larger trout disappear completely in the "varying mist of gravel and sand raised ... by the current" (209). It is only "the shadow of the

Kingfisher" that he perceives moving up the stream to become lost in the sun and swift current.

Nick's epistemological dilemma is further complicated by contradictions in his own soul—the tendency to gentleness and compassion versus the impulse to cruelty. The same grasshoppers with which he empathizes he later uses for bait, crushing or slamming them with his hat (222), "threading the hook under his chin, down through his thorax and into the last segments of his abdomen." Nick's schizophrenic sensibility, half primitive, half civilized, allows him to feel happy about the trout he releases into the stream, whose pain Nick has caused.

It is both Nick's inability to know reality for sure, as he can only "wonder" about the fire-scarred town of Seney, the sooty grasshoppers that whirl up in front of him, or the long-range implications of his own psychic wound, and his willful flight from such realities that Nick must confront to progress beyond the emotional holding pattern of "Big Two-Hearted River." The inner equilibrium Nick seeks awaits not in distancing himself from the emotional baggage he has left home from his trip, baggage the reader will bring to the reading, the conjunctive experience alongside the reader's own intrapersonal river, but by eliciting the moral courage and imaginative presence of the maturing artist in "On Writing."

NOTES

1. Mark Schorer, "The Background of a Style, "*Ernest Hemingway: Critiques of Four Major Novels*, ed. Carlos Baker (New York: Charles Scribner's Sons, 1962) 88.

2. E. M. Halliday, "Hemingway's Narrative Perspective," in *Critiques of Four Major Novels*, 175.

3. Halliday, 177.

4. Harry Levin, "The Style of Hemingway," in *Hemingway and His Critics*, ed. Carlos Baker (New York: Hill & Wang, 1961) 111, 113.

5. John Graham, "Ernest Hemingway: The Meaning of Style," in *Critiques of Four Major Novels*, (184).

6. Graham's observation that the subject is "aware of his act of perception" is a major tenet of postmodern fiction (184).

7. Ernest Hemingway, *Green Hills of Africa* (New York: Charles Scribner's Sons, 1935) 37.

8. Ernest Hemingway, *Death in the Afternoon* (New York: Charles Scribner's Sons, 1932) 2.

9. Cited in *Ernest Hemingway: On Writing*, ed. Larry Phillips (New York: Charles Scribner's Sons, 1984) 153.

10. See Malcolm Cowley, "Nightmare and Ritual in Hemingway," in *Hemingway: A Collection of Critical Essays*, ed. Robert P. Weeks (Englewood Cliffs: Prentice Hall, 1962) 40–52, and Philip Young, *Ernest Hemingway*, Pamphlets on American Writers 1 (Minneapolis: U of Minnesota P, 1959).

11. Cowley, 51. Studies as recent as those by Jeffrey Meyers and Kenneth Lynn stress the writing as the product more of private hurts than of artistic ingenuity.

12. Ernest Hemingway, "On Writing," in *The Nick Adams Stories*, ed. Philip Young (New York: Charles Scribner's Sons, 1972) 233–41. All further references to "On Writing" are to this edition.

13. James Nagel points out that while little understood by modern scholars, Hemingway's mode was basically impressionistic as early as 1920. Impressionism was a movement Hemingway could hardly have avoided. Nagel discusses the "epistemological distortions" that keep Nick's perceptions in a constant state of flux. The alleged objective narrator must continuously struggle with problems of truth and illusion, and finally the reader must rely on his *own* perception and sensitivity to reveal the psychic drama. See "Literary Impressionism and *In Our Time*," *The Hemingway Review* (Spring 1987): 17–26. For other commentary on epistemological complexity in Hemingway's work, see Emily Stipes Watts, *Ernest Hemingway and the Arts* (Urbana: U of Illinois P, 1971); Richard Peterson, *Hemingway: Direct and Oblique* (Paris: Norton, 1969); Raymond Nelson, *Hemingway; Expressionist Artist* (Ames: Iowa State UP, 1979); Sheldon Norman Grebstein, *Hemingway's Craft* (Carbondale: Southern Illinois UP, 1973).

14. Death in the Afternoon, 191.

15. Ernest Hemingway, *A Moveable Feast* (New York: Charles Scribner's Sons, 1964) 13.

16. Mario Praz, "Hemingway in Italy," in *Hemingway and His Critics*, 118.

17. Ernest Hemingway, *The Garden of Eden* (New York: Charles Scribner's Sons, 1986) 174, 211. As early as *Death in the Afternoon*, Hemingway remarks that the only reality is what one remembers, and "Memory, of course, is never true" (100).

18. See Joseph M. Flora, *Hemingway's Nick Adams Stories* (Baton Rouge: Louisiana State UP, 1982).

19. I am indebted to Constance Pedoto for her insights into Hemingway's postmodern tendencies. See her dissertation, "*Il Gioco del Nulla*: Ernest Hemingway and Italo Calvino's Construction of Nothingness" (U of South Florida, 1988).

20. Patricia Waugh, Metafiction: The Theory and Practice of Self-Conscious Fiction (London and New York: Methuen, 1980) 8.

21. Catherine Belsey, *Critical Practice* (London and New York: Methuen, 1980) 104.

22. Philip Young, "Big World Out There: The Nick Adams Stories," in *The Short Stories of Ernest Hemingway: Critical Essays*, ed. Jackson J. Benson (Durham: Duke UP, 1975) 39.

23. Sheridan Baker, "Hemingway's Two-Hearted River," in Benson, 158.

24. Baker, 151, 157.

25. See the aforementioned essays by Cowley, Young, and Baker.

26. *The Short Stories of Ernest Hemingway* (New York: Charles Scribner's Sons, 1966) 209. All further references to "Big Two-Hearted River" are to this edition.

27. Young, "Big World Out There," 42.

KENNETH S. LYNN

The Troubled Fisherman

T he longest of the fishing trips he took in the summer of 1919 was into
the woods in the upper peninsula of Michigan near the town of Seney, about
fifteen miles south of Lake Superior. In seven days of casting in the Big Fox
and Little Fox rivers, Ernest and two friends, Al Walker and Jock Pentecost,
caught about two hundred trout. One of the fish pulled in by Jock was fifteen
and a half inches long, but it was Ernest who almost landed what would have
been the prize catch. "I lost one on the Little Fox below an old dam," he
wrote to Howie Jenkins, "that was the biggest trout I've ever seen. I was up
in some old timbers and it was a case of horse out. I got about half of him out
of wasser and my hook broke at the shank!"[1] He did, however, gather in the
materials for a notable piece of fiction.

In the fish story he had just finished writing, he told Gertrude Stein
and Alice B. Toklas on August 15, 1924, he had been "trying to do the
country like Cézanne and having a hell of a time and sometimes getting it a
little bit. It is about 100 pages long and nothing happens and the country is
swell. I made it all up, so I see it all and part of it comes out the way it ought
to, it is swell about the fish, but isn't writing a hard job though?"[2] His sense
that the story was swell about the fish was not mistaken. ("He watched them
holding themselves with their noses into the current, many trout in deep, fast
moving water, slightly distorted as he watched far down through the glassy

From *New Critical Approaches to the Short Stories of Ernest Hemingway*, edited by Jackson J.
Benson: 149–155. © 1990 by Duke University Press.

convex surface of the pool, its surface pushing and swelling smooth against the resistance of the log-driven piles of the bridge.")[3] Nor was he speaking idly when he suggested that his recreations of landscape were like a series of pictures by Cézanne. ("Ahead of him, as far as he could see, was the pine plain. The burned country stopped off at the left with the range of hills. On ahead islands of dark pine trees rose out of the plain. Far off to the left was the line of the river.")[4] In two respects, that is to say, his letter furnished the Misses Stein and Toklas with an accurate sense of what he had accomplished. But interestingly enough, he made no mention of the most difficult of all the objectives he had been seeking to attain in "Big Two-Hearted River": to endow a story in which "nothing happens" with an inner drama of terrific intensity.

As the solitary Nick Adams leaves the train station at Seney and walks across a "burned-over country" toward "the far blue hills that marked the Lake Superior height of land,"[5] he feels a wonderful sense of release. "He felt he had left everything behind, the need for thinking, the need to write, other needs. It was all back of him."[6] Toward the end of the day he pitches his tent and crawls inside, noting with pleasure how "homelike" the space seems. At last, he thinks, "he was settled. Nothing could touch him. It was a good place to camp. He was there, in the good place. He was in his home where he had made it."[7]

From this point forward the story abounds in details of how splendid the fishing is and of what a good time Nick is having. Nevertheless, dark thoughts of some sort are lurking on the margins of his consciousness. While he is finishing his supper the first night, he suddenly becomes aware that his mind is "starting to work," but because he is tired he is able to "choke it."[8] The next day his happiness is again interrupted. An arduous battle with the biggest trout he has ever seen ends with the trout's escape, and as Nick is reeling in his line he feels "a little sick, as though it would be better to sit down."[9] To avoid the possibility of a second defeat in one day, he thereupon modifies his plans. Instead of plunging into the armpit-deep water of a swamp overshadowed by big trees, where he might hook big trout in places impossible to land them, he decides to postpone the adventure. "There were plenty of days coming when he could fish the swamp," he says to himself, as the story ends.[10]

What are the "other needs" Nick feels he has put behind him as he heads off toward the river? Why does he more than once refer to his tent as his home, and why does he feel so pleased to be in it? Why is it that failure to kill the big fish makes him feel sick? With the exception of "The Battler," "Big Two-Hearted River" raises more tantalizing questions than any other Hemingway story.

Plausible answers to these questions may be found by placing the story in its biographical context. Ernest spent the summer of 1919 thinking and writing. He also spent it in bitter contention with his mother. The following summer the ill will between the two of them exploded into open warfare when she expelled him from Windemere within days of his twenty-first birthday and presented him as he was leaving with a letter that was indisputably the masterpiece of her epistolary career. Consequently, by the time he wrote the story about his fishing trip to Seney he was not only burdened by upsetting memories of the first summer after the war, but by even more upsetting memories of the second. Perhaps, then, the "other needs" Nick feels he has put behind him include a need to please his mother, while his talk of his tent as his home may represent a reaction to being thrown out of his parents' summer cottage. Perhaps, too, the burned-over country and the grasshoppers that have turned black from living in it constitute tacit reminders to him of his mother's penchant for burning things. And finally, the activity of his mind that keeps threatening to overwhelm his contentment could be rage.

The angler on the bank of the Big Two-Hearted River is clearly a man with a divided heart—but the precise nature of the division is never identified. "In the swamp the banks were bare, the big cedars came together overhead, the sun did not come through, except in patches; in the fast deep water, in the half light, the fishing would be tragic."[11] The words apply well to the fisherman's efforts to shun the murky depths of his troubled inner life. First and last, Nick remains an enigma.

But to many readers in the twenties, Nick was not an enigma. For these people assumed that the key to Nick's secret was the fact that his creator was the archetypal representative of a war-scarred "lost generation." Ultimately, this assumption crept into formal assessments of the story. The experience that has given Nick "a touch of panic," Edmund Wilson announced in "Ernest Hemingway: Bourdon Gauge of Morale" (1939), is "the wholesale shattering of human beings in which he has taken part."[12] Leading up to and away from this statement, "Bourdon Gauge" contains some wonderfully appreciative comments about the stifled pangs and undruggable disquiet that lurk beneath the most innocent surfaces in Hemingway's stories. In the case of "Big Two-Hearted River," however, Wilson felt a need to specify the malaise underlying it, and in doing so he could only think that it had to do with World War I. He cited no textual evidence in support of this diagnosis for the simple reason that there was none. Not a single reference to war appears in the story, and it is highly doubtful, furthermore, judging by what can be observed of Nick's behavior, that panic is the feeling that he is fending off. Nor does battlefield trauma bear any discernible relation to those vague "other needs" that he feels he has put behind him or to his strong expressions of contentment with his "homelike" tent.

Half a decade after "Bourdon Gauge," Wilson's interpretation was reinforced by Malcolm Cowley's introduction to the Viking *Portable Hemingway* (1944). To Hemingway this essay could not have come as a surprise. For in *Exile's Return* (1934) Cowley had already proclaimed that the young American writers born in the years around 1900 were a lost generation, inasmuch as the war had shattered their relationship with the country of their boyhood and they had become attached to no other. That Hemingway felt precisely the way he himself did about the war was one of Cowley's cardinal beliefs, and he delighted in drawing other parallels between their lives. The equivalent for him of Hemingway's Michigan was Cambria County, Pennsylvania, on the western slope of the Alleghenies, where he had spent his boyhood summers fishing and shooting and walking in the woods, and his equivalent of Oak Park was a residential section of Pittsburgh, where his father practiced medicine, just like Dr. Hemingway. When America entered World War I, Cowley had wanted to join an ambulance corps in France, but because the demand for drivers had slackened by the time he got to Paris, he ended up driving a camion for the French military transport—which in his retrospective view was not all that different from driving a Red Cross truck in Italy. So closely did he identify himself with Hemingway that in his *Portable Hemingway* introduction he erroneously asserted that the novelist had been born in 1898, the year of his own birth. Hemingway's awareness of Cowley's habit of superimposing his own life on his was made explicit by him more than once. Thus, in a letter to Harvey Breit of the *New York Times* five years before his death, he sardonically observed that "Malcolm thot I was like him because my father was a Dr. and I went to Michigan when I was 2 weeks old where they had Hemlock trees."[13] That Cowley would someday go on from the lost-generation argument of *Exile's Return* to a lost-generation interpretation of "Big Two-Hearted River" must have seemed to him like an inevitable development.

In the *Portable Hemingway* Cowley argued, not so much by direct statement as by artful implication, that Hemingway's fisherman, like Hemingway himself, was a war veteran who was trying to block out fearridden recollections of being wounded. Proof of Nick's state of mind was not to be found in the story, to be sure, but that didn't bother Cowley. Hemingway's stories "are most of them continued," he said, by which he meant that the emotions underlying "Big Two-Hearted River" could be understood in the light of the emotions expressed in "Now I Lay Me," written three years later.[14] Since the hero of the latter story is an American lieutenant in war-time Italy who is afraid to close his eyes at night, "Now I Lay Me" has the effect, said Cowley, of giving readers "a somewhat different attitude toward the earlier story" and of drawing attention to something that "we probably missed at first reading; that there are shadows in the background and that part of the story takes place in an inner world."[15]

In stressing an emotional consistency between "Big Two-Hearted River" and "Now I Lay Me," Cowley neglected to point out that the most emotional moment in the latter story is set in the hero's childhood and involves a confrontation between his parents. Nevertheless, Cowley's endorsement of the war-trauma argument soon became an inspiration to other critics, most notably to an impressionable young man named Philip Young, who "ported a *Portable Hemingway* halfway across Europe during World War II."[16] In 1952 Young projected the admiration he felt for the Cowley introduction, amplified by his own reactions to war, into a book that proclaimed that the wound suffered by Hemingway in 1918 had so deeply affected him that he had spent his whole life as a writer composing variations on the story of the psychically crippled "sick man" in "Big Two-Hearted River."[17] Ten years later Mark Schorer spoke for what was now a critical cliché when he characterized Hemingway as the lifelong victim of the events that had befallen him at Fossalta di Piave. "Nothing more important than this wounding was ever to happen to him," Schorer sweepingly declared.[18]

Thus, the war-wound interpretation of the story was established not by textual evidence, but by what the critics knew about the author's life—or rather, by what they thought they knew about his life. And after he was dead, they eagerly seized on his posthumously published comment in *A Moveable Feast* that "Big Two-Hearted River" was about "coming back from the war but there was no mention of the war in it" as clinching proof that they were right.[19] They would have been better advised to wonder if a master manipulator was not making fools of them from beyond the grave, as he so often had in life.

For a quarter of a century after the story was published, Hemingway kept his own counsel about it. But in the aftermath of World War II he made a number of statements in which he related it to World War I. In all likelihood, though, these revelations reflected latter-day events. The late forties marked the beginning of the end for Hemingway. Fantasies of suicide thronged his mind, intermingled with fears of insanity, and his friend Buck Lanham saw him writing in the morning with a drink in his hand. For years he had been given to saying that the first war had cost him a lot of sleep, but he had usually been careful to couple such confessions with manly assertions that he had finally put insomnia behind him and was once again in wonderful shape. The breathtaking tragedy that took form in the late forties exposed the hollowness of that boast. All too keenly aware of his problems and yet adamantly opposed to seeking professional help in understanding them, he more than ever felt the need of a heroic explanation for his life. In an effort to account for his imperiled sense of himself, as well as to preserve his macho reputation, he turned once more to Fossalta.

Thus, in a letter dated August 25, 1948, he informed Malcolm Cowley that he could now see that in the first war he had been hurt very badly in body, mind, and spirit and also morally, that "Big Two-Hearted River" was about a man who was home from the war, and that he, the author, was still hurt in that story. The real truth about himself, he assured Cowley, was that in the war "I was hurt bad all the way through and I was really spooked at the end."[20] And in another letter a few years later to the *New York Times's* Charles Poore, he again characterized "Big Two-Hearted River" as "a story about a boy who has come back from the war. The war is never mentioned though as far as I can remember. This may be one of the things that helps it."[21] Private communications, however, were merely warm-ups for the gloss he offered the public at large in *A Moveable Feast*.

The book was written between 1957 and 1961, during which time the author's long debate with himself about self-destruction was moving inexorably toward violent resolution, despite his terrifying belief that suicide was a cowardly, unmanly act. In the wake of his death his enemies in the critical world took the same line toward it, as he had feared they would. To these commentators his life had ended with a whimper, not a bang. After 1930 he just didn't have it any more, Dwight Macdonald fairly gloated in the pages of *Encounter* in January 1962, and by the summer of 1961—the critic savagely continued—the position was outflanked, the lion couldn't be stopped, the sword wouldn't go into the bull's neck, the great fish was breaking the line, it was the fifteenth round and the champ looked bad, and the only way out was to destroy himself.

Even a Hemingway fan like Norman Mailer felt moved to confess in a troubled essay in *Esquire* entitled "The Big Bite" that his suicide had been "the most difficult death in America since [Franklin] Roosevelt's."[22] What made it difficult for Mailer was that in taking his life Hemingway had seemed to call into question all that he had represented. Consistently, he had presented himself as the champion of whatever endeavor he had undertaken; consistently, he had proclaimed that the great thing was to last and get your work done. How could such a life be reconciled with such a death?

Mailer's ultimate answer to this question was that "It is not likely that Hemingway was a brave man who sought danger for the sake of the sensations it provided him. What is more likely the truth of his own odyssey is that he struggled with his cowardice and against a secret lust to suicide all his life, that his inner landscape was a nightmare, and he spent his nights wrestling with the gods. It may even be that the final judgment on his work may come to the notion that what he failed to do was tragic, but what he accomplished was heroic, for it is possible that he carried a weight of anxiety with him which would have suffocated any man smaller than himself."[23]

As a hypothesis, Mailer's comment was marvelously suggestive and ought to have inspired searching examinations of the dynamics of Hemingway's early life. But it did not. Old habits of mind prevailed. Fossalta had been the break-point in a gallant hero's history. By seeming to imply in *A Moveable Feast* that "Big Two-Hearted River" was about a man who was doing his best to defend himself against memories of a dirty war, Hemingway himself helped to buttress that assumption.

NOTES

1. EH to Howell Jenkins, c. September 15, 1919, in *Ernest Hemingway: Selected Letters*, 1917–1961, ed. Carlos Baker (New York: Scribner's, 1981), p. 29.

2. EH to Gertrude Stein and Alice B. Toklas, August 15, 1924, *Selected Letters*, p. 122.

3. Ernest Hemingway, *The Complete Short Stories of Ernest Hemingway: The Finca Vigia Edition* (New York: Scribner's,) p. 163.

4. *Short Stories*, p. 164.

5. *Short Stories*, pp. 163, 164.

6. *Short Stories*, p. 164.

7. *Short Stories*, p. 167.

8. *Short Stories*, p. 169.

9. Short Stories, p. 177.

10. *Short Stories*, p. 180.

11. *Short Stories*, p. 180.

12. *The Portable Edmund Wilson*, ed. Lewis M. Dabney (New York: Viking press, 1983), p. 399.

13. EH to Harvey Breit, July 23, 1956, *Selected Letters*, p. 867.

14. Malcolm Cowley, ed., *The Viking Portable Hemingway* (New York: Viking Press, 1944), p. ix.

15. *Portable Hemingway*, p. x.

16 Philip Young, *Ernest Hemingway: A Reconsideration* (University Park: Pennsylvania State University Press, 1966), p. 5.

17. *A Reconsideration*, p. 47.

18. Mark Schorer, "Ernest Hemingway," in *Major Writers of America*, ed. Perry Miller (New York: Harcourt Brace & World, 1962), p. 675.

19. Ernest Hemingway, *A Moveable Feast* (New York: Scribner's, 1964), p. 76.

20 Malcolm Cowley, "Hemingway's Wound," *Georgia Review* 38 (Summer 1984): 229–30.

21. EH to Charles Poore, January 23, 1953, *Selected Letters*, p. 798.

22. Norman Mailer, "The Big Bite," *Esquire* 58 (November 1962), p. 134.

23. Norman Mailer, "Punching Papa," *New York Review of Books* 1 (August 1963): 13.

PAUL SMITH

Who Wrote Hemingway's In Our Time?

T here was a time when I thought I knew the answer to the question in this title, back in the early 1980s when most of us assumed the obvious: It was Ernest Hemingway, of course, although we recognized the intricate web linking him with his character, Nick Adams, and we had been instructed by a number of persuasive studies of the various narrative points of view in the 1925 collection, *In Our Time*.[1]

Between then and now, a decade later, that seemingly simple question has been asked again, and asked in a way that makes the answer a good deal less obvious. A new generation of critics has returned to the issue of the unity of *In Our Time* and, with some of the evidence from Hemingway's manuscripts, has argued for the hypothesis of *a* Nick Adams as the implied author of the stories in that book, and not only those that concern *another* Nick Adams, the character from "Indian Camp" to "Big Two-Hearted River."[2] That's my concern here, and in particular, the evidence for that hypothesis and the consequences for the interpretation of the crucial story, "Indian Camp."

The several arguments for Nick Adams as the implied author of *In Our Time* are complex, so for time's sake I will depend on the one that ranges the farthest and dares the most: Debra A. Moddelmog's 1988 essay "The Unifying Consciousness of ... *In Our Time*."[3] And with an apology for summarizing, I take this to be its general structure.

From *Hemingway Repossessed*, edited by Kenneth Rosen: 143–150. © 1994 by the Ernest Hemingway Foundation.

First, the importance of Moddelmog's hypothesis. Reading Nick Adams as the "author" of the *In Our Time* stories may resolve confusions about the book's "unity, structure, vision, and significance," and cast "new light on Nick Adams as a character, both separate from and an extension of Ernest Hemingway" (592).

Second, an admission that although at the time of writing these stories Hemingway did not plan to "attribute any of them to Nick," he realized— sometime in the summer of 1924, one presumes—that since "Nick shared so much of [his] personality and experience that turning him into the author of the stories *ex post facto* required very little work. All Hemingway had to do was supply Nick with the relevant background, specifically a writing career and some post-war history" (594).

Third, the evidence for Hemingway's intention to give Nick a career as a writer in the post-war period is there in the story's original conclusion, later published as "On Writing" in *The Nick Adams Stories* (*NAS*, 1972). It begins with the remark from "On Writing" that, "Nick in the stories was never himself" (*NAS* 238); that is, Nick-as-author was never Nick-as-character in the Nick Adams stories; but since he cites "My Old Man" and refers to only one of the Nick Adams stories ("Indian Camp"), those "stories" might include any or all of those alluded to in the "On Writing" conclusion in addition to those that have Nick as a character. To count: first, the Nick Adams stories "The End of Something," "The Three-Day Blow," "Cross-Country Snow;" and "The Doctor and the Doctor's Wife." Those without Nick as a character but with linking allusions or thematic similarities are "A Very Short Story," "Soldier's Home," "Mr. and Mrs. Elliot," "Cat in the Rain" and "Out of Season." That list includes all of the 1925 edition of *In Our Time*, with the exception of the Nick Adams story "The Battler," written after "Big Two-Hearted River," and "On the Quai of Smyrna," and substituted as an "introduction" in the winter of 1926–1927.[4]

Here the argument deserves a review and a comment on its evidence.

First, it interposes between the reader and the conventional narrator an implied author named Nick Adams. That implied author is, in his own words, *never* the character he creates, whether that character bears his name or not.[5] Thus everything that happens to the character Nick, or anything he thought or imagined, would seem to be un-attributable to the narrator Nick, with the exception of those in "On Writing" in which he claims or implies authorship.

To evaluate this assumption, consider Nick's claim to have written a story called "My Old Man" and then his offer to prove his fine and prescient eye with the remark that "the next week Georges Parfrement was killed at that very jump [where the jockey Butler was killed] and that was the way it looked" (*NAS* 237).

Here, at the outset, we must make a decision. The argument maintains that "we cannot pin down the precise date when Nick wrote any particular story in *In Our Time*" (595). However, we can "pin down" the precise date "Nick Adams" wrote "My Old Man" with a fact discovered by Michael Reynolds—Reynolds reads the papers, all of them. There was a Georges Parfrement who was killed on or about 18 April 1923, which might place Nick's "composition" of the story in early April of that year, at least six months after Hemingway wrote his version (Reynolds 1989, 105).

Now this may be a trivial fact of history, but I note it since we are told later of our inability to discover the implied author's "actual history ... because we lack the biographical evidence (letters, memoirs, interviews) that usually fill the gap between an author's life and his fiction, [and] we are left wondering where we might find the real Nick Adams" (596). To speak of an implied author's "actual history" or of him as the "real Nick Adams" is to suggest a rather curious ontology. An "implied author" is, one would suppose, a fictive figure, whether he "exists," so to speak, in the text or not, or has been inferred from evidence in a manuscript, rejected by its "other author with the not uncertain term, 'shit'" (*LTRS* 133). What's troubling is to be asked to imagine what sort of documents would serve as "biographical evidence" of that "real" Nick Adams: a letter from him, but to whom; one of his memoirs, but of what; an interview, but where and when and, indeed, how?

If Nick Adams wrote Hemingway's "My Old Man" and cited Georges Parfrement's death as evidence of "the way it looked" a week or two later, then either Parfrement is a fictive construct, or he is not. If he is, then everything the implied author claims (including, by the way, his writing a story called "My Old Man") is, at most, as fictive as that hapless rider. If, however, the name Parfrement refers to a French jockey who really died in April 1923, then everything else Nick Adams recalls is, at least, as suspect as that evanescent fact from a defective memory.

But for this argument, such questions are quibbles—and, perhaps, rightly so, for neither Hemingway nor his manuscripts suggest that either ontology or epistemology were much on his mind. So the argument moves from matters of "biographical evidence" to the next point.

Since "our main interest is Nick's psyche, we need not worry too much about our inability to sort reality from imagination [for by] looking for repeated patterns and by studying the subjects that Nick chooses to develop as well as his manner of presenting those subjects, we should uncover those fixations of his imagination that reveal his basic outlook on life" (596).

Here, another comment is warranted, for this is the crucial point of the argument. Relieved of the burden of sorting "reality from imagination," we are free to consider those epistemic choices that reveal Nick, in the role of implied author, through his imaginative obsessions and to discover his vision of life.

And that seems fair enough, if only because it has been done before with Joyce's *Dubliners* and Anderson's *Winesburg, Ohio*, two story collections that laid influential hands on Hemingway's. But it seems just as fair to observe that to raise the distinction between "reality and imagination" (whatever those terms mean) in an argument for an implied author of *In Our Time*, and then to dismiss it, is to work both sides of the critical street. If that distinction is troubling, it should be resolved; if it is not, it should not be raised. But since it has been raised, we should recall that the critical concept of an "implied author" was not originally meant to be fleshed out with a life, a wife, or whatever.[6]

These are troubled waters, and not easily bridged; nor, I suspect, will they be until we understand why we want to cross them. It was tried briefly at the 1990 International Hemingway Conference in Boston with a panel discussion gathered to consider the topic of "Nick as Narrator of *In Our Time*." Debra Moddelmog introduced the discussion with these questions: "Why should we want to find ... self-reflexivity in Hemingway's fiction? Are we trying to make him 'one of us'? ... [And] do the conceptions of Nick as a novelist of Hemingway as a meta-fictionist make the fictions more complex and interesting; and if so, are we perhaps being New Critics with a vengeance?"[7]

I was on that panel and mumbled, mainly; yet I do not recall any precise answers to those questions. But now, armed with a script, I bring them up again, with my own, I trust, more audible answers.

First, yes, we are trying to make Hemingway "one of us," as every critical generation has, and *has* to, to earn its critical stripes.

Second, yes, the conceptions of Nick as novelist make the fictions more complex and interesting, but only in the way that we, with our meta-fictional bent, define complexity or interest.

And third, yes, the aesthetic criteria the New Critics assumed half a century ago still underlie the assumptions of the meta-fictionist generation. Once again, the intent of the hypothesis that Nick Adams is the implied author of the *In Our Time* stories is to resolve "many confusions about the book's unity, structure, vision, and significance" (592). *Unity* and *structure* are old formalist terms, and they beg the same questions they did 50 years ago: What is so sacrosanct about *unity*? Why do we fix our gaze on the structure of the collection rather than on the individual structures of the stories? Would the force of each of those stories be diminished if each was read as randomly as they were written, as most of us do? And how does their cumulative "vision and significance" differ from a set of stories written by an "implied author," or even an incipient novelist?[8] That's a raft of questions—surely too many even to contemplate here—so I will consider one matter in a crucial case, the enigmatic ending of "Indian Camp."

For such a mysterious story, there is a remarkable unanimity among its commentators: with varying emphases, all recognize it as an initiation story. And all but a few see that initiation as a failure, for Nick's certainty that he "would never die" is patently illusory, innocent, romantic, or all three.[9]

With the publication of the story's original manuscript's first eight pages, given the title "Three Shots," the two manuscript halves were joined by most readers to mark the ending as doubly ironic, for Nick seems to regress to his state of innocence before he fired the three shots.[10] But one critic, agreeing that Nick only sensed death "in the abstract" in "Three Shots," and then came to "know its reality," saw something more: When Nick comes to realize his father's love, "that love reinforces his sense of being, and of immortality. Thus the ending is neither illusory nor ironic" (Penner 202).

Each of these interpretations assumes that the story is told by an *undramatized narrator*—again, Booth's term. The narrator is familiar with events of the past three days and remarks four times on the characters' emotional states before the ending: once on Nick's, once on the Indian wife's, and twice on Nick's father's; but in each instance the remark does not depend on much more than what is apparent in the character's behavior of speech—indeed, they seem almost redundant.[11] But it is precisely that redundancy that suggests a narrator, however undramatized.

Very little of what I have summarized from earlier critics is necessarily incompatible with the later position of those who argue that Nick Adams is the implied author of "Indian Camp." That argument simply interposes Nick Adams between the reader and the story's narrator, and makes the younger Nickie Adams his own fictional projection. But that authorial Nick Adams is a far from simple figure, and what is attributed to him radically changes our reading of the story.

The invention of Nick as the implied author begins with the remark in "On Writing" that he "had never seen an Indian woman having a baby [but that] he'd seen a woman have a baby on the road to Karagatch and tried to help her"; and it adds that the sentence in chapter 2 of *In Our Time*, "Scared sick looking at it" describes Nick's reaction (596). This conflation of the two texts transfers the authority and something of the event in the *In Our Time* chapter to the memory in "On Writing"; but in chapter 2, there is no engaged narrator who "tried to help" the woman in labor, and the person "scared sick looking at it" was the young girl holding the blanket (*SS* 97).[12]

From this it is concluded that Nick, in writing "Indian Camp," changed the "witness of the delivery from an adult immersed in war and evacuation to a child involved with family life and night-time adventures." Furthermore, this implies that "the older Nick views his meeting with the woman on the road to Karagatch as an initiation of the innocent," and then projects himself as a young boy present at a difficult childbirth "[who] is both victimized by the exigencies of the adult world ... [and has] a lingering inability to accept suffering and dying." This leads to the conclusion that the story Nick Adams wrote is permeated with a "strong degree of self-pity" in his projection of himself as its victim; but that "self-indulgence" is then repudiated with "self-irony [in] the child's denial of his own mortality, a denial that he, a war veteran and a writer, now knows to be a lie" (596–597).

Whether as author or implied author, the older Nick Adams interposed between the reader, the narrator, and the younger Nick Adams, reduces the boy's feeling "quite sure he would never die," first, to a youngster's lie; second, to an authorial projection's self-delusion; and finally, to a fictive author's ironic dismissal of that self-delusion.

This strategy to explain a boy's lie as an older person's self-delusion to be repudiated by an author's ironic honesty certainly satisfies a meta-fictional need, but in so doing it trivializes the immediate, profound, and enigmatic question of how that boy could lie, how he could have "felt quite sure that he would never die."

Most of our explanations of Nick's final certainty explain it away with something between indulgence and sanctimony. We wink at his feeling as a childhood fantasy, an understandable delusion, a romantic impulse, for we know—don't we?—that he will die, as will we—or *because* we will. Or from our superior position we say that he lied. But what Nick feels is not a lie. Neither we nor any fictive author can invoke any truth-conditions to deny the boy's feelings, any more than you can tell me that I do not feel quite sure that most critics of this story are dead wrong. *What* I feel may be wrong, but *that* I feel it is incontestable. Not, of course, that I do.

Finally, imagine for a moment that what Nick felt was a truth of a sort that is strange to us. In "The Art of the Short Story"—that rough, suspect, and self-serving memoir—there is a mysterious remark, only part of which has raised comment. Hemingway maintained that the title "Big Two-Hearted River" was substituted for the Fox River, the setting of the story, because "Big Two-Hearted River" is poetry, and because there were many Indians in the story, just as "the war was in the story, and none of the Indians nor the war appeared" (3). "Indian Camp" begins the *In Our Time* collection and "Big Two-Hearted River" ends it, and both are set in the same locale, a morning's train ride west from St. Ignace in Michigan's Upper Peninsula.

The last story is so resonant with rituals linking Nick Adams to the natural world—like his offering of the trout's offal to the mink, the local spirits of the tragic swamp—that although there are, indeed, no Indians in the story, there is no need for them, or perhaps there is only one. They are there in "Indian Camp"; and although some have hinted at it, no one has yet wondered whether the initiation we all agree Nick Adams has endured follows an Indian ritual, the end of which, if he survives it, rewards the young initiate with the profound and undeniable feeling that "he will never die."

If it turns out that some native American ritual is closer to the informing source of "Indian Camp," we may well seem to be so engaged in our reasonable world, with its logical laws, that we have forgotten, as Hemingway once said, "what mysteries were in the woods ... that we came from" (*FWBT* 176–177).

NOTES

1. The most accessible collection of these is *Critical Essays on Ernest Hemingway's "In Our Time,"* ed. Michael S. Reynolds (1983). It includes Robert M. Slabey, "The Structure of *In Our Time,*" *South Dakota Review* (August 1965): 28–52; Clinton S. Burhans, Jr., "The Complex Unity of *In Our Time,*" *Modern Fiction Studies* (1968): 313–328; Jackson J. Benson, "Patterns of Connection and Their Development in Hemingway's *In Our Time,*" *Rendezvous* (Winter 1970): 37–52; Linda W. Wagner, "Juxtaposition in Hemingway's *In Our Time*" *Studies in Short Fiction* 12 (1975): 243–252; and David J. Leigh, S. J., "*In Our Time*: The Inter-chapters as Structural Guides to Pattern," *Studies in Short Fiction* 12 (1975): 1–8; see also David Seed, "The Picture of the Whole: *In Our Time,*" in *Ernest Hemingway: New Critical Essays*, ed. Robert A. Lee (1983).

2. Of those critics who have entertained this hypothesis, the two most challenging have been Elizabeth Dewberry Vaughn and Debra A. Moddelmog; I focus on the latter article since it offers a practical example of its theoretical position with an interpretation of "Indian Camp."

3. Debra A. Moddelmog, "The Unifying Consciousness of a Divided Conscience: Nick Adams as Author of *In Our Time,*" *American Literature: A Journal of Literary History, Criticism & Bibliography* 60 (Dec. 1988): 591–610.

4. Yet the argument includes "The Battler" to demonstrate Nick's learning "about the cruelty of society..., a lesson which ends ... in confused escape" (598) and "On the Quai ... ," as evidence of Nick's obsession with "the violence and senselessness of war" (599).

5. Note that the argument begins with Nick identified as an "implied author" on p. 592; on p. 594 Hemingway "surrenders authorship to Nick"; and from there to the end there are eight overt references to Nick as author, although on p. 609 Nick becomes a "fictional persona." On Nick as author and Nick as character, the argument opens with the distinction between the two, but thereafter it attributes details of the life of the character to that of the author. Near the conclusion of the essay, after we are told that Nick was "writing about himself" in "Cross-Country Snow," we are warned to be "careful not to confuse Nick the writer with Nick the character" (606).

6. As noted earlier, Moddelmog begins with the term *implied author*, continues with *author, writer,* and *fictional persona*; and I, perhaps too assiduously, have assumed that the latter terms were shorthand references to the first. In *The Rhetoric of Fiction* (1961) Wayne

Booth was, I believe, the first to consider the concept of an "implied author" systematically and at length. He defined it as the author's "implied version of himself," as a "presence," a "second self," that is always distinct from both the "real" author and the narrator and that will differ in different works. "Our sense of the implied author includes not only the extractable meanings but also the moral and emotional content of each bit of action and suffering of all the characters. It includes, in short, the intuitive apprehension of a completed artistic whole; the chief value to which *this* implied author is committed" (70–73, 151).

7. Undated letter from Debra Moddelmog to the panelists, which was read in part at the conference, 10 July 1990.

8. Booth used the term *self-conscious narrator* to distinguish between those conscious of their roles as writers and those narrators who seem unaware that "they are writing, thinking, speaking, or 'reflecting' a literary work" (155). One or another of those terms might be more appropriate in this discussion.

9. For Joseph DeFalco, Nick's certainty is "illusory and childlike" (32); for Arthur Waldhorn, Nick, like the newborn, is still protected by the "caul of innocence" (54); and several suggest that when Nick trails his hand in the morning lake there is at best the potential for a later recognition of "renewal and reassurance" (Waldhorn 55). Yet they all consider this a romantic, even Wordsworthian, response to experience (DeFalco, Waldhorn, and Oldsey [217–218]). Some interpret Nick's feeling in rather more narrow or conditional ways: having witnessed only a suicide, Nick feels he will never die *that* way (Monteiro 155); or that *only* in the early morning *and* on the lake *and* sitting in the stern *and* with his father rowing could Nick feel "*quite* sure that he would never die" (Smith 39).

10. Larry Grimes ("Night Terror and Morning Calm: A Reading of 'Indian Camp' as sequel to 'Three Stories.'" *Studies in Short Fiction* 12 [1975] 413–415), for example, argues that "Three Shots" dramatizes Nick's fear of death, common to a child's "fantasy life," and that Nick's experience of the "raw and grotesque" evidence of death can be ignored only "in the reassuring presence of his father" adds to the story's concluding irony (414).

11. They occur when the narrator notes that Nick's "curiosity had been gone for a long time," the Indian wife "did not know what had become of the baby or anything," and Nick's father "was feeling exalted and talkative as football players in the dressing room after a game" and, later, "all his post-operative exhilaration [was] gone" (*SS* 93–94).

12. That it was the girl who was "scared sick" is explicit in Hemingway's *Toronto Daily Star* dispatch of 20 October 1922, titled "A Silent Ghastly Procession," the source for chapter 2 (*Dateline Toronto*).

PAUL WADDEN

Barefoot in the Hemlocks: Nick Adams' Betrayal of Love in "Ten Indians"

"*Ten Indians* has received considerable attention for its alleged "castration scene" in which Doctor Adams, wielding a literal and symbolic knife, informs Nick of the infidelity of his son's first girlfriend. Despite the possibility that this may have been the cruelest cut of all—from father to son, no less—critics have almost universally misread the closing of the story as yet another decisive step forward in the *Bildungsroman* of young Nick Adams. Joseph Flora, for instance, asserts that Nick's "quick rebounding from his 'heartbreak' over the faithless Prudence suggests that there is a healthy resilience in Hemingway's hero" (50); Jan Bakker likewise contends that the ending indicates in Nick "a healthy ability to digest and outgrow emotional shocks" (5); Wirt Williams suggests that Nick's failure the next morning to remember that his heart has been broken indicates "a transcendence is made" (93); Jarvis Thurston deduces that Nick's memory lapse "symbolizes his reconciliation with an unjust and ugly reality" (176); and Philip Young summarily concludes that Nick "has learned another lesson" (48).

Notwithstanding the near unanimity in interpretive commentary that "Ten Indians" represents yet another successful initiation for Nick, a more careful reading of the story—and an array of manuscript, biographic, and intertextual evidence—suggests to the contrary that Nick's first experience of sexual betrayal is much deeper than has been critically acknowledged, and

From *The Hemingway Review* 16, no. 2 (Spring 1997): 3–18. © 1997 by the Ernest Hemingway Foundation.

that his absorption of this "lesson" is far from complete—better characterized by "denial" than "transcendence." Indeed, far from suggesting a "quick rebound," "Ten Indians" conforms more to the pattern of failed or ineffectual initiations evident in two other prominent Nick Adams stories between which this episode in Nick's life is positioned: the aborted initiation of "Indian Camp" and the arrested initiation of "The Killers."

"Ten Indians" opens as Nick and the Garner family return in the evening from Fourth of July festivities in nearby Petoskey. As the horse-drawn wagon bounces down the road, Joe Garner stops the team from time to time to pull drunken Indians—nine in all—from the wagon's path. Nick and the Garners indulge in light-hearted banter, and when young Carl and Nick tangle in a knowledge-display over whether raccoons or skunks were foraging by the lake the night before, Carl teasingly concedes the point by retorting that Nick ought to "know skunks" since he has "an Indian girl." Mrs. Garner upbraids her son for the racial slur but Mr. Garner continues the line of questioning:

> "Have you got an Indian girl, Nickie?" Joe asked.
> "No."
> "He has too, Pa," Frank said. "Prudence Mitchell's his girl."
> "She's not."
> "He goes to see her every day."
> "I don't." Nick, sitting between the two boys in the dark, felt hollow and happy inside himself to be teased about Prudence Mitchell. "She ain't my girl," he said.
> "Listen to him," said Carl. "I see them together every day."
> Carl can't get a girl," his mother said, "not even a squaw."
> Carl was quiet. (CSS 254)

Mrs. Garner then moves closer to Joe in the wagon and her husband advises Nick to "watch out to keep Prudy," ending the exchange by declaring that "Nickie can have Prudence ... I got a good girl" (254).

Critical discussion of this passage has largely focused on the implicit juxtaposition of the Garner family (good-humored, well-adjusted, and intact) with the troubled single parent home to which Nick is returning. Yet another significant effect of the exchange, as Paul Smith notes, is to "invest Nick's affair with maturity and seriousness" (*Reader's Guide* 56), for Nick's relationship with Prudy is fully acknowledged, even dignified, by its explicit comparison with the marital union of the Garners. The Garners clearly regard the link between the two as significant enough to offer their advice and moral support to the young man. The "hollow and happy" feeling Nick experiences when teased about Prudy—the exact phrase he will use years later in "Fathers and Sons" to recall his romantic fulfillment with his Indian lover—further intimates his deeply felt attachment to her. As Jarvis Thurston observes of Nick in this opening scene, "His love for Prudence is simple and admirable, the love of a boy for a girl, unconscious of racial distinctions or assumptions of superiority and inferiority" (174).

In terms of the narrative, however, this opening dialogue does not bode well for Nick and his Edenic maiden so ironically named "Prudence." Joe Garner's admonition for him to "watch out to keep Prudy" and Nick's inability to "smell a skunk" even when he claims "I know skunks," foreshadows his lover's faithlessness. More seriously, though, Nick's own words—and silences—implicate him in the impending betrayal, for he repeatedly fails to acknowledge his bond with Prudy, three times denying that he "knows" her. Nick's own actions, then, set into motion a form of literary (and psychological) cause and effect, beyond the constraints of linear time, which can end in no other way than in his banishment from the Garden of pure and unreflective love.

A second key passage in the middle of the story is also essential for understanding the state of Nick's mind and the effect that the news of Prudence's infidelity will have on him. Upon reaching the Garners' home, Nick declines Mrs. Garner's invitation to stay for a warm dinner and sets off through the woods for home:

> Nick walked barefoot along the path through the meadow below the barn. The path was smooth and the dew was cool on his bare feet. He climbed a fence at the end of the meadow, went down through a ravine, his feet wet in the swamp mud, and then climbed up through the dry beech woods until he saw the lights of the cottage. (255)

Nick's transit evokes the image of a young man at home in both civilization and nature. He is equally comfortable in the communal glow of the Garners' kitchen or solo in the natural world—nature's son at one with settlers and natives, effortlessly civilized and polite in his comportment with the Garners, yet Indian-like in the barefoot ease with which he crosses the smooth path through the dewy countryside. The young man is shown easily circumventing conventional boundaries—climbing a fence and slipping through a ravine. And unlike the war-wounded older Nick who fishes for a return to psychic wholeness in "Big Two-Hearted River" and who apprehensively avoids the swamp and its "tragic adventure" (180), the young Nick of "Ten Indians" freely wets his feet in "the swamp mud" before ascending through the dry woods to glimpse the cabin lights. Nick's heightened state of awareness and integration are not to last, however; the revelation that his father has in store for him will very shortly shatter his well-being.

The story reaches its climax as Nick's father invites him into the kitchen for a supper of "cold chicken" (in contrast to the warm dinner promised by the Garners). The "big shadow" Doctor Adams casts on the wall portends their exchange (255):

> "I saw your friend, Prudy."
> "Where was she?"
> "She was in the woods with Frank Washburn. I ran onto them. They were having quite a time."
> His father was not looking at him.
> "What were they doing?"
> "I didn't stay to find out."
> "Tell me what they were doing."
> "I don't know," his father said. "I just heard them threshing around."
> "How did you know it was them?"
> "I saw them."
> "I thought you said you didn't see them."
> "Oh, yes, I saw them."
> "Who was with her?" Nick asked.
> "Frank Washburn."
> "Were they—were they—"
> "Were they what?"
> "Were they happy?"
> "I guess so." (256)

Extensive scholarly debate has already examined the question of Doctor Adams' motivation for apprising Nick of what he observed by the Indian camp (and why he might have been there in the first place)[1]; namely, whether as an emasculated husband he is passing on his condition by ritually castrating his son or whether he is a surgeon who out of fatherly concern plies the wounding steel. I shall not re-open that controversy here but focus instead on the symptoms of Nick's psychological trauma, too often downplayed or overlooked by critics. First, Nick is so stunned by his father's revelation that the series of questions he asks is halting and repetitious. Second, in his disorientation, the young man claims his father said that he "didn't see" the couple, even though Doctor Adams has referred to them explicitly several times. Third, in disbelief if not denial, Nick presses his father to tell him who Prudy's companion was, despite the fact that he has already been identified as "Frank Washburn." Fourth, Nick cannot bring himself to utter the words that would force his father to reconfirm the act that he has observed in the woods, but is reduced to stuttering—"Were they—were they—." Fifth, when his father mercifully excuses himself to give Nick a chance to compose himself, the young man breaks down and cries— the *only* time in any of the Nick Adams stories that the hero weeps. At last, all that remains for Nick is to verify whether his erstwhile love has gone so far as to profane their own trysting place, and when his father returns he learns that she has indeed.

The closing of the story has been the object of repeated misunderstanding as critics have made light of Nick's mental distress and read simple irony into his effort to comprehend his experience. At his father's bidding, Nick goes back to his room where he "undresses," and physically and emotionally naked to his wound, lies with his face in the pillow. In a daze, he reasons: "My heart's broken.... If I feel this way my heart must be broken" (257). Although this attempt to make sense of his pain apparently has seemed comic to some critics, adolescents are forced to use just such shaky deductive logic in negotiating new experience as they compare their inner feelings to states they have only heard others tell of. The experience is hardly a laughing matter to Nick.

Notably, in the closing paragraph that immediately follows, the narration suddenly shifts into the first extended omniscient passage in the story—a sign of the psychological slippage that has taken place in Nick's mind. After a long time with his face in the pillow, Nick "[forgets] to think about Prudence" and finally falls asleep. But a gale continues to rage in his unconscious and during the night he awakens to hear the wind in "the hemlock trees," with their connotations of mortality and darkness, and "the waves of the lake coming in on the shore." The story concludes:

> In the morning there was a big wind blowing and the waves were running high up on the beach and he was awake a long time before he remembered that his heart was broken. (257)

Given the battering Nick's young psyche has undergone, the "big wind blowing" and the waves "running high up on the beach," is it credible that he has recovered so quickly? Is this swift "forgetting" of psychological trauma an indication of a "quick rebound" and "healthy resilience" (Flora 50), "a transcendence" (Williams 93), or a "reconciliation with an unjust and ugly reality" (Thurston 176)? Or is it instead an indication of deep denial and forceful repression? In other words, has Nick simply "learned another lesson" (Young 48) or has his learning been decisively deferred, suppressed, or even aborted?[2] Lewis epitomizes the critical dismissal of Nick's trauma when he dryly notes—à la Shakespeare—that men have died from time to time and worms have eaten them, but not for love (*Hemingway on Love* 10), and yet Hemingway's young hero nonetheless does suffer a kind of death with the loss of his first and only Eden. To give further support to the claim that Prudence's infidelity was not something to be shrugged off after a night's sleep, nor Nick's forgetfulness merely an upbeat indication of health and resilience, I turn now to manuscript evidence.

Hemingway's writing tactic of "strategic omission," excising key scenes or information in the belief that the missing material would deepen the characterization and heighten the dramatic tension of a story, suggests that manuscript versions of "Ten Indians" may shed important light on the tale's ending. To begin, the penultimate manuscript version of "Ten Indians" (the so-called second "Madrid version")[3] was entitled by Hemingway "A Broken Heart." Unless the author intended it to be completely sardonic (and other manuscript evidence to be discussed shortly suggests that he did not), this title indicates that Nick's experience was more than just a surface scratch. Nick is portrayed in "Ten Indians"—and throughout the Nick Adams stories—as a very sensitive young man, perhaps even too sensitive for his own good. Manuscript versions of the story reveal that Doctor Adams, for one, believed that learning of Prudence's infidelity would prove deeply distressing to his son. In the drafts of the story Hemingway wrote in Madrid, it is not Nick, but Dr. Adams who returns to his room and undresses; he then kneels beside his bed, and prays, "Dear God, for Christ's sake keep me from ever telling things to a kid.... For Christ's sake keep me from ever telling a kid how things are" (Smith, "Tenth Indian" 61).

The anguish of Nick's father over his son's state of mind is similarly evident in his bungled attempt—in manuscript versions—to account for Nick's betrayal, an episode included in the Madrid versions but cut from later drafts. After informing Nick of what he has seen in the woods, his father tells him by way of explanation:

> "I'm sorry, Nickie," his father said, looking at Nick, "But that's the way people are."
> "They don't have to all be rotten," Nick said. His voice hurt him to talk.
> "Just about," his father said. "It's a fairly rotten place, Nick."
> "I guess it's so," Nick said. He choked.
> "No, it's not so," his father said. "Everybody's not rotten."

"Oh, it's so all right," Nick said. "You said it. You can't take it back now."

"I was just bitter when I said it, Nick," his father said.

"You know how I talk when I'm bitter. I just shoot my mouth off. People aren't all really rotten."

"They are. They're all rotten to hell." (Smith, "Tenth Indian" 61)

Nick's trepidation is roundly evident in the exchange as he chokes and his voice hurts to talk. Further, his father belatedly realizes that his convenient justification for Prudence's behavior—"that's the way people are"—has backfired, for in his agitation Nick is only too willing to jump to the conclusion from his experience with one girl that people are "all rotten to hell." In the manuscript passage that follows this exchange, it is Nick's father rather than Nick who cannot sleep. As Smith observes, in this version both Nick and his father are "men without women, and the title, 'A Broken Heart,' refers as much to the father as to the son ("Tenth Indian" 62). In this respect, there is little evidence that comic irony is intended in Nick's appraisal of his "broken heart," or that sarcasm was implied in the manuscript title.

Manuscript endings to the story also provide convincing support for the interpretation that Nick does not simply shrug off his betrayal. Hemingway's drafts of the closing paragraph occupy three notebook pages of the final handwritten version of the manuscript. The first attempt ends with the lines "Nick lay for a long time with his face in the pillow and [finally] after a while he went to sleep. It had been a long day." Other variants, all later canceled, include the closing lines, "It had been a very long day" and "Ah, little lad, you've had a long day." These discarded versions underscore, however imperfectly, the trial that the young man has been through. Still unsatisfied with their emotional effect, however, Hemingway tried the opposite tack—reverse psychology so to speak—and wrote a series of alternate closing sentences that suggest an amnesia on Nick's part: "He did not remember what he had felt badly about"; "He did not think about anything... and he went back to sleep"; "He was happy and went back to sleep" (Smith, "Tenth Indian" 63–64). It was only after these repeated experiments that Hemingway composed the paragraph, incorporating elements of both variants, that he included in the final draft.

Because of this extensive revision, "Ten Indians" was the last story to be completed for the collection fittingly entitled *Men Without Women*. Smith speculates that one of the causes for the delay (that is, Hemingway's difficulty in "getting it right") might have been the image of his own deteriorating marriage that he saw reflected in his depiction of Nick's father and absent mother (*Reader's Guide* 198). Also plausible, however, is the possibility that Hemingway had difficulty in coming to terms with the Prudence in his own past. That a girl distinctly resembling the Prudence of "Ten Indians" figured prominently in Hemingway's adolescent life—at least as conceived by his adult imagination—is beyond question. And it is to this historical young woman, also named Prudence, that my argument now turns.

In *Ernest Hemingway: A Reconsideration*, Philip Young observes that "many of the stories about Nick are very literal translations of some of the most important events in Hemingway's own life" and "remarkably little has been changed in the telling" (63). Few stories appear to be more sharply autobiographical in their details than "Ten Indians." In "The Bacons and Prudence," a chapter of a biographical study focusing on Hemingway's life in northern Michigan, Constance Montgomery re-travels the route from the small town of Petoskey to the Hemingway cabin that appears in "Ten Indians." She identifies particular men and women in the area who peopled the story (many with the same first name) and interviews Joe Bacon (a.k.a. Joe Garner), a neighbor of the Hemingway family who recalls making such evening wagon trips from town and whose son Carl was a summer companion of young Ernest. She distinguishes specific landmarks in the story—the incline where the boys climbed out of the wagon and it was "hard pulling" for the horses (253), the hilltop near the schoolhouse from which Nick glimpses the lights of Petoskey. Montgomery also spoke to a retired teacher from the one-room schoolhouse where an Indian girl named "Prudence Boulton," two years younger than Ernest, had attended class. Her teacher remembered that Prudy had "nice skin" and "long, black hair" and was "pretty" (100).

In a similar journey to northern Michigan several years later, David St. John interviewed two Ottawa Indians who lived near the Boultons when Prudence was young and her family's shanty was a short walk from the Hemingway cabin. The elderly Indians similarly remembered Prudy as being "very pretty," a "very fine girl," and "very sweet" (82, 84). St. John researched the local school records and found that Prudence had a brother Richard who was three years younger than she, and a brother Edward who was five years older. The Prudence of "Ten Indians" makes a dramatic appearance in "Fathers and Sons," an episode which I shall come to shortly, and from this story her age can be dated as between that of her fictional older brother Eddie and younger brother Billy, which corresponds well with the actual age differences among the real-life Prudence Boulton, her older half-brother Edward, and her younger brother Richard. This chronology would make Prudence two years younger than Ernest. The Ottawa Indians interviewed by St. John and the retired school teacher interviewed by Montgomery both recalled that Prudence Boulton had died when she was still a young woman (one local rumor had it that she perished giving birth to Ernest's baby), and St. John had the distinct feeling that his questions about Prudence made the two Indians feel downcast—that they, indeed, were "holding something back" (84). More recent research has perhaps supplied the reason. A 15 February 1918 announcement in the *Petoskey Evening News* reports the double suicide of Richard Castle and "a young Indian girl with whom he had been living," identified as Prudence by local police (Smith, "Tenth Indian" 73–74).[4]

Though it is, of course, impossible to determine whether the events described in "Ten Indians" actually occurred, circumstantial evidence suggests a strong possibility. In his biography of Hemingway, Carlos Baker indicates that Ernest and Prudence came into close contact when she worked as a domestic helper for Ernest's mother. Baker, however, dismisses any romantic relationship between the two teenagers and asserts that "Ernest's fictional accounts of sexual initiation with Prudy Boulton were more likely the product of wishful thinking than of fact" (26). Hemingway's widow, in contrast, held a far different view of her husband's relationship with Prudence and regarded Nick's experiences as "a reflection of real-life fact" (Lynn 52). Mary Hemingway also records in her autobiography that during Hemingway's courtship of her, the author told her that her legs were "like Prudy Boulton's ... the brown Chippewa girl who was the first female he had ever pleasured" (103).

Beyond this speculation about historical events, it is clear that Prudence—real, imagined, or a combination of both—was vividly alive in Hemingway's mind. As James Mellow surmises, she became "an enduring symbol of indulgent and gratifying female sexuality.... [which] haunted Hemingway's fiction through nearly every decade of his adult life" (31). In fact, so "real" was this female who "did" with the young Hemingway "what no one has ever done better" ("Fathers and Sons," *CSS* 375) that he compared other women—including his future wife Mary—to her. On his ill-fated African safari of 1953, for instance, Hemingway became enamored of a native girl named Debba that he described as "a cross between Prudy Boulton and an impudent, dark, short-haired version of Marilyn Monroe" (Meyers 502). With his wife Mary away in Nairobi, he "began an elaborate courtship of his African 'fiancée'" which culminated in a celebration so "energetic" that it broke Mary's camp bed (Baker 518). As in Hemingway's relationship with Prudence, whether an actual consummation occurred or not is open to question. In this instance, however, the return of Mary Hemingway to the camp put an end to Ernest's liaison with his born-again Prudence.

Notwithstanding the eroticism that Prudy appears to have been imbued with—in both Hemingway's own life and that of his alter-ego Nick—critics have too frequently placed the relationship on the Procrustean bed of "socioeconomic exploitation." Theodore Bardacke's dismissal of Nick's relationship with Prudence, for example, as "an adolescent union with a little Indian girl who is submissive and devoid of any real individual personality" (348) is characteristic of this short shrift. Yet such readings not only fail to attend carefully to the stories (Prudence seems far more worldly and in control of the relationship than Nick, for instance) but also do not take into account Hemingway's deeply felt, though by no means simple, primitivism.

Baker observes that as a boy Hemingway "was constantly aware of [the Indians'] presence, like atavistic shadows moving along the edges of his consciousness" (13); throughout his life Hemingway sometimes even pronounced that he was "one-eighth Indian," with no basis other than imagination for his claim (Lewis, "Long Time Ago Good" 203). Although a full discussion of Hemingway's view of the aboriginal and autochthonic is beyond the scope of this essay,[5] let it suffice to point out here that in such atavistic pursuits as camping, hunting, fishing, and fighting, as well as in human relationships, Hemingway appraised the primitive as no less than "the substitution of the authentic for the inauthentic" (Lewis, "Long Time Ago Good" 207). In this regard, Prudy was hardly a member of a benighted race over which Hemingway could exert his superior economic and racial status. Rather she was a flesh-and-blood manifestation of a dimension of human experience that he believed to be more real and rich than life within the confines of well-mannered civilization. Given Hemingway's relationship with the complex site—philosophical, psychological, autobiographical—that Prudence occupied in his psyche, and its influence over him, it is perhaps not surprising that years after writing "Ten Indians" Hemingway recalled in an interview that he had felt "very sad" after drafting the story (Plimpton 131).

The final evidence for a different interpretation of "Ten Indians" is found intertextually in other Nick Adams stories. "Indian Camp" and "The Killers" present some of the clearest examples of comparable experiences that Nick cannot come to grips with and instead retreats from or flees. In "Indian Camp," Nick as a young boy accompanies his father to an Indian settlement where a woman has been in labor for three days. As Nick looks on, his father performs a Caesarean, with no anesthesia, using a jackknife for a scalpel and fishing line for sutures. Before the operation is over, Nick no longer watches, for his "curiosity had been gone for a long time" (CSS 69). In the meantime, to make matters worse, the woman's husband, who has been confined to the shanty with a foot injury, commits suicide by cutting his throat with a razor. After seeing the birth by backwoods Caesarean and the bloody corpse of the new Indian father, Nick asks his own father as they return home in a rowboat whether "dying is hard"; he then arrives at the childish conclusion that "he would never die" (70). In *The Tip of the Iceberg: Hemingway and the Short Story*, Johnston perceptively observes that "Indian Camp" is "the story of an abortive initiation of a sensitive boy who is not able to cope with, nor to learn from, the violent lessons of the night. At the moment of truth, he flinches. Rather than taking a step toward maturity, Nick, figuratively speaking, stumbles back into the sheltering arms of his father" (54).

In "The Killers" an older Nick similarly evades the implications of his experience but this time with physical rather than psychological flight. In this story Nick happens to be in the wrong place at the wrong time—chatting with his friend George at Henry's Lunch-Room—when he is bound and gagged by two professional hit-men. They have been contracted to kill a retired prizefighter who eats supper every night at the diner. That night, the boxer doesn't show up and because Nick has "a lot of luck" in the words of one of the killers, he experiences nothing more than a brush with a violent death. His first response when the hit-men leave is to "swagger it off," for as the narrator explains, "He had never had a towel in his mouth before" (*CSS* 220). But after warning the intended victim—and seeing the boxer's resigned acceptance of his slaying—Nick decides as the story ends to "get out of this town" (222). Both of his reactions, the initial swagger and the later flight, indicate his refusal to realize the implications of his experiences. As DeFalco notes, "The choice of flight merely reflects his unwillingness to face the consequences of his knowledge" (64). "Indian Camp" and "The Killers" thus illustrate the psychological mechanism of denial similarly at work in "Ten Indians," where Nick buries in his unconscious the infidelity of his first lover.

In two stories besides "Ten Indians"—"The Last Good Country" and "Fathers and Sons"—Prudence also plays a role, though she is referred to as "Trudy" rather than "Prudy."[6] In "The Last Good Country" she is a highly charged though physically absent character (as in "Ten Indians") whom Nick's younger sister names as her rival for Nick's affection as the brother-and-sister pair strike out to "the last good country": "You don't mind you're with me instead of going to Trudy?" Nick's sister asks (513), implying that her brother might prefer a sexual liaison with Prudence rather than his sister's companionship. Only after a prickly exchange in which they agree to no longer refer to Nick's romantic interest are Nick and Littless able to settle into a comfortable partnership. The original manuscript version of the story contains a more sexually explicit exchange about Prudy/Trudy between Nick and his sister; this was deleted by editors for matters of "taste." The manuscript from which the posthumously published story was adapted reads:

"'You wouldn't go and make her another baby?' Littless asked. To which Nick replied, 'I don't know'" (Smith, *Reader's Guide* 312). Thus, in "The Last Good Country" Prudence remains a haunting presence if only for the reason that Nick has previously consummated with her the sort of sexual attraction that remains unacted upon in his flirtations with his sister.

It is, however, "Fathers and Sons" which presents the missing puzzle-piece for a full-fledged revision of conventional readings of "Ten Indians." As the final story of *Winner Take Nothing*, it supplies "the thing omitted"—the lost center to the earlier story. In "Fathers and Sons," Nick as the grown-up "Nicholas Adams," drives through the fall countryside with his son beside him in the car; his thoughts stray to his own father, their relationship, and his father's Victorian injunctions about sex. As Nick enters a reverie, the third person narration becomes subjective:

> Nick's own education in those earlier matters had been acquired in the hemlock woods behind the Indian camp. This was reached by a trail which ran from the cottage through the woods to the farm and then by a road which wound through the slashings to the camp. Now if he could still feel all of that trail with bare feet. First there was the pine-needle loam through the hemlock woods behind the cottage where the fallen logs crumbled into wood dust and long splintered pieces of wood hung like javelins in the tree that had been struck by lightning. You crossed the creek on a log and if you stepped off there was the black muck of the swamp. You climbed a fence out of the woods.... (371–72)

Nick's rumination takes him into the very terrain of "Ten Indians"—along a path he likewise trod "with bare feet" through "the hemlock woods behind the cabin," along the "black muck of the swamp," crossing identical boundaries as he "climbed a fence." The same Edenic details link the two stories and locations, like landmarks of a forgotten Paradise, such that Nick's buried desire awakens and he muses, "Now if he could still feel all that trail with bare feet..." he might once again re-enter the Garden. Yet this time, Nick's initial recollection of his first good country contains barely concealed hints of wounding and trauma, for he now recalls that the road "wound through the slashings" and "long splintered pieces of wood hung like javelins in the tree that had been struck by lightning." He continues down the path, nevertheless, and dreamlike, enters the forest primeval, the sacred time and place in which he knew Prudence:

... there was still much forest then, virgin forest where the trees grew high before there were any branches and you walked on the brown, clean, springy-needled ground with no undergrowth and it was cool on the hottest days and they three lay against the trunk of a hemlock wider than two beds are long ... (372)

In the prelapsarian state, under a hemlock whose trunk was "wider than two beds are long," Nick partakes of unlimited and uninhibited sexuality with his dusky Eve. Even the presence of Prudence's younger brother Billy presents no obstruction to them: "I no mind Billy. He my brother" says Trudy. In the aftermath of sexual union, Nick feels "hollow and happy" (273) as he did in "Ten Indians" when teased about Prudy. A gruesomely comic interlude (with admittedly dark overtones) follows in which Nick threatens to scalp and kill Trudy's brother Eddie if he attempts to steal into Nick's sister's bed, as Billy says he intends.[7] But soon all is forgiven and the young couple is once again making love on the forest floor. The interlude comes to a close when Trudy says, "Give me kiss on the face" (374).

Having come face to face with his first love—and having kissed her again—Nick is suddenly back in the car driving once more through the evening fields, his thoughts returning to his father and the conflicts between them. Only when Nick's own son unexpectedly asks him—sensing somehow the scenes that have passed before his father's eyes—what the Indians of his father's childhood "were like to be with," does Nick's mind venture to the heart of that experience and the object of his long-ago amnesia:

Could you say she did first what no one has ever done better and mention plump brown legs, flat belly, hard little breasts, well holding arms, quick searching tongue, the flat eyes, the good taste of mouth, then uncomfortably, tightly, sweetly, moistly, lovely, tightly, achingly, fully, finally, unendingly, never-endingly, never-to-endingly, suddenly ended, the great bird flown like an owl in the twilight, only it was daylight in the woods and hemlock needles stuck against your belly. (375–76)

Nick's recollection of Prudence is surely the most poetical and moving of Hemingway's descriptions of the sexual act. Nick *does* once again tread the path through the hemlocks and lie in the forest bed. Moreover, he comes to momentarily realize that some element of this experience has not been lost in spite of its suppression and ache:

... all the empty pain killer bottles and the flies that buzz do not kill the sweetgrass smell, the smoke smell and that other like a fresh cased marten skin. Nor any jokes about [Indians] nor old squaws take that away.... (376)

Yet the fruits of Nick's reveries and the story of his subsequent fall from grace are challenging lore to transmit to the son whose question has prompted Nick's memories. He is not equal to the task—indeed, to this potential initiation, for if the son is old enough to ask perceptive questions he is old enough to learn. With a chin as weak and tutoring as ineffectual as his own father's, Nick reduces his experience of "the Indians" to the evasive reply, "You might not like them.... But I think you would" (376).

Nick's failure to impart to his son anything but the vaguest generalities about his past suggests that his wound has not healed and that the inexorable post-Edenic sins of the father will visited upon the son in yet another generation. Nick's pattern of concealment and silence, betrayal and denial, begun long ago in a wagon on a summer evening, still mars his apprehension of an original love that was "unconscious of racial distinctions or assumptions of superiority or inferiority" (Thurston 174). Nowhere in the Nick Adams stories is there evidence that Nick ever again sustained a romantic relationship with a woman. Like the hemlocks whose bark has been peeled and the splintered tree struck by lightning, Nick's course—the same as his father's—leads unremittingly toward his own mortality. Thus, as the story closes, his son asks by way of innocent but prescient reminder, why they never "pray at the tomb" of his grandfather (376). And he expresses hope that his own father's grave will not be far away so that he can pray at it when Nick is dead.

Notes

I would like to thank Ray Lewis White and Professor Stanley Renner of Illinois State University for their comments on an earlier draft of this essay.

1. Robert Fleming's "Hemingway's Dr. Adams—Saint or Sinner?" aptly summarizes the various points of view expressed in this exchange.

2. Only Joseph DeFalco, in the chapter "Initiation Experiences" in *The Hero in Hemingway's Short Stories*, appears to recognize in a passing comment the nature of Nick's response as "a childish denial of the efficacy of the experience as a step towards maturation" (52), though he undermines his observation with the dubious assertion that "[t]he tone of this tale makes it impossible to interpret the 'hurt' Nick receives from the affair in any fashion other that it is bathetic" (50).

3. My discussion of these manuscript versions is indebted to Paul Smith's authoritative article on the composition history of "Ten Indians" entitled "The Tenth Indian and the Thing Left Out."

4. In his biography of Hemingway, Peter Griffin writes, without specifying his sources, that "Prudence Boulton, three months pregnant by a French-Canadian

lumberjack ... committed suicide. Both had taken strychnine, the Indians said, and their screams had been heard for hours across Susan Lake" (53).

5. This topic is treated thoughtfully and thoroughly in Robert Lewis' " 'Long Time Ago Good, Now No Good": Hemingway's Indian Stories."

6. The fact that Prudence is referred to as "Trudy" in "The Last Good Country" and "Fathers and Sons" has caused at least one critic, Roger Whitlow, to make the curious claim that they are "different girls" (101). Notwithstanding this conjecture, the two ostensibly different girls are conjoined by age, race, location, time, description, personality, Nick's relationship with them, and even by name—for "Trudy" is a shortened form of Prudence. Moreover, earlier drafts of "Fathers and Sons" refer to "Trudy" as "Prudy," indicating beyond a doubt that Hemingway had the same character in mind for all three stories.

7. For reasons of space I cannot examine the implications of this scene. See Ann Boutelle's "Hemingway and 'Papa': Killing of the Father in the Nick Adams Fiction" for an insightful discussion of Nick's sudden display of Victorian honor and the overtones of incest and violence in the exchange.

WORKS CITED

Baker, Carlos. *Hemingway: The Writer as Artist.* Princeton: Princeton U P, 1952.

Bakker, Jan. *Fiction as Survival Strategy: A Comparative Study of the Major Works of Ernest Hemingway and Saul Bellow.* Amsterdam: Rodopi, 1983.

Bardacke, Theodore. "Hemingway's Women." In *Ernest Hemingway: The Man and His Work.* Ed. John McCaffery. New York: Cooper Square, 1950. 340–51.

Boutelle, Ann. "Hemingway and 'Papa': The Killing of the Father in the Nick Adams Fiction." *Journal of Modern Literature* 9 (1981): 135–36.

DeFalco, Joseph. *The Hero in Hemingway's Short Stories.* Pittsburgh: U of Pittsburgh P, 1963.

Fleming, Robert. "Hemingway's Dr. Adams—Saint or Sinner?" *Arizona Quarterly* 39.2 (Summer 1983): 101–10.

Flora, Joseph. *Hemingway's Nick Adams.* Baton Rouge: Louisiana State U P, 1982.

Griffin, Peter. *Along With Youth: Hemingway, The Early Years.* New York: Oxford U P, 1985.

Hemingway, Ernest. *The Complete Short Stories of Ernest Hemingway: The Finca Vigía Edition.* New York: Scribner's, 1987.

Hemingway, Mary. *How It Was.* New York: Knopf, 1976.

Johnston, Kenneth. *The Tip of the Iceberg: Hemingway and the Short Story.* Greenwood, FL: Penkevill, 1987.

Lewis, Robert W. *Hemingway on Love.* Austin: U of Texas P, 1965.

_____. "Long Time Ago Good, Now No Good: Hemingway's Indian Stories." *New Critical Approaches to the Stories of Ernest Hemingway.* Ed. Jackson Benson. Durham: Duke U P, 1990. 200–12.

Lynn, Kenneth. *Hemingway.* New York: Simon & Schuster, 1987.

Mellow, James. *Hemingway: A Life Without Consequences.* Boston: Houghton Mifflin, 1992.

Meyers, Jeffrey. *Hemingway: A Biography.* New York: Harper & Row, 1985.

Montgomery, Constance Cappel. *Hemingway in Michigan.* Waitsfield: Vermont Crossroads, 1977.

Plimpton, George. "An Interview with Ernest Hemingway." In *Modern Critical Views: Ernest Hemingway.* Ed. Harold Bloom. New York: Chelsea House, 1985. 119–36.

Smith, Paul. *A Reader's Guide to the Short Stories. of Ernest Hemingway.* Boston: G.K. Hall, 1989.

_____. "The Tenth Indian and the Thing Left Out." In *Ernest Hemingway: The Writer in Context*. Ed. James Nagel. Madison: U of Wisconsin P, 1984. 53–74.

St. John, Donald. "Hemingway and Prudence." *Connecticut Review* 5.2 (April 1972): 78–84.

Thurston, Jarvis. *Reading Modern Short Stories*. Chicago: Scott, 1955.

Whitlow, Roger. *Cassandra's Daughters: The Women In Hemingway*. Westport, CT: Greenwood, 1984.

Williams, Wirt. *The Tragic Art of Ernest Hemingway*. Baton Rouge: Louisiana U P, 1981.

Young, Philip. *Ernest Hemingway: A Reconsideration*. University Park: Pennsylvania State U P, 1966.

DAVID J. FERRERO

Nikki Adams and the Limits of Gender Criticism

Hemingway is the perfect straw man for feminist critics. And in many ways he was asking for it. Witness his sometimes self-parodic *machismo*; his preoccupation with war, boxing, hunting and bullfighting; his string of divorces; his celebration of the masculine in much of his writing after 1930. Yet this view distorts our understanding of much Hemingway fiction. This is especially true of the Nick Adams stories from *In Our Time*. I am thinking in particular of "The End of Something" and "The Three-Day Blow," which concern Nick's efforts to define and negotiate relationships with men and women, and "Cross-Country Snow," which explores Nick's attempt to come to terms with the demands of paternity within the institution of monogamous marriage. In "The End of Something" Nick awkwardly, abruptly, and somewhat cruelly breaks up with his girlfriend Marjorie. In its sequel, "The Three-Day Blow," Nick's friend Bill helps him work through the breakup by getting him drunk and taking him hunting; the story ends with Nick getting over Marjorie and re-establishing camaraderie with his male companions. In "Cross-Country Snow" Nick and his friends ponder the threat that Nick's impending fatherhood poses to their friendship and Nick's freedom. These stories continue to be cited along with the others for misogyny and homoerotic male fantasizing about living a life of "men without women."

From *The Hemingway Review* 16, no. 2, Spring 1997. © 1997 by the Ernest Hemingway Foundation.

The accusations of misogyny in these stories rest upon a number of complaints: that Marjorie is simple and undeveloped, and that her growing expertise in manly pursuits threatens Nick; that Nick's rejection of her and rediscovery of male comradeship constitute desire to erase women from his life; that Nick's ambivalence about, and muted sense of entrapment by his wife's pregnancy betrays yet another fantasy of male freedom from women and paternal obligation.[1] Even the new school of Hemingway-friendly scholars who acknowledge the sympathetic treatment of Marjorie and other women in Hemingway's fiction tend to take some of these charges for granted.[2] In recent years, however, this second strand of scholarship has produced a small body of work that uses the tools of feminist criticism and gender studies to rethink the assumptions behind the charges. Mark Spilka,[3] Nancy Comley, and Robert Scholes[4] have done some of the most ambitious work in this area. Out of their work has a emerged a semi-rehabilitated Hemingway who grasped the socially constructed nature of gender, boldly explored the limits of conventional gender categories, and experimented with alternatives.

I want to take their work a step further, and use their portraits of a gender-bending Hemingway more literally (and playfully) to suggest that these stories resist the misogynist tag. I hope my method will expose the inconsistencies and double standards that mar current critical discourse on gender and power. Then I will demonstrate through more conventional close reading how these early stories present a remarkably critical interrogation of hard-boiled masculinity while recovering those elements of traditional masculinity most useful in an age of shifting gender relations.

For the first part of this analysis I propose a simple gender-bending exercise of my own, one that transposes gender categories in a rewriting of these Nick Adams stories. Let us imagine the publication of a collection of short stories by an exciting new woman writer about a young woman's coming of age, circa 1998. The protagonist in the story is a young woman, Nikki Adams (the name "Adams" being the female author's conscious attempt to reappropriate R.W.B. Lewis's "American Adam," while creating a symbolic feminine progenitor disassociated from the traditional Edenic taint). Some of the stories deal with her early relationships with boys, and her discomfort as she becomes aware of society's expectations of her as a woman. With the help of a reliable female companion who provides her with temporary sanctuary and sage advice, she manages to grope her way toward the understanding that comes from courageously facing the hardships imposed on women under patriarchy.

In one story, an adolescent Nikki breaks off a relationship with her boyfriend. One passage describes her handling of the break-up and her boyfriend's reactions:

Mark unpacked the basket of supper.

"I don't feel like eating," said Nikki.

"Come on and eat, Nik."

"All right."

They ate without talking, and watched the two rods and the firelight on the water.

"There's going to be a moon tonight," Mark said happily.

"You know everything," Nikki said.

"Oh Nikki, cut it out! Don't be that way!"

"I can't help it," Nikki said. "You do. You know everything. That's the trouble. You know you do."

Mark did not say anything.

"I've taught you everything. You know you do. What don't you know, anyway?"

"Oh, shut up," Mark said. "There comes the moon."

They sat on the blanket without touching each other and watched the moon rise.

"You don't have to talk silly," Mark said. "What's really the matter?"

"I don't know."

"Of course you know."

"No I don't."

"Go on and say it."

Nikki looked at the moon, coming up over the hills.

"It isn't fun any more."

She was afraid to look at Mark. Then she looked at him. He sat there with his back toward her. She looked at his back. "It isn't any fun any more. Not any of it."

He didn't say anything. She went on. "I feel as though everything was gone to hell inside of me. I don't know Mark. I don't know what to say."

She looked on at his back.

"Isn't love any fun?" Mark said.

"No," Nikki said. Mark stood up. Nikki sat there with her head in her hands.

"I'm going to take the boat," Mark called out to her. "You can walk back to the point."

"All right," Nikki said. "I'll push the boat off for you."

(adapted from *IOT* 34–5)

It is not difficult to imagine the feminist reception of such a story. The problematizing of gender representations in fiction would likely be forgotten, and Mark would emerge in the critical discourse as the typically self-absorbed adolescent male. Having forgotten that it was his independent, free-spirited girlfriend who taught him how to catch and clean fish—the threat this poses to his masculine construction of self has perhaps caused him to repress the memory—he now attempts to assert dominance. Facing such masculinist impudence perhaps for the first time, Nikki bristles. Confused, she lashes out at him, calling him a know-it-all. He tells her to "cut it out," which attempts to silence her while denying the legitimacy of her feelings. When she presses the issue he tries to silence her again by telling her to "shut up." He follows up by trying to assert his knowledge and regain control the conversation by pointing again to the moon. After a few moments' silence, Mark belittles her, calling her outburst "silly." Her laconic "It isn't fun anymore" speaks volumes about her growing awareness of just how unsatisfying heterosexual monogamy is for a woman of dawning confidence and self-possession like herself. Mark's behavior this evening drives the point home. He responds with the platitude, "Isn't love fun?"—a lame attempt to reinscribe her within the structures of patriarchal romance while exploiting her feelings of guilt. Wounded by her flat "No," he retaliates by taking the boat and leaving her behind. Being a gracious, maturing woman who even now feels compelled to put his needs before hers, she actually helps him take it.

The next story in the collection picks up where the breakup story left off. Nikki's tougher, wiser friend Billie (a sexually ambiguous name suggesting a subtext of lesbian bonding), has taken her back to her father's cabin where they can be alone for awhile. Billie knows what has just happened and tries to console Nikki. So she raids her father's liquor cabinet and suggests they get drunk together. As they drink they discuss baseball, books, and drinking etiquette. They revel in the transgression of being young women who drink whiskey and talk about sports, just like Billie's father, who is "out with the gun." With the oppressive father/phallus safely out sight for awhile, Billie speaks openly to Nikki:

> "You were very wise, Nikker," Billie said.
> "What do you mean?" asked Nikki.
> "To bust off that Mark business," Billie said.
> "I guess so," said Nikki.
> "It was the only thing to do. If you hadn't, by now you'd be back home working trying to get enough money to get married."
> Nikki said nothing.
> "Once a woman's married she's absolutely bitched," Billie went

on. "She hasn't got anything more. Nothing. Not a damn thing. She's done for. You've seen the gals that get married."

Nikki said nothing.

"You can tell them," Billie said. "They get this sort of fat married look. They're done for."

"Sure," said Nikki.

"It was probably bad busting it off," Billie said. "But you always fall for somebody else and then it's all right. Fall for them but don't let them ruin you."

"Yes," said Nikki.

"If you'd have married him you would have had to marry the whole family. Remember his mother and the guy she married?"

Nikki nodded.

"Imagine having them around the house all the time and going to Sunday dinners at their house, and having them over to dinner and him telling you all the time what to do and how to act."

Nikki sat quiet.

"You came out of it damned well," Billie said. "Now he can marry somebody of his own sort and settle down and be happy...."
(adapted from *IOT* 46–7)

Billie's advice and the grim picture of marital life that she paints would be applauded as a kind of manifesto for women's emancipation from the constraints of patriarchal domination. Nikki's tacit ambivalence about what she hears would be read as a sign that she has not yet raised her consciousness fully. Yet when the two finally leave the confines of the cabin, Nikki has an epiphany: "Outside now the Mark business was no longer so tragic. It was not even very important. The wind blew everything like that away" (49). That moment would perhaps be hailed as Nikki's first conscious awareness of her right to forge an existence outside the cultural and institutional structures designed by men to circumscribe and subordinate her. Billie would emerge as a tough feminist role model, and Nikki as a heroine for our times.

A later story in the collection finds Nikki on a ski trip in the Alps with some expatriate friends of hers. She has apparently achieved the dream of feminist sisterhood and independence from patriarchal authority, as symbolized by the pristine mountain landscape. She and her friends rest after a day of skiing and talk about their futures. The scene is idyllic. Then, abruptly, one of her friends, Geri, shatters the reader's illusion:

"Are you going to have a baby?" Geri said, coming down to the table from the wall.

"Yes."

"When?"

"Late next summer."

"Are you glad?"

"Yes. Now."

"Will you go back to the States?"

"I guess so."

"Do you want to?"

"No."

"Does Henry?"

"No."

Geri sat silent. She looked at the empty bottle and the empty glasses.

"It's hell, isn't it?" she said.

"Not exactly," Nikki said.

"Why not?"

"I don't know," Nikki said.

"Will you ever go skiing together in the States?" Geri said.

"I don't know," said Nikki.

... "Maybe we'll never go skiing again, Nikki," Geri said.

"We've got to," said Nikki. "It isn't worth it if you can't."

"We'll go, all right," Geri said.

"We've got to," Nikki agreed.

"I wish we could make a promise about it," Geri said.

... "There isn't any good in promising," Nikki said. (adapted from *IOT* 111–12)

Patriarchy returns with a vengeance. Just when our heroine seems to have learned Billie's lesson and carved out an alternative lifestyle, nature and culture conspire to ensnare her. This turn of events could be read as a flaw in the story or an authorial copout, an unnecessary capitulation to the cultural expectation that children be raised by a monogamous heterosexual couple. Or, it might be read as a brilliant stroke of understatement. That no one even suggests she transgress such powerful normative expectations (or risk economic hardship) by raising the child outside the confines of heterosexual monogamy speaks volumes about patriarchy's iron grip. So powerful are such norms, so menacing the sanctions for breaching them, that the alternative cannot even be spoken. They are once again silenced. The vision of homosocial utopia is shattered for all of them. The critics turn the story sequence into a clarion call for women readers.

These scenarios reveal the double standard that clouds many of our analyses of gender and power. When a male author interrogates the social institutions that obligate men to women, he is a misogynist. When a woman writes of women imposed upon by men and the same institutions, she is a feminist. In a sense, there is no contradiction here. The only difference is what the terminology foregrounds and erases. The term "misogynist" is negative; it focuses on what the writer is *against*. The term "feminist," on the other hand, is positive, focusing on what the writer is *for*. If our vocabulary included the term "misandroist," and if the term "masculinist" had positive connotations, we could pair our terms symmetrically. But the asymmetry exists, and therein lies the double-standard: Writing that concerns itself with defining the masculine and that explores the problematic role of women within that definition is oppressive; that which concerns itself with defining the feminine and that explores the the problematic role of men in such a definition is emancipatory.

If this double standard was ever justified, it certainly is not today. The Nick Adams stories of *In Our Time* have nothing to do with misogyny; they are about a boy's efforts to define himself as a man. That young men need to learn to negotiate relations with women and other men, and to accept adult responsibilities is a condition created by life, not by patriarchy, or capitalism, or male fiction writers. And as the above experiment in gender transposition suggests, a sympathetic, nuanced response to the work can emerge once we lay aside ironclad preconceptions and ideological axe-grinding.

Nick does not hate women. He is an adolescent who gropes awkwardly with them and his feelings for them. When he breaks things off with Marjorie he botches it. He broods, then snaps, then broods and evades, before finally uttering a lame "It isn't fun anymore." Sensitive readers are justified in sympathizing with Marjorie, who until now has thought everything was fine, and who was more likely to expect a marriage proposal at this point than a breakup. But if Nick looks bad—and to Hemingway's credit he does look bad—we are allowed to see why in "The Three Day Blow." Nick is despondent after the breakup. Bill tries to make him feel better with some tough guy platitudes about male emasculation in marriage. But the narration does not encourage us to accept Bill's world view. Nick certainly doesn't. Nick's silence throughout most of Bill's monologue suggests that his words are falling on deaf ears. The next paragraph confirms Nick's indifference to Bill's bombast:

> Nick said nothing. The liquor had all died out of him and left him alone. Bill wasn't there. He wasn't sitting in front of the fire or going fishing tomorrow with Bill and his dad or anything. He wasn't drunk. It was all gone. All he knew was that he had once

had Marjorie and that he had lost her. She was gone and he had sent her away. That was all that mattered. He might never see her again. Probably he never would. It was all gone, finished. (47)

Despite Bill's diatribe, Nick feels the loss deeply and begins to understand painfully the finality of what he has done. Worse, he does not know yet whether he has done the right thing. The story's ending seems to undercut this interpretation when the wind blows away his angst and he re-establishes fellowship with the men. But to read this as misogynist (or latently homosexual) is absurd. Breakups happen. And when they do, those involved seek solace with friends or family members, usually of the same sex, because that is where they will likely find their most sympathetic hearing. Nick doesn't have to hate women and love men to break off his relationship and start over. He only has to be confused about what he wants.

If this reading of "Three-Day Blow" seems thin at first, it gains strength when read in the context of "Cross-Country Snow." Here Nick clearly has misgivings about leaving his friends and starting a family. Domesticity and fatherhood will take him away from the idyllic life he has enjoyed with his friends. But the writing is on the wall even before we learn of Helen's pregnancy. George has to go back to school, which interferes with Nick's desire to ski another day. George himself wishes he didn't have to return. He says to Nick: "[D]on't you wish could just bum together ... and not give a damn about anything?" (145). The young men have already become aware that they will have to separate. Nick's paternity is just one of the adult responsibilities intruding on their world. Their awareness that this ski trip will likely be their last carefree time together provokes understandable melancholy and uncertainty.

Nick does not rebel against Helen or the child. He says he doesn't feel bad about what was clearly an unintended pregnancy, though he feels the pang of separation from George. If Nick seems unenthusiastic, it is because he is scared. Marriage and family loom ominously for a young man who has only in the past few years enjoyed freedom from familial constraints. Nonetheless, his friends speak of Helen as if she were a familiar part of Nick's life. No one blames Helen or curses her, least of all Nick. The conversation is very matter of fact. Nick has consciously chosen domesticity and his friends accept it without comment, making clear the rejection of Bill that may seem unconvincing at the end of "Three-Day Blow." Nick does not resent his wife or his life. He merely feels a deep melancholy about trading the carefree security of youth for the burdens and uncertainty of maturity. Yet he does accept the obligation. Nick's feeling of resignation expresses not misogyny, but stoic acceptance of his duty to Helen and their child.

This reassertion of heterosexual monogamy plays into the hands of critics who see heterosexual monogamy as part of the problem in the first place. Once again, though, Hemingway is caught in a double bind. When he seems to eschew women and family, he is pilloried for being a misogynist man-child. (Even the supposed homoerotic subtext of "Three Day Blow" fails to exonerate him.) If he reaffirms heterosexual monogamy he is accused of reinscribing heterosexist, patriarchal oppression. How can both be offensive? Are such interrogations and outcomes really so hostile to women's or feminists' concerns?

We have already seen that charges of misogyny stem from a too narrow reading of Nick's experience and awareness. Feminists who define heterosexual monogamy as oppressive might celebrate the challenge to domesticity that the stories offer, but the feminist double standard requires them to see Nick's misgivings as a threat. They could just as well lament the provisional acceptance of marriage and family as foreclosing the alternatives the text opens up, because Nick's resignation defuses the text's own transgressive potential, reinscribing and reinforcing the norms it initially challenges.

But for Nick to do otherwise would leave us with a single mother, an abandoned child, and a deadbeat dad. Thus, the message of stoic acceptance of paternal responsibility seems ultimately to be a congenial one for those feminists concerned about the frequent abdication of paternal responsibility in late 20th-century America and its impact on the condition of women. In an age of single, teenage mothers and child-support scofflaws, the Hemingway code seems a good place to start in reconstructing a version of masculinity that stresses fulfillment of these and other social obligations. This may do little to usher in the lesbian utopia dreamed of by the most radical gender theorists, but for more sober-minded feminists, it can provide a realistic avenue through which to construct a more equitable model of male-female interdependence.

Of course, we cannot reassert the code naively. The Hemingway code has its dark side, as evidenced by Hemingway's own life, which illustrates how difficult the code is to live up to. But this is where the insights of modern feminism step in—if its excesses can be curbed. If we can move beyond the dogmatism, distrust, and acrimony that pervade so much feminist criticism and pedagogy, we can situate writers like Hemingway in conversations that explore with greater nuance the various constructions and negotiations that shape gender relations. This dialogue can lead toward alternative approaches to gender relations that celebrate both worlds and allow them to commingle in an environment of mutual sympathy. We cannot do this without voices such as Hemingway's, for they remain resonant to many men, including those who never experienced his world. To simply ridicule male voices, to dismiss their culture and deny them the fraternity that women have learned to cultivate among themselves, only exacerbates the antagonism. Backlash in this context is inevitable. Hemingway's fiction can provide models for that, too. But the searching introspection and eventual conscious commitment that Nick brings to his relationships points to a better way: a stoic, clear-headed, and tough-minded middle ground for both men and women, free from archaic social codes and strident ideological posturing.

NOTES

1. Actually, the indictment precedes feminism. Conventional wisdom has tended to take Hemingway's alleged misogyny for granted. As early as 1940 Edmund Wilson, one of Hemingway's early admirers, criticized him for his "growing antagonism to women" (276). Even in these pre-feminist days, critics such as Wilson and Leslie Fiedler concluded that Hemingway could not depict women sensitively, or claimed that he preferred to depict men without women. These critics began early to reduce Hemingway's women into two categories: "love-slaves" and "bitches." It was decades before Roger Whitlow recognized these categories as products of the critics' biases rather than Hemingway's (10–15). The rise of feminism in the 1960s further tarnished Hemingway's reputation on this score. Katherine Rogers' *The Troublesome Helpmate: A History of Misogyny in Literature* picked up where Wilson and Fiedler left off and turned their criticism into a full-blown assault on Hemingway, as well as others in the male-defined canon. By the time Judith Fetterley's infamous "*A Farewell to Arms*: Hemingway's Resentful Cryptogram" was first published in 1976, Hemingway's academic reputation had suffered considerably (enough that Carole Carpenter could design critical thinking assignments using *The Sun Also Rises* as a primer in sexist thought and language in her undergraduate writing courses), and he was showing up less and less often on high school and college syllabi.

2. As Susan Beegel has noted, the backlash against Hemingway may have had more to do with reaction against his critical champions of the 1950s and 1960s than with Hemingway himself. "When potential readers reject Hemingway as indifferent to minorities and hostile to women," she says, "they are often responding not to Hemingway's fiction, but to the indifference and hostility of some of his early critics, and the negative image of the author those influential first admirers unintentionally first projected" (277). Beegel's claim is confirmed by a survey of feminist considerations of Hemingway's fiction since the early 1980s, the impact of which was surprisingly positive mainly because they opened up new ways of appreciating Hemingway's treatment of women. Joyce Wexler's "E.R.A. for Hemingway: A Feminist Defense of *A Farewell to Arms*," Charles J. Nolan's "Hemingway's Women's Movement," and Robert Merrill's "Demoting Hemingway: Feminist Criticism and the Canon," challenged the early feminist pillorying of Hemingway, while studies such as Peter Balbert's "From Hemingway to Lawrence to Mailer: Survival and Sexual Identity in *A Farewell to Arms*," Wendy Martin's "Brett Ashley as New Woman in *The Sun Also Rises*," and Linda Wagner's "'Proud and Friendly and Gently': Women in Hemingway's Early Fiction," re-examined Hemingway's representations of women and construction of gender. These critical reassessments, of course, produced spirited rebuttals, but it is safe to say along with Robert Lewis that, at the very least, "the only safe conclusion one can reach about Hemingway's

depiction of women in general ... is that it is complex, and preconceptions of Hemingway's attitudes have almost certainly impeded careful reading and understanding of his work" (22).

3. Mark Spilka's heavily biographical *Hemingway's Quarrel with Androgyny* shifted the emphasis away from an exclusive concern with Hemingway's women toward a more comprehensive consideration of Hemingway's treatment of gender. Drawing on what we know of Hemingway's childhood, and equipped with a fully developed arsenal of new critical methodologies, Spilka examined Hemingway's family life and childhood reading preferences, and found tensions between Victorian and modern values that reflected those in the culture at large. Despite their strait-laced, Protestant, Midwestern values, Hemingway's parents raised him and his sisters androgynously, teaching all of them both domestic and outdoor skills, and going so far as to dress them and cut their hair alike. Hemingway was therefore particularly well-suited to explore the shifting definitions of gender that characterized the 1920s, and conditioned to view them favorably, if ambivalently. (Spilka concurs with Rena Sanderson, however, that after 1930 Hemingway—like American culture itself—eventually hardened into the masculinist pose he is now famous for before softening again toward the end of his life.) His analysis of Hemingway's early and late novels in light of his speculations about Hemingway's possible androgyny produces some persuasive readings of the fiction that point toward a Hemingway deeply sensitized to issues of culture and gender and the ways that the two interact, often to the detriment of the both men and women.

4. In *Hemingway's Genders*, Comley and Scholes take Spilka's androgyny thesis a step further, arguing that Hemingway actively sought out men and women who transgressed conventional gender roles, and covertly celebrated them in his fiction while scrupulously maintaining a macho, homophobic facade. However, they soberly pull up short of suggesting that Hemingway himself was a latent homosexual. In fact they argue quite the contrary: "The ability to enter into subject positions different from his own and to distance himself from his own views with mockery is one of Hemingway's strong qualities as a writer, and one for which he is seldom given sufficient credit" (129). They note for example that with the bitches in his fiction come the "rude writers" (41). In other words they argue that even Hemingway's seemingly most unrelenting bitches—most notoriously Margaret Macomber and Helen Walden—turn out to be bitches mainly in the minds of his male protagonists, whom Hemingway wants us to see as pathetic and unreliable, despite his identification with them—a striking display of self-criticism. Rena Sanderson makes the point as well:

> Although Hemingway has been condemned for depicting women as "bitches" very few such women actually appear in his writings, and almost exclusively during the 1930s. The few times Hemingway embodies his fears of powerful women in a fictive "bitch", he is attacking not only or primarily the woman but rather male passivity and dependence on women—traits he found in himself. Writing retrospectively in 1943, he admitted: "Take as good a woman as Pauline—a hell of a wonderful woman—and once she turns mean. Although, of course, it is your own actions that turn her mean. Mine I mean." (185)

In these studies Hemingway emerges as much more nuanced, self-critical, and sympathetic to the experiences of women and the problematics of traditional gender construction than once assumed. These qualities naturally show up frequently in his writing.

Works Cited

Balbert, Peter. "From Hemingway to to Lawrence to Mailer: Survival and Sexual Identity in *A Farewell to Arms." The Hemingway Review* 3.1 (Fall 1983): 30–43.

Beegel, Susan E "The Critical Reputation of Ernest Hemingway." *The Cambridge Companion to Hemingway.* Ed. Scott Donaldson. New York: Cambridge U P, 1996. 269–99.

Carpenter, Carol. "Exercises to Combat Sexist Reading and Writing." *College English* 43.3 (March 1983): 293–300.

Comley, Nancy R. and Robert Scholes. *Hemingways Genders: Rereading the Hemingway Text.* New Haven: Yale U P, 1994.

Fetterley, Judith. *"A Farewell to Arms*: Hemingway's 'Resentful Cryptogram.'" *The Resisting Reader: A Feminist Approach to American Fiction.* Bloomington: Indiana U P, 1987. 46–71.

Fiedler, Leslie A. *Love and Death in the American Novel.* Rev. edn. New York: Dell, 1960.

Hemingway, Ernest. *In Our Time.* 1930. New York: Macmillan, 1986.

Lewis, Robert W. *A Farewell to Arms: The War of the Words.* New York: Twayne, 1992.

Lewis, R.W.B. *The American Adam.* Chicago: U Chicago P, 1955.

Martin, Wendy. "Brett Ashley as New Woman in *The Sun Also Rises." New Essays on The Sun Also Rises.* Ed. Linda Wagner-Martin. Cambridge: Cambridge U P, 1987. 65–82.

Merrill, Robert. "Demoting Hemingway: Feminist Criticism and the Canon." *American Literature* 60.2 (May 1988): 255–68.

Nolan, Charles J., Jr. "Hemingway's Women's Movement." *Ernest Hemingway: Six Decades of Criticism.* Ed. Linda W. Wagner. East Lansing: Michigan State U P, 1987. 209–19.

Rogers, Katherine M. *The Troublesome Helpmate: A History of Misogyny in Literature.* Seattle: U of Washington P, 1966.

Sanderson, Rena. "Hemingway and Gender History." *The Cambridge Companion to Hemingway.* Ed. Scott Donaldson. New York: Cambridge UP, 1996. 170–96.

Spilka, Mark, *Hemingway's Quarrel with Androgyny.* Lincoln: U Nebraska P, 1990.

Wagner, Linda W. "'Proud and Friendly and Gently': Women in Hemingway's Early Fiction." *Ernest Hemingway: The Papers of a Writer.* Ed. Bernard Oldsey. New York: Garland, 1981. 63–71.

Wexler, Joyce. "E. R. A. for Hemingway: A Feminist Defense of *A Farewell to Arms." Georgia Review* 35.1 (1981): 111–23.

Whitlow, Roger. *Cassandra's Daughters: The Women in Hemingway.* Westport, CT: Greenwood, 1984.

———. "The Destruction/Prevention of the Family Relationship in Hemingway's Fiction." *Literary Review* 20 (1976): 5–16.

Wilson, Edmund. *The Wound and the Bow.* New York: Oxford U P, 1947.

HOWARD L. HANNUM

"Scared sick looking at it": A Reading of Nick Adams in the Published Stories

Nick Adams, like Huck Finn, Jay Gatsby, or any other major character in American literature, is entitled to a life of his own, but Nick is seldom allowed such imaginative separation from Ernest Hemingway. Autobiographical assumption is virtually automatic among those who write about Nick. On the other hand, those who read the Nick stories generally become caught up in his experience, and eschew the vast Hemingway scholarship, for the time, to respond to Nick as his own person. This, of course, is the Nick Adams that Hemingway, with his disdain for academics, wanted to present to us.[1]

Hemingway's future readers will surely remember him for his short stories, whose style of writing and subject matter won him his initial fame and played such a large part in the development of the modern short story. Although Hemingway has a thriving society of scholars to celebrate his achievements, he must ultimately depend on general readers for his fame. This latter group is far less likely than the scholars to remember his work after 1945, whose structural flaws, intrusive ego, and swollen prose at times make it seem the antithesis of the early great fiction.

The short stories centering on Nick have often been seen as the loose configuration of a novel: creative writers from D. H. Lawrence to Joyce Carol Oates have so viewed them. Further, Philip Young's collection, *The*

From *Twentieth-Century Literature* 47, no. 1 (Spring 2001): 92–113. © 2001 by Hofstra University.

Nick Adams Stories, though fleshed out with unpublished narratives, offered most of the published "Nick materials" in one volume. A popular college textbook, it has prompted many readers to treat the stories as stages of a novel. That is the general approach taken here.

"Indian Camp," with the devastating trauma of its Caesarian section and the suicide of the Indian father, not only scarred Nick Adams for life but also provided Hemingway with the framework of his metaphor in developing Nick. The stark realism of the first story was not something he used once and discarded. It went a long way toward explaining Nick, and Hemingway was not about to pass over it. What appears at first to be Hemingway's realistic detail in describing the Caesarian is in fact the basis for an extended system of metaphor, running through all of the stories and contributing greatly to their unity. Hemingway returned to the details, supplying new ones and integrating those of 1927 (*Men Without Women*) and 1933 (*Winner Take Nothing*) with the original ones of 1922–25 (*In Our Time*). He took each important detail of the Caesarian and began a sequence of images with it, story by story, in what Frank O'Connor called "elegant repetition" (159), a series of leitmotifs, of incremental metonymies, whose contexts he juxtaposed and superimposed, in ever-complicating patterns, with Nick always the true center of experience but never escaping the Indian camp. The night of horror inflicted "the wound" that never healed; the physical wound at Fossalta came too late for such effects. The girl watching a childbirth on the Karagatch Road (71)[2] at least got to cry, and might well have recovered, but Nick appears never to have done so.

The boy Nick's first sight of a naked woman involved, in rapid succession, the full form with its burgeoning abdomen, pubes (resembling a beard), and confusing absence of a penis; then, the piercing cut and explosion of blood, the laying bare of internal organs, and the tissue placed in his basin (68–69). Later, wounded by shrapnel at the Piave River (276), he identified with the Indian woman being held down for penetration by the steel of his father's knife. The Caesarian had to be severely damaging, intensifying his natural fear of castration. Followed immediately by the Indian father's gory throat-slashing, the Caesarian fixed Nick's association of blood and death with sex, and his obsession with the separation of body and soul, particularly at night. While life had come into the world from the mother's body in birth, it had gone out of the father's in suicide. Nick's mind had apparently blocked out much of the Caesarian, but he had clearly seen the father's head tilted back. Finally, Nick would later recognize, sexual treachery also seemed involved, in the never-resolved implication of Uncle George's paternity of the Indian child,[3] one possible cause of the father's suicide and of George's abrupt disappearance. The laughter of one of the young Indians when the mother bit George's arm was not lost on Nick, who was to know, in "Ten Indians" (254), the piercing laughter of the Garners at his own betrayal on July 4 a few years hence.

The surgery and the site haunted Nick long afterward. His association of sex with death was so strong that he went beyond the Elizabethan notion of *dying* (the fall of the blood) at the point of orgasm, to suppose an actual separation of his soul from his body. This occurred in his first sexual experience with Prudie Mitchell: "something inside Nick" had "gone a long way away"—and this happened, significantly, in the woods up near the Indian camp. In his reverie of Prudie (renamed Trudy) in "Fathers and Sons," Nick recalled, at the point of orgasm, "the great bird flown like an *owl* in the *twilight, only it was daylight in the woods*" (376; emphasis added). He had thus psychologically relocated his first adolescent experience of sex in the night of the Indian camp (the setting of the Caesarian). The notion of the soul's flight at the climax of sex was paralleled by its flight at the threat of death. Nick's soul did once leave him, but returned, as he was wounded in "Now I Lay Me" (276). After this, he had to sleep with a light on, for fear it would happen again (in the same story and in "A Way You'll Never Be"), until he dropped into the fetal slumber at the end of "Big Two-Hearted River," part 1. The Indian camp, meanwhile, continued to figure traumatically as the place Nick visited to get rid of the smell of his father, after the episode of the "lost" underwear in "Fathers and Sons" (375) and, again, as the site of Prudie's infidelity with Frank Washburn in "Ten Indians."

Hemingway was indeed integrating the key images in "Indian Camp" and the stories of 1925 with images in the stories of 1927 and 1933. Thus, for example, he had not provided evidence that Nick had served in the war, from which he claimed Nick was returning in "Big Two-Hearted River" (1925), until "In Another Country" and "Now I Lay Me" (both 1927), and had not provided evidence of the mental break-down strongly implied by his state of mind in "Big Two-Hearted River" until "A Way You'll Never Be" (1933). Likewise, the important detail of Nick's introduction to sex with Prudie Mitchell, as background for "Ten Indians" (1927), did not appear until "Fathers and Sons" (1933), the same story that filled in Nick's relationship with Dr. Adams prior to the rupture that occurred in "Ten Indians." Perhaps the clearest case of Hemingway's fictional backfilling involved the "medium brown" grasshoppers, which Nick the soldier extolled as the very best trout bait, in both "Now I Lay Me" (1927) and "A Way You'll Never Be" (1933), *after* he had already used them in "Big Two-Hearted River" (1925). In his later two collections, Hemingway either worked up to, or out from, an *In Our Time* story, to round out Nick's chronology and character. A loose analogy with T. S. Eliot's notion of how a new classic affects the canon of a literature might be drawn here. Eliot wrote in "Tradition and the Individual Talent":

> The existing order is complete before the new work arrives; for order to persist after the supervention of novelty, the whole existing order must be, if ever so slightly, altered; and so the relations, proportions, values of each work of art toward the whole are readjusted.... (*Sacred Wood* 50)

Thus, "The Light of the World" (1927) and "Fathers and Sons" (1933) filled important gaps in Nick's character and actually strengthened earlier stories like "The Battler" and "Big Two-Hearted River" (both of 1925).[4]

Since Hemingway's stress on key images was not immediately apparent to the reader, his new fictional prose looked more like Daniel Defoe's than it did the prose of the traditional eighteenth- and nineteenth-century novelists. In a style conspicuously free of allusion or the familiar poetic figures, Hemingway relied on the implied metaphor, often in its limited form of metonymy (for example, "the blanket" or "the bunk" representing the Caesarian). The choice was thoroughly consistent for him and the theory of the iceberg he would later articulate, metonymy representing after all the tip of the metaphorical iceberg. Metonymy was the figure implied in Ezra Pound's formula for the new poetry, and seemed a natural outgrowth of his conviction that the proper and perfect symbol is the natural object (Pound 9), a conviction Hemingway, then so closely associated with Pound, obviously shared.

By his repetition and integration of the basic images of the Caesarian, Hemingway made them into haunting metonymies, leitmotifs that never released Nick, but in fact were complicated by a wide accretion of associations as they were repeated. Thus, the blanket (and its surrogate the quilt) thrown back to reveal birth and death in the Indian cabin carried additional associations of camping, love, and war by the time Nick spread his blankets at the Big Two-Hearted River. The bunk was associated with the Caesarian and the suicide in "Indian Camp," with Nick's retreat from his betrayal by Prudie in "Ten Indians," and with these matters plus his military experience in "A Way You'll Never Be."

As Carlos Baker recognized in an early study of the fiction, Hemingway made many of his images into "objective correlatives," which Eliot had defined as "a set of objects, a situation, a chain of events" (100) that constituted "the formula of a particular emotion," so that when the external details were given, the emotion was immediately evoked. Baker noted "Eliot's practice of fashion[ing] his objective correlatives into a series of complex literary symbols ... designed to elicit a more or less controlled emotional response from the reader" (56; like the Wagnerian passages in *The Waste Land* and its images of women: Isolde, the lady in the boudoir, the whores on Thamesbank, the typist home at teatime). Hemingway's correlatives, Baker said, "could be traced back, not [as could Eliot's] to anterior literature or art objects, but to things actually seen and known by direct experience of the world" (56). Hemingway was setting up sequences of correlatives, or leitmotifs, out of his own text—single details in the case of the Caesarian, incidents out of Nick's boyhood and youth—with the detail or incident traced through several stories, and complicating with each repetition.

The horrors of the Caesarian had long been buried in Nick's unconscious until set off by his wounding at Fossalta in "Now I Lay Me," with the flight and return of his soul (276). In that instant, as indicated above, he identified with the Indian mother, penetrated by the steel knife, but perhaps more with her husband, penetrated by the steel razor blade, and losing his soul. In the story, Nick also lay on a blanket in the middle of the night. He did not call the Caesarian fully back to consciousness in this story of 1927, but he came much closer in "A Way You'll Never Be" (1933).

In the latter story, Nick, still suffering brief mental breakdowns from his head wound, returned to Fossalta from the hospital. Though under control at first, he had to retreat to a bunk with a long hallucination that included both memories of combat before his wounding and a nightmare that he suffered every night at this stage of his recovery. In this nightmare he associated the place where he had been wounded with a composite of what seemed the cabin in "Indian Camp" and a house of indeterminate form from his military experience:

> the nights the *river ran so much wider and stiller than it should* and outside of Fossalta there was a *low house painted yellow* with *willows all around* it and a low *stable* and there was a *canal*, and he had been there a thousand times and never seen it.... *That house meant more than anything* ... but it *frightened him especially* when the *boat lay there* quietly in the willows. (310; emphasis added)

The river that "ran so much wider and stiller than it should" was in one sense Walloon Lake, which he had been rowed across to the Indian camp on the night of the Caesarian. The low house, which he had "never seen," though he was so often there, was in one sense the Indian cabin; in another, it was the house he could not visualize near the place of his wounding. Nick realized that

He never dreamed about the front now any more but *what frightened him* was that long yellow *house* and the different *width of the river*. Now ... he had gone through the same town and there was no house. Nor was the river that way. (311; emphasis added)

What he dreamed about now was in large part the Indian cabin and the lake. He was *frightened especially* by the *boat*.

Near the end of the story his hallucination intensified again, and he returned to the bunk and faced the climax of his nightmare, in the form of an Austrian soldier:

Nick shut his eyes, and *in place of* the *man with the beard* who looked at him over the sights of the *rifle*, quite calmly before squeezing off ... he *saw* a long *yellow house* with a low stable and the *river* so much *wider than it was and stiller*. (314; emphasis added)

Nick substituted the house for the man with the beard; metaphorically, he replaced the Austrian soldier about to shoot him with the house and its more terrifying threat of his father (with beard) and the Caesarian. In this confused dream context, the beard identified his father and recalled the Indian mother's pubes, the house was the Indian cabin, and his bunk again recalled the full horror of the Caesarian and the suicide,[5] and echoed his retreat to bed, broken-hearted, at the end of "Ten Indians."

The image of the Caesarian had become confusingly intertwined with two traumatic incidents of sexual treachery in Nick's youth: his betrayal by Prudie Mitchell in "Ten Indians" and his own jilting of Marge in "The End of Something." He had retired with his face in the pillow (257) in the first story, with his face in a blanket (82) in the second. In his extended hallucination in "A Way You'll Never Be," Nick's memory picked up both incidents; it roamed back through a series of experiences that involved climbing a hill: leading the infantry attacks up Mount Grappa with Captain Paravicini, driving an ambulance up the mountain to retrieve wounded, and ascending the hill of Montmarte to the Sacre Coeur in a taxi, but having to step out when it got steep. ("Sometimes his girl was there and sometimes she was with someone else" [310]—for it was really the area near the Indian camp where Prudie was with Frank Washburn.)

The Paris part [of his dream] came earlier and he was not frightened of it *except when she had gone off with someone else* and the *fear* that *they might take the same driver twice*. (311; emphasis added)

Nick's fear of the driver's recognition traced back to climbing another hill, in "Ten Indians" on his ride home from Petoskey with the Garners on July 4 years earlier and having to step out of the wagon "when it got steep" (253), with Nick tortured by the whispered comments and laughter of Joe Garner and his wife at the mention of Prudie (254), whom Nick no doubt already feared to have lost to Frank Washburn. In his haste to learn of Prudie he forgot his shoes. His fear in Paris was that the driver would have seen his girl with another man and would laugh, as Garner had.

In his effort to break with Marge, Nick had been unable to go beyond sulking conversation, so that she took the initiative and immediately and decisively rejected him when he said that love wasn't fun anymore (81–82). The switching of traditional masculine and feminine roles is striking (for 1916) and clearly warrants the reference in Nick's reverie in "A Way You'll Never Be" to "the great Gaby" and "the far side of the taxi" (obvious plays on E. Scott Fitzgerald's *The Great Gatsby* and *This Side of Paradise*). For Nick's loss of masculine drive seemed to match what Hemingway saw as a similar loss in Jay Gatsby and other Fitzgerald characters. Nick's irresolution with Marge continued a pattern of passive conduct with women. His divided sympathies for the Indian mother and father, as well as the pattern of his own parents' marriage, had surely helped to paralyze him.

Beyond the images of the surgery, Nick's fears of explosion, evacuation, and castration provided Hemingway with objective correlatives that he reiterated many times throughout the stories. He involved Nick in all three fears by the masterstroke of having the quilt suddenly thrown back from the Indian mother, opening before Nick the explosion of blood, the Caesarian, and the absence of a male organ, all at once. Hemingway's deliberate stress on these elements in "On the Quay at Smyrna" seems an anticipation of what the reader will find in the cabin. Explosion was part of Nick's earliest recorded memory (278): the jars popping when his mother burned his father's snake specimens, probably even before the Caesarian. The sudden incision with the doctor's pen-knife produced the most traumatic explosion, of course. Hemingway used the threat of artillery, in Smyrna and again on the Karagatch Road, to enforce this fear of explosion early in *In Our Time*. More artillery was delivered or threatened at Fossalta, including Nick's various woundings: in the spine ("Nick sat against the wall"), in the leg ("In Another Country"), unspecified ("Now I Lay Me"), and climactically, in the head, in "A Way You'll Never Be." Nick's obviously shaky condition in "Big Two-Hearted River" seems to be the result of his wounds and the explosions that caused them. Many gun—or shotgun—blasts sound through other Nick stories.

Both Nick's fixation on evacuation and his natural fear of castration may well have begun to surface with the burning of the snake specimens, but the two fears certainly were accentuated by the Caesarian. Evacuation had a powerful effect on Nick. The brutal, gory evacuation, of the harbor, and of the wombs, at Smyrna, with the screams and repressive lights, was hardly worse than that on the Karagatch Road—with birth still asserting itself in the midst of the retreat (and in the latter case the scared girl who had lifted a blanket upon it). These apparently "normal" deliveries, one reported, one observed, after the war, sandwiched the long spectacle in the Indian cabin for the young boy who should not even have been present. The total evacuation of the lumber mill at Hortons Bay by schooner, and of Nick's love with Marge by rowboat, reinforced the notion. So did the eviscerated deer hanging in Milan. The Austrian retreat from Fossalta left carnage and debris on the same scale as Smyrna and the Karagatch Road. And of course the town Nick expected to find at Seney had been shockingly evacuated because of the fire.

Nick's natural fear of castration was exacerbated certainly by his father's castration in front of his son—double castration as it turned out—in the episode with Dick Boulton and the logs and in Mrs. Adams's failure to support him in "The Doctor and the Doctor's Wife." His mother's two "house-cleanings" (disposing of the snake specimens [277] and the arrowheads [278]) added to the problem. Further suggestions of castration abound in Hemingway's stories. At the start of *In Our Time*, Smyrna recalls for many readers the reputedly Turkish form (severing the penis only). The more prevalent form was suggested, surely, by Dick Boulton's hanging his saw in the crotch of a tree near the logs he was to cut up. The references to cutting in "The Battler" contributed to Nick's fear: his slicing bread, Bugs's "cuttin' a man" (103), and Ad's desire for Nick's knife. Nick's first sight of the Indian mother without a penis was confusing, and his identification of her pubes with his father's beard (to cover his weak chin and its suggestive impotence) still troubled Nick as late as the war stories.

The beard provides a transition to Nick's own approaching puberty: he is already unconsciously pursuing the female when he leads his father in search of "black squirrels" at the end of "The Doctor and the Doctor's Wife" (*squirrel* was a nineteenth-century term for a prostitute). Nick is dumping his mother and her authority at the end of this story; he will have dumped both parents in favor of pursuing the female by the end of "Ten Indians." Hemingway will add to this sequence with the skunks and Prudie's smelling like one ("Ten Indians" 254) and the references to the black squirrels in "Fathers and Sons": Nick having intercourse with Trudy (earlier Prudie) while waiting for a black squirrel to show itself as Billy Mitchell takes Nick's shotgun and goes off to shoot another black squirrel (372–74).

While the Caesarian was largely submerged beneath consciousness during Nick's boyhood and youth, Hemingway introduced new objective correlatives alongside those already operating from the Caesarian. Many of the new ones were incidents centered in Nick's relationship with his father, particularly in the doctor's cowardice in the face of Boulton and Mrs. Adams in "The Doctor and the Doctor's Wife" and the rupture caused by his snooping into Nick's affair with Prudie in "Ten Indians." After that episode, Nick was without parents, depending on a succession of surrogates: at Hortons Bay, on the road across northern Michigan, and in wartime Italy. As with the details of the Caesarian, Hemingway used these correlatives in incremental repetitions to reveal Nick's character. Since they were for the most part incidents, rather than single details, they did not lend themselves so readily to patterns like leitmotifs in music, as the details of the Caesarian did.

The trial of courage Nick so often faced had begun at least by the time of the Boulton episode. The doctor's backing down before Boulton no doubt spurred Nick's long fascination with boxing (his immediate recognition of Stanley Ketchel, Ad Francis, and Ole Andreson in the road stories) and his own concern with fistfights (the brakeman and Ad) and other challenges to his own courage. In "The Light of the World" he flinched and put up money when the bartender threatened Tom and him (292); in "The Battler" he smarted under the brakeman's trick punch, then found himself briefly overmatched in the near-fight with Ad (101–02), but in "The Killers" he risked his life to warn Ole Andreson. In "In Another Country" Nick considered himself a dove in contrast to his "hunting-hawk" (208) comrades in Milan, though he learned a new courage from the Italian major whose wife died of pneumonia, and in "A Way You'll Never Be" puked and fell back in his first infantry attack (314), but thereafter found courage in grappa.

The challenge of the female, another set of correlatives, was forcefully dramatized for Nick by his mother's embarrassing his father in the Boulton episode. Perhaps even earlier, her "burnings" (278) of the doctor's mementos and specimens showed her disregard for him. Whether or not Nick heard his parents' argument over Boulton, the boy Nick well knew the pattern (and who won and who lost). His respect for his father never recovered. He had no positive role model for relations with women. Nick lost his original advantage with Prudie, who dropped him for Frank Washburn, and with Marge, who walked away with dignity from the vacillating and soon-sorry Nick. In "A Very Short Story" he was jilted by Luz. Similarly, "his girl" in Paris went off with someone else; and in the later stories his wife was never at his side. In "Big Two-Hearted River" he has no thought of women for himself, and in "Fathers and Sons" his wife is in some manner estranged.

The challenge of authority began for Nick when he was too young to protest being subjected to the Caesarian. Thereafter, his father's intrusions into his life finally ruined their relationship. What I have termed elsewhere "the doctor's obsession with the task at hand"[6] led him to engage with Boulton and incur his insults, drove him into domestic quarrels with a woman he could not face down, and led him to spy on Prudie. It carried him to excess in the dispute over the underwear. Nick's final rejection of him occurred in the dialogue of "The Three-Day Blow," with Nick's tepid "My old man's all right," which hardly matched his compliment to Bill's dad, "He's a swell guy" (88). Nick showed a touch of real sympathy in the admission "He's missed a lot" [being a doctor and never having had a drink], but there was nothing here or in any of the stories after "Ten Indians" to match the spontaneous "*Let's* take the guns and *go ... look for your dad*" (92; emphasis added). No one would want the doctor to overhear that. On the road or at war, Nick seldom thinks of his parents, and still has trouble assessing them in "Fathers and Sons."

The need for approval, another correlative, naturally focused on Nick's relation to Dr. Adams in the early stories. Nick had chosen his father's approval over his mother's after the Boulton episode. His only recorded memories of his mother were her headaches and her burnings. His need for approval, still evident in his conduct toward Mrs. Garner, in "Ten Indians," just before the break with his father, marked his character for years afterward. His reverence for Bill's dad was unfortunate. So was his dependence on the unwholesome Bill, and his advice about Marge. He needed Bill's insincere flattery, even though he was only partly swayed by it. Despite flying in the face of conventional conduct for the time by leaving home, Nick continued to show a need for approval. His youthful adventures did not yield a mentor. On the road, Tom and later George the counterman were mere advisors (sometimes ignored). He was all too quick to sense the lack of approval by the "hunting-hawks" with their "real" medals in Milan. He studied Italian grammar to win the approval of the major in the hospital and courted the favor of Captain Paravicini.

Hemingway continued to develop correlatives out of familiar details in Nick's experiences. After the Boulton episode, he developed the shotgun into a powerful leitmotif, layering context upon context in succeeding stories: not just the doctor's frustration and impotence regarding his wife but indeed some joy for Nick in hunting with his father and pride in the man's phenomenal eyesight (370), then the unhappy lecture on sex (371), in hunting with Prudie and Billy Mitchell (and sex with Prudie [373]), in more hunting with Bill and Bill's dad, anxiety with Al and Max, drawing enraged aim on his father over the "lost" underwear (375), and seeing in the Austrian soldier at Fossalta both his father and himself taking aim, just before he puked on his first attack (314). And all of this renewed by his own son's impatience for a shotgun—fed partly by Dr. Adams's gift of an air rifle (376) and the still unassimilated shock of his father's death (with face disfigured). Details that Hemingway used less often than the bunk or the shotgun from story to story nevertheless had effects similar to leitmotifs, in view of his general technique. These include the knife and cutting, the swamp, and logs and railroad tracks, all analyzed below as they are extended into the climactic "Big Two-Hearted River."

One instance of Nick's need for approval (Bill's, in the Marge business) saved Nick from his unofficial "engagement" and what might have followed, but he did not choose his own time for the break. The full impact of the step did not hit him until the next day. Only after Bill had gotten him drunk (Nick realized this [89]), then pumped him about Marge,[7] did Nick realize how unhappy he had made himself ("he had lost her ... that was all that mattered"). But Bill overplayed his hand when he said, "You don't want to think about it. You might get back into it again." The uncertain Nick could not let go of this possibility: "He might go into town Saturday night ... he could always go into town Saturday night" (92). Nick would enter many towns, but none would be Petoskey on a Saturday night.

Hemingway had carried the Nick stories beyond straight realism with this scene. Nick had had seven very large drinks—fifteen ounces of whiskey by conservative estimate—not over the course of a few hours even, but steadily in the course of what seemed more like one hour. Realistically, Nick would have been asleep or poisoned long before Bill opened the topic of Marge. Nick's sudden, shocked return to sobriety ("The liquor had all died out of him ... he wasn't drunk" [91]) was also beyond credibility in realistic terms. After three drinks, Nick began losing his identity with his sobriety when he looked in a mirror in the dining room:

> His face looked strange. He smiled at the face in the mirror and
> it grinned back at him. He winked at it and went on. It was not
> his face but it didn't make any difference. (89)

As if by some trick of refraction in the mirror, as Hemingway launched into multiple representation,[8] Nick's identity took a number of forms "on the road" and still more "in the war" (*Nick Adams* 37, 135), before he emerged at Seney, in a naturalistic passage worthy of Frank Norris or John Steinbeck, in the opening of "Big Two-Hearted River," the passage signaling a return to realism generally, as Nick walked out of the blackened landscape into the green land.

"Certified as nutty" and treated like a child by Captain Paravicini, Nick is as close to mental collapse in "A Way You'll Never Be" as we ever see him, and, correspondingly, as close to identifying the yellow house and the river of his nightmare as he ever comes. However, as he had submerged the trauma of the Caesarian throughout his youth, he has submerged both the Caesarian *and* Fossalta by the time we meet him in "Big Two-Hearted River." This could not be more than a matter of months after "A Way You'll Never Be"— unless the reader assumes that Nick recovered from the war, for the skiing stories, then suffered another breakdown before "Big Two-Hearted River," or lived for an indefinite time in a psychoneurotic state that would have prohibited the early writing career assumed for him in some analyses of the stories. Of course, Hemingway told us that this story was "about a boy coming home beat to the wide from a war" ("The Art of the Short Story" 130–31).

In "Big Two-Hearted River" Hemingway extended the central trope of the stories—Nick's fear of the soul's departure and return at the approach of death. First fully articulated in "Now I Lay Me" (1927), as Nick's soul did go off and come back, the trope obviously derived in part from the Indian father's suicide in "Indian Camp," and in part from the arrival of the Indian baby's soul. As the following pages will develop, Hemingway integrated details from the later war stories with those in *In Our Time* to develop the trope. "Big Two-Hearted River" had thus stood as a finely crafted "work in progress" for some eight years, until the new Nick stories were fitted to it. The fear that had haunted Nick since the suicide had resurfaced in the dream sequence at Fossalta. "Fathers and Sons" revealed that the fear had become confused with sexual climax as Nick reached puberty. On this fishing trip to the river, he clearly sought to escape the fear in a safe, boyhood activity that excluded the war, Dr. Adams, and "girls." But that was not to be: Hemingway introduced all of these, just beneath Nick's consciousness.

The fire at Seney plunged the returned soldier back into the devastation of war when he arrived (as if at the front) by train, dressed in khaki, carrying a pack, and a fishing rod in the manner of a rifle. Destruction was everywhere around him. However, Nick's retreat to the railroad bridge began a chain of naturalistic implication that informed the rest of the story, as the trout steadied themselves in the current.

Hemingway returned to the central trope when Nick noticed an arcing trout, its shadow lost to its substance (its soul to its body) as it left the water, recalling both Nick's wounding and the Indian father's suicide, with all the psychological associations that bunks and penetrating steel involved for Nick. But Hemingway complicated the metaphor this time with a kingfisher and its threat to snatch the trout and carry it off:

> As the shadow of the kingfisher moved up the stream, a big trout
> shot upstream in a long angle, only his shadow marking the angle,
> then lost his shadow as he came through the surface of the water,
> caught the sun, and then, as he went back into the stream under
> the surface, his shadow seemed to float down the stream with the
> current, unresisting, to his post under the bridge where he
> tightened facing up into the current. (163–64)

Nick's fear of losing his own soul was briefly revived, even though the trout
regained his shadow safely.

Hemingway had actually initiated this trope in the jump of the bass at
the end of "Indian Camp":

> They were seated in the boat, Nick in the stern, his father
> rowing. The sun was coming up over the hills. A bass jumped,
> making a circle in the water. Nick trailed his hand in the water. It
> felt warm in the sharp chill of the morning. In the early morning
> on the lake sitting in the stern of the boat with his father rowing,
> he felt quite sure that he would never die. (70)

The bass had made an untroubled flight and return, stirring a circle in
the water, which was warm with life to Nick's touch. But in its arc the bass
gave a form and structure to the soul's departure and return. The arc of the
bass's flight also became for Nick the parabola of an artillery shell, with life
and death in the balance until it landed, during the war, and later at Smyrna
and on the Karagatch Road. It was the shape of the soul's flight after sex with
Prudie. Ironically, the arc was also the form of the fly-cast, which had caught
so many fish, and the form of the shriek of a shell or a fishing reel, rising and
subsiding. What terrified Nick after "Indian Camp" was the possible failure
of the soul to return. His own wounding at night lent an added horror to
darkness, and the need for light, which plagued him in "Now I Lay Me" and
"A Way You'll Never Be."

In "The Art of the Short Story" Hemingway, writing of "Big Two-
Hearted River," stated that boys coming home from the war in Nick's
condition

> could not suffer that it be mentioned in their presence. So the
> war, all mention of the war, anything about the war, is omitted ...
> there were many Indians in the story, just as the war was in the
> story, and none of the Indians nor the war appeared. (130–31)

The presence of the war and the Indians would thus have to rest on implications in the details of the text. This suggests that Hemingway composed his story not only with leitmotifs and correlatives but also with key phrases identifying other Nick stories, and that he expected the reader to find them. These phrases were part of his calculated repetition, and often involved the leitmotifs and correlatives already stressed in "earlier" stories. Evidence of the war was clear in Nick's arrival in the burned town and in the blackened hoppers. Evidence of the Indians seemed quite strong when he napped, after leaving the blackened land and in the logs so prominent later in the story. Lying in the grove of pine trees surely recalled hunting with Billy Mitchell and sex with Prudie, recounted in "Fathers and Sons" (the earth was brown and soft, the trees grown high above ground without branches, in both settings [163,239]). In fact, Hemingway seems to have worked in references to many of the "earlier" stories. Nick could hardly have failed to mark the contrast between this arrival at Seney and being knocked from the train in "The Battler." Walking into and out of Seney must have reminded him of walking into and out of the hellishly black town in "The Light of the World" and the war-ravaged Fossalta. He had walked along tracks in "The Battler" and "The Killers," as well. The chipped and split stone foundations of the Mountain House surely suggested those of the lumber mill at Hortons Bay—"our old ruin" (79) to Marge, in "The End of Something." The stone should also have suggested his father's burned arrowheads, from "Now I Lay Me."

The fire at Seney had turned Nick's favorite fishing bait, the medium-brown grasshoppers, completely black, just as it had the "burned over" (163) ground around the town, as Hemingway extended his naturalism. When Nick wondered how long the hopper "would stay that way" (165), implying recovery, he implied his own recovery from the "blackening" of the war. Nick's identification with the hopper was clear when he tossed it to a stump across from the one he sat against (165). Nick's position, with his legs extended in front of him, showed his physical recovery since "Nick sat against the wall" and "In Another Country," but his psychological recovery was evidently not so far advanced. He had "left everything behind him," including the unspecified "other needs" (164) and the things he could "choke" on his way to sleep the first night. But healing was in progress, for the ground did yield to sweet fern and pine plain.

From the time he entered the green land until his battle with the giant trout, Nick's fishing trip became the idyllic one he had imagined for himself on the nights of "Now I Lay Me." His effort to get back to an idealized youth of flawless camping and fishing was working out beautifully: he hit the river at the right spot, found a good campsite, pitched his tent tight as a drum, and cooked his dinner. He had not relished food this way since Bugs cooked the ham and egg sandwiches in "The Battler." He had worked feverishly but quite happily against the oncoming darkness. Most significantly, Nick had been genuinely happy for a matter of hours, for the first time since we have known him, and would remain so until he woke to the new day. He seemed to have escaped the Caesarian; its destructive metonymies had been suspended. Burning the mosquito showed his full control over the environment. Even the blankets, potentially so charged with meanings for him, did not disturb him. The embers of his fire gave him light enough to keep off any fear of losing his soul.

Fishing was the avowed purpose of the trip, and Nick took as much pleasure in readying his gear as he had in making camp. He had begun again in the morning, catching his hoppers, cooking breakfast, and threading his line. Still, his silhouette, with so many straps and pouches, and his rod, was like that of an infantry soldier; his khaki shirt and his wading in the river (like the Austrians in the Piave) were repressed reminders of the war. At first, he fished confidently, aggressively, as he had in his dreams in "Now I Lay Me." Freed from his familiar fear and anxiety, he delighted in his practice of the sport. This was the way he would have fished with Chesterton and Hugh Walpole at Charlevoix, with Bill and his dad in "The Three-Day Blow." He caught and released a small trout. But then he encountered the giant trout that went high out of the water, and his nerve suddenly broke: "the rod came alive and *dangerous*," he felt "a heavy, *dangerous*, steady pull." All at once he was back in the war: "The reel ratcheted into a *mechanical shriek* as the line went out in a rush ... the *reel note rising*" (176; emphasis added). Nick heard the artillery. At the same time, the shriek recalled the Indian mother and the Caesarian (the screams his father could not stop). The Big Two-Hearted River had become the Piave and then instantaneously Walloon Lake, as in his nightmares. Nick had gone to pieces. As the giant trout nearly completed his arc, he broke the leader. Like a soul not returning, he broke the familiar pattern, and this disturbed Nick. He felt "a little sick" and had to retire from the stream. Once again he was not a "hunting-hawk," like the Italian soldiers in Milan ("Nick's hand was shaky ... it would be better to sit down" [193]).

Nick had been scared sick again; he had looked away in the Indian cabin, felt sick at Ad's maimed ear, at the underwear, at the quarrel with Luz in Milan, and had puked at Mount Grappa (108). The girl on the Karagatch Road would indeed become a correlative. He was too good a fisherman to be so upset at the loss of the trout. The bad luck, or even a mistake, involved in losing the fish would not have shocked him so. Nick's "other needs," those things he could "choke" the night before, had suddenly come back upon him. He had not come so far from Fossalta as he had hoped. As the final challenge to his courage, the trout overwhelmed him.

The Caesarian had damaged him permanently, Fossalta had retraumatized him, and now the wound had been reopened. His joy in the fishing had gone; his anxiety was back. When he returned to the stream, he fished timidly. He did not fish "the turns of the bank and the deep holes" he had fished in "Now I Lay Me," (276). He let the larger trout stay in the shadows near the banks and fished the middle of the stream in journeyman fashion. Such fishing had to be disappointing, after his long anticipation.

In his imaginary fishing trips Nick had stopped for lunch at noon, as he did here, sitting on a log like the one he now sat on, a log with no bark (238). He was also virtually surrounded by logs, which must have recalled his various trips to the Indian camp, the bark-peelers' camp, and the Chippewas he had known there, including Dick Boulton. Nick had fished a swamp before the war, as he told us in "Now I Lay Me," the day he cannibalized a trout for bait (276). But as he finished his lunch, he focused uneasily on the swamp before him. Obviously suggesting the threatening and the unknown, the swamp and the deep holes around him seem vaginal:

> Ahead the river narrowed and went into a swamp ... [which] looked solid with cedar trees ... trunks close together ... branches solid ... banks ... bare.... You would have to keep almost level with the ground to move at all. (179)

Wading through water "up to his thighs," holding "the rod pumping alive" against his abdomen, a trout threshing heavily" on the line, between river banks that "narrowed and went into a swamp," and forced to a prone position to enter, Nick certainly prefigures sexual activity,[9] but clearly is not yet ready for this.

Nick's mind-set during this trip tempts the reader to assume that he was the unfortunate fiancé of Luz in "A Very Short Story," recovering from the shock of his "Dear Nick" letter. As partial motivation for the trip, this would explain his absorption in the physical details and his complete exclusion of sexual thoughts. The rejected lover had reached back to the masculine activities of his prewar days. The assumption that he was recovering from Luz would also strike a kind of narrative balance, if not provide justice, for Nick's own broken "engagement" to Marge.

As he prepared to kill and clean the two trout he had caught, Nick underwent a considerable change of role. Back at the railroad bridge he had sympathized with the arcing trout against the kingfisher, but here he killed his trout in the way a kingfisher would, whacking them against the log; in doing this, he unwittingly assumed his father's role and reenacted a crude Caesarian. He slit the trout from the vent to the tip of the jaw: "All the insides and the gills and tongue came out in one piece." It wasn't "one for the medical journals" (69), but it was a good job, and like the doctor putting a final "something" into young Nick's basin, Nicked tossed the offal to the minks. Also like the doctor, he used a jackknife, washed his hands, and cleaned the knife. But, reenacting the trauma of the Indian cabin, himself in the role of "surgeon," Nick still had not escaped it.

A swamp had threatened him on his walks to the Indian camp to meet Prudie—crossing a log, he must avoid falling into the black muck (372)—and a big swamp had threatened Nick on his nightwalk in "The Battler." In the swamp before him, fishing would be "tragic," "a tragic adventure" (180), wading in water ... under his armpits, like the Austrians holding their rifles high before they fell in the Piave (311). Hemingway had mentioned the swamp four times in part 1, fourteen times in part 2. Nine of the mentions are in the last seven paragraphs, as Nick backs away from fishing the swamp: he will not fish it "this afternoon" or "tomorrow." "There were 'plenty of days' (180) when he could fish the swamp." Hemingway could not have made the threat any stronger, since this is a periodic story and the last word is *swamp*.

Nick's idyllic fishing trip had collapsed. He had failed his latest trial of courage with the trout, and he is evading the challenge of the female in the swamp. His problem seems clear. He is growing toward his father's station in life, but has never really escaped his own crippling trauma in the Indian cabin. Faced with the intolerable affront of the Caesarian, Nick learned early the defense mechanism of submergence ("he would never die" [70]). And he used it, after the Boulton incident and after Fossalta, and is using it again after the giant trout. On the threshold of adult life, he has not yet learned that submergence merely shelves problems, without solving them for him. Submergence has kept him in bondage to the past; the swamp would involve Nick in his future.

Nick has not "fished the swamp" with any remarkable success, in the postwar skiing stories and "Fathers and Sons." "Cross-County Snow" shows him greatly recovered physically and associates him with the leg wound in "In Another Country," for while he can ski, he "can't telemark with my leg" (144). But he can make an arc of his own on skis, and endure having his mind plucked out of his body by a downhill drop, without any fear that "his soul is going out of his body" (143). The "rush and sudden swoop" (like an incoming artillery shell) of his drop excited no anxiety. Nick's capacity to submerge traumatic experience is operating again. But he comes off as a somewhat immature young man, here and in "An Alpine Idyll," indulging himself on the ski slopes, away from his wife and her pregnancy (he did not at first notice that the waitress in "Cross-Country Snow" was pregnant, and wondered afterward why he had not [145]). Nick had a long experience of turning away from pregnancy.

If the metonymies of the Indian camp and Fossalta have retreated from memory, the challenges posed by the female and authority remain unmet, as does Nick's need for approval. In "Fathers and Sons" he is divorced or separated from his wife, but he is enjoying a visit from his young son. This stirs uneasy memories of Dr. Adams, who has suffered a disfiguring death (assumed in the criticism to reflect Clarence Hemingway's suicide by gunshot). Nick's protestations of love for the man who taught him to fish and to hunt seem somewhat hollow. Although he had loved him "very much and for a long time" (371), he "had shared nothing with him" after he was fifteen (375). At thirty-eight, Nick is still too angry to show insight to the doctor's problems with Mrs. Adams (whom Nick never mentions). A rhapsodic passage about his father's being with him in outdoor places is undercut by his comment that "even remembering the earliest times was not good remembering" (371). His escape for the time being from a sex talk with his own son does not soften his harsh memory of the doctor's talk with him. He even takes a final stab at his father's pride in the Caesarian: "the undertaker had been both proud and smugly pleased" at the job he had done on the doctor's face. Nick's final comment to his son, "I can see we'll have to go [to the doctor's grave]" (377) trades his need of his father's approval for the need of his son's.

NOTES

1. This analysis draws on the fifteen published Nick stories and the vignettes of *In Our Time* that reflect Nick's war experience (I regard "A Very Short Story" as Nick's). I am concerned with the experience as Nick's, not as Hemingway's. I deliberately avoid references to Hemingway biographies and hold reference to critical works to a very bare minimum. Nick is in some ways a more interesting character when freed from the autobiographical assumption.

2. Page references are to *The Complete Short Stories of Ernest Hemingway: The Finca Vigia Edition*. By its very nature, this analysis requires frequent citation of supporting incident or detail. To avoid excess, I have relied on the reader's general memory of principal characters and events.

3. The critical controversy over this question was for a time stilled by Philip Young's facetious claim that he had sired the child (*Studies*). But the question is still very much open, as Gajdusek shows (56).

4. Nick Adams obviously lived intently in Hemingway's imagination from 1922 to 1933 (less intently into the 1950s). That Hemingway continued "working on" Nick's experience is clearly demonstrated in the integration of stories in three collections.

5. The house and the expandable river/lake (311, 314) are the constant details in Nick's recollections here. The canal derives from Nick's stay in Milan ("always you crossed ... a canal to enter the hospital" in "In Another Country" [206]), and the stable might well be the one he knew with the Garners and their rich family life in "Ten Indians" (6).

6. In "The Case of Dr. Henry Adams" I contend that the doctor has an excessive,

unreflecting self-absorption in the task at hand, an obsession, with a buoyant enthusiasm, but at the same time a failure to consider effects or the rights of others. It is rigid and Puritanical and cannot brook opposition. (Hannum 42)

7. Nick has seven large drinks in all. Bill appeared not to pour a second for himself, and had "only a shot" for his fourth. Of *his* fourth drink, Nick observed, "That's an awfully big shot." Bill did not open the subject of Marge until Nick had his sixth drink (85–90).

8. Hemingway's multiple representation sends Nick through similar experiences without causal or chronological relation, in a mode beyond realism. For this analysis, I have assumed an order that places Nick "on the road" in "The Light of the World," "The Battler," and "The Killers," then at war in "In Another Country," "Now I Lay Me," "A Way You'll Never Be," and "Nick sat against the wall," with varied aspects of Nick's personality under scrutiny from story to story. No one could survive his four wounds in such a short time, of course.

9. Hovey notes "certain analogies to the female organs" and "yielding, fertile softness, symbolizing femaleness" (35–36); Twitchell finds Nick distorting the swamp to make it "more female" (275–76); elsewhere I cite both of these and note that "the stretch of river" Nick fished appeared vaginal as it "narrowed and entered a swamp" that "looked solid with cedar trees, their trunks close together, their branches solid" ("Soldier's Home" 11).

WORKS CITED

Baker, Carlos. *The Writer as Artist*. Princeton: Princeton UP, 1972.

Eliot, T. S. *The Sacred Wood*. London: Methuen, 1920.

Fitzgerald, F. Scott. *The Great Gatsby*. New York: Scribner's, 1925.

———. *This Side of Paradise*. New York: Scribner's, 1920.

Gajdusek, Robert E. "False Fathers, Doctors, and the Caesarean Dilemma: Metaphor as Structure in Hemingway's *In Our Time.*" *North Dakota Quarterly* 65.3 (Summer 1998): 53–61.

Hannum, Howard L. "The Case of Dr. Henry Adams," *Arizona Quarterly* 44.2 (Summer 1988): 39–57.

———. "Soldier's Home: Immersion Therapy and Lyric Pattern in 'Big Two-Hearted River.'" *The Hemingway Review* 3:2 (Spring 1984) 2–13.

Hemingway, Ernest. "The Art of the Short Story." *Ernest Hemingway: A Study of the Short Fiction*. Ed. Joseph M. Flora. Boston: Twayne, 1989. 129–44.

———. *The Complete Short Stories of Ernest Hemingway: The Finca Vigia Edition*. New York: Macmillan, 1987.

———. *The Nick Adams Stories*. Ed. Philip Young. New York: Scribner's, 1972.

———. *The Sun Also Rises*. New York: Scribner's, 1926.

Hovey, Richard B. *Hemingway: The Inward Terrain*. Seattle: U of Washington P, 1968.

O'Connor, Frank. *The Lonely Voice*. New York: World, 1962.

Pound, Ezra. "A Retrospect." *Literary Essays of Ezra Pound*. Ed. T. S. Eliot. London: Faber, 1954. 3–14.

Twitchell, James. "The Swamp in Hemingway's 'Big Two-Hearted River.'" *Studies in Short Fiction* 9 (1972): 275–76.

Young, Philip. "Comment." *Studies in Short Fiction* 3.2 (Fall 1965). ii–iii.

Character Profile

Nick Adams appears in more than a dozen of Ernest Hemingway's short stories. He ranges in age from a relatively young boy to a man at least thirty-eight years old with a son. We are given no physical description of him but are led to associate him with our images of America's rugged individualism. With the exception of his drinking, we can assume that he is in good shape as he enjoys arduous hiking in the sun and swift skiing. He says he is from Chicago, and given that his father is a doctor, we might assume that his family is not impoverished. Nick loves nature; is an expert hunter and fisherman; is preoccupied with notions of toughness; likes being alone and free; and becomes wounded physically and psychologically, to the point of being labeled mentally unbalanced.

Nick is content when he is outdoors. He teaches his one girlfriend, Marge, about fishing, and enjoys watching trout in the river, making camp, and feeling the ground beneath his back when he lies down. He is "excited" when he sees morning outside his tent. He knows what bait to use, where to stand in the river, where he is without consulting a map, and how to touch a fish without causing it to develop a deadly fungus. Growing up, Nick tries to be tough, but throughout his life he also appears sensitive. At a young age, he is brought along with his father to an Indian camp where a woman is struggling to have a baby. Upon entering the room with the pregnant woman, Nick immediately is disturbed by her screams and asks his father if he can't give the woman something for the pain. Nick's father has Nick assist while he performs a Caesarean birth, but the boy does not watch the process. However, he does look when his father checks on the pregnant woman's husband and finds him in a pool of blood. Unable to tolerate his wife's screams and probably foreseeing a deadly outcome, the man has slit his throat. After this dreadful experience, young Nick tells himself he will never die, the first of his mechanisms for handling a ruthless world.

Similarly, Nick's toughness is later questioned when he is thrown from a train by its brakeman. Now he is an older boy freely wandering, yet freedom incurs its own costs. He is angry that the brakeman tricked and mistreated him, and when he meets up with a man in the woods, he explains his need to get revenge:

> "The bastard!"
> "It must have made him feel good to bust you," the man said seriously.
> "I'll bust him."
> "Get him with a rock sometime when he's going through," the man advised.
> "I'll get him."
> "You're a tough one, aren't you?"
> "No," Nick answered.
> "All you kids are tough."
> "You got to be tough," Nick said.

The issue of toughness reappears when Nick says he must leave town because a man he knows is doing nothing about the fact that thugs are looking to kill the man. Nick says he can't stand to think about it. "It's too damned awful," he says. Two others know of the situation, and their responses contrast Nick's more sensitive perspective. One man, a cook, walks away so he cannot hear all the details of the situation; the other man, George, suggests that Nick not think about it; neither the cook nor George feel they need to leave town. In a later story, Nick admits his lack of toughness to a commander. Nick tells him he has never been in a battle without being drunk (one of the methods he uses to escape), although the commander responds that Nick was "much braver in an attack" than he was. Nick admits to himself that he could never have done the brave things his fellow soldiers had done to earn their medals.

Another aspect of Nick's personality is that he likes being alone and free. He has some friends and some women along the way who enjoy his company, yet he likes camping by himself and does not like to fish when others are on the river, unless they are part of his party. When he visits his friend's house, he asks him if he has anything to read, seemingly preferring this to conversation and companionship. Also, Nick talks to another friend about how great it would be "to bum" around and ski in some of the most beautiful places, free to just enjoy nature.

Yet as much as Nick seems to value feeling free, he does tell a major in the service that he wants to get married. Also, after he splits up with his girlfriend, he talks to his friend, Bill, and is secretly relieved to hear that nothing is final, that it is possible to still get back with the woman. "He felt happy now," we read. "There was not anything that was irrevocable…. Nothing was finished. Nothing was ever lost." This concept is comforting, not only in relation to his girlfriend but in other aspects of life.

Another key component that shapes Nick's identity, is the fact that he is wounded on the battlefield and forced to try to rehabilitate his one leg. He is haunted by war-time memories, must sleep with a light on, and wakes up from dreams "soaking wet, more frightened than he had ever been in a bombardment." We also see other unpleasant experiences that have psychologically wounded Nick, and when he is with his son he starts remembering how poor his own childhood had been as well. "Now, knowing how it had all been, even remembering the earliest times before things had gone badly was not good remembering. If he wrote it he could get rid of it. He had gotten rid of many things by writing them." Here, then, he turns to another mechanism to handle the pain. This time, though, the method won't just block the pain, but will let it out, seemingly a much healthier goal. Yet, we learn, Nick thinks it is still too soon to write about his childhood.

Ultimately nature provides another avenue for handling pain. When Nick is camping and fishing, we are told, "He had not been unhappy all day." The question remains, though, whether nature provides a healthy repairing or is just another vehicle for escape. "He felt he had left everything behind, the need for thinking, the need to write, other needs. It was all back of him," we read. Indeed, the instances where Nick is described as happy almost all have to do with being outdoors, yet in the most extensive description of camping and fishing, in "Big Two-Hearted River," we are also told that Nick is holding back bad experiences: "His mind was starting to work. He knew he could choke it because he was tired." Nick's suffering, then, seems stronger than his happiness. We are reminded of the short story "The Battler," when Nick is still young and asks a man he met in the woods about his ex-prizefighter friend:

"What made him crazy?" Nick said.
"Oh, a lot of things," the negro answered from the fire….
"He took too many beatings, for one thing…."

Contributors

HAROLD BLOOM is Sterling Professor of the Humanities at Yale University and Henry W. and Albert A. Berg Professor of English at the New York University Graduate School. He is the author of over 20 books, including *Shelley's Mythmaking* (1959), *The Visionary Company* (1961), *Blake's Apocalypse* (1963), *Yeats* (1970), *A Map of Misreading* (1975), *Kabbalah and Criticism* (1975), *Agon: Toward a Theory of Revisionism* (1982), *The American Religion* (1992), *The Western Canon* (1994), and *Omens of Millennium: The Gnosis of Angels, Dreams, and Resurrection* (1996). *The Anxiety of Influence* (1973) sets forth Professor Bloom's provocative theory of the literary relationships between the great writers and their predecessors. His most recent books include *Shakespeare: The Invention of the Human* (1998), a 1998 National Book Award finalist, *How to Read and Why* (2000), *Genius: A Mosaic of One Hundred Exemplary Creative Minds* (2002), and *Hamlet: Poem Unlimited* (2003). In 1999, Professor Bloom received the prestigious American Academy of Arts and Letters Gold Medal for Criticism, and in 2002 he received the Catalonia International Prize.

PHILIP YOUNG taught at Penn State University. He is the author of *Ernest Hemingway: A Reconsideration* and *American Fiction, American Myth*.

HORST H. KRUSE is the author of *Mark Twain and "Life on the Mississippi."* Dr. Kruse is a former professor of English at Okayama University and is now President of Kobe Women's University Seto Junior College in Japan.

JOSEPH M. FLORA teaches at the University of North Carolina at Chapel Hill. He is the author of *Ernest Hemingway: A Study of the Short Fiction* and a joint editor of *The Companion to Southern Literature*.

NICHOLAS GEROGIANNIS was a professor at Auburn University. He is the editor of *Complete Poems: Ernest Hemingway*, as well as of a book of Hemingway's.

KENNETH G. JOHNSTON has been Professor of English at Kansas State University. He is the author of several dozen essays on Hemingway's fiction and has published *The Tip of the Iceberg: Hemingway and the Short Story*.

LAWRENCE BROER is Professor of English at the University of South Florida. His publications include *Hemingway's Spanish Tragedy* and *Hemingway and Women: Female Critics and the Female Voice*.

KENNETH S. LYNN is Professor of History Emeritus at Johns Hopkins University. He has published *Hemingway* as well as several other titles.

PAUL SMITH was James J. Goodwin Professor of English at Trinity College, Connecticut and has been described as the preeminent scholar of Hemingway's short fiction and manuscripts. He was the founding president of the Hemingway Society. His published work includes *A Reader's Guide to the Short Stories of Ernest Hemingway*. He is also the editor of *New Essays on Hemingway's Short Fiction*.

PAUL WADDEN has taught at Illinois State University and has translated, written, or edited various titles. Dr. Wadden is currently a senior researcher at Wadden Writing and Research Associates.

DAVID J. FERRERO has taught at Harvard University.

HOWARD L. HANNUM is retired from the English department at La Salle University. He has published on Hemingway in various journals and in collections of critical essays.

Bibliography

Baker, Carlos, ed. *Hemingway and His Critics: An International Anthology*. New York: Hill and Wang, 1961.

Beebe, Maurice and John Feaster. "Criticism of Ernest Hemingway: A Selected Checklist." *Modern Fiction Studies* 14, no. 3 (Autumn 1968): 337–69.

Benson, Jackson J., ed. *New Critical Approaches to the Short Stories of Ernest Hemingway*. Durham and London: Duke University Press, 1990.

———. *The Short Stories of Ernest Hemingway: Critical Essays*. Durham: Duke University Press, 1975.

Boutelle, Ann Edwards. "Hemingway and 'Papa': Killing of the Father in the Nick Adams Fiction." *Modern Literature* 9, no. 1 (1981–82): 133–46.

Carabine, Keith. "Hemingway's *In Our Time*: An Appreciation." *Fitzgerald/Hemingway Annual* (1979): 301–26.

Clifford, Stephen P. "Hemingway's Fragmentary Novel: Readers Writing the Hero in *In Our Time*." *The Hemingway Review* 13, no. 2 (Spring 1994): 12–23.

Civello, Paul. "Hemingway's 'Primitivism': Archetypal Patterns in 'Big Two-Hearted River.'" *The Hemingway Review* 13, no. 1 (Fall 1993): 1–16.

Cooley, John R. "Nick Adams and 'The Good Place.'" *Southern Humanities Review* 14 (1980): 57–68.

DeFalco, Joseph M. *The Hero in Hemingway's Short Stories*. Pittsburgh: University of Pittsburgh Press, 1968.

"Ernest Hemingway." *Modern Fiction Studies* 14, no. 3 (Autumn 1968).

Fenton, Charles A. *The Apprenticeship of Ernest Hemingway: The Early Years.* NY: Farrar, Straus, and Young, 1954, 1958.

Flora, Joseph M. "Saving Nick Adams for Another Day." *South Atlantic Review* 58, no. 2 (May 1993): 61–84.

Gifford, William. "Ernest Hemingway: The Monsters and the Critics." *Modern Fiction Studies* 14, no. 3 (Autumn 1968): 255–70.

Gordon, David. "The Son and the Father: Patterns of Response to Conflict in Hemingway's Fiction." *Literature and Psychology* 6 (1966): 122–36.

Gurko, Leo. *Ernest Hemingway and the Pursuit of Heroism.* New York: Crowell, 1968.

Hays, Peter L. "Hemingway, Nick Adams, and David Bourne: Sons and Writers." *Arizona Quarterly* 44, no. 2 (Summer 1988): 28–38.

Lee, A. Robert, ed. *Ernest Hemingway: New Critical Essays.* Totowa, N.J.: Barnes and Noble, 1983.

Lewis, R. W. B. *The American Adam: Innocence, Tragedy, and Tradition in the Nineteenth Century.* Chicago: University of Chicago Press, 1955.

McCaffery, John K. M., ed. *Ernest Hemingway: The Man and His Work.* Cleveland: World, 1950.

Muller, G. H. "*In Our Time*: Hemingway and the Discontents of Civilization," *Renascence* 29 (1977): 185–92.

Nagel, James. "Hemingway's *In Our Time* and the Unknown Genre: The Short-Story Cycle." In *American Literary Dimensions: Poems and Essays in Honor of Melvin J. Friedman*, ed. Ben Seigel and Jay Halio. Newark, DE and London: University of Delaware Press and Associated University Press, 1999, 91–98.

O'Faolain, Sean. *The Vanishing Hero: Studies in Novelists of the Twenties.* Boston: Little, Brown, 1956, 112–45.

Reynolds, Michael S. *Critical Essays on Ernest Hemingway's* In Our Time. Boston: G. K. Hall, 1983.

Robinson, Forrest. "Hemingway's Invisible Hero of 'In Another Country.'" *Essays in Literature* 15, no. 2 (Fall 1988): 237–44.

Rovit, Earl. *Ernest Hemingway.* NY: Twayne, 1963.

Ryan, Frank L. *The Immediate Critical Reception of Ernest Hemingway.* Washington, D.C.: University Press of America, 1980.

Scafella, Frank. "'I and the Abyss': Emerson, Hemingway, and the Modern Vision of Death." *The Hemingway Review* 4, no. 2 (Spring 1985): 2–6.

———. "Imagistic Landscape of a Psyche: Hemingway's Nick Adams." *Hemingway Review* 2 (1983): 2–10.

Schwenger, Peter. *Phallic Critiques.* London: Routledge and Kegan Paul, 1984.

Sempreora, Margot. "Nick at Night: Nocturnal Metafictions in Three Hemingway Short Stories." *Hemingway Review* 22, no. 1 (Fall 2002): 19–33.

Smith, Paul. *A Reader's Guide to the Short Stories of Ernest Hemingway.* Boston: G. K. Hall & Co., 1989.

Smith, Ronald. "Nick Adams and Post-Traumatic Stress Disorder." *War, Literature, and the Arts* 9, no. 1 (Spring-Summer 1997): 39–48.

Strong, Paul. "The First Nick Adams Stories." *Studies in Short Fiction* 28, no. 1 (Winter 1991): 83–91.

Strychacz, Thomas. "Dramatizations of Manhood in Hemingway's *In Our Time* and *The Sun Also Rises*." *American Literature* 61, no. 2 (May 1989): 245–60.

———. "'You Know Me, Don't You?' Role Reversal in the Nick Adams Stories." *North Dakota Quarterly* 62, no. 2 (Spring 1994–1995): 132–39.

Vaugh, Elizabeth Dewberry. "*In Our Time* as Self-Begetting Fiction." In *Ernest Hemingway: Seven Decades of Criticism.* East Lansing, MI: Michigan State University Press, 1998, 135–47.

———. "*In Our Time* as Self-Begetting Fiction." *Modern Fiction Studies* 35, no. 4 (Winter 1989): 707–16.

Wagner, Linda Welshimer, ed. *Ernest Hemingway: Five Decades of Criticism.* East Lansing: Michigan State University Press, 1974.

Waldhorn, Arthur. *A Reader's Guide to Ernest Hemingway.* Syracuse, NY: Syracuse University Press, 2002.

Weeks, Robert P., ed. *Hemingway: A Collection of Critical Essays.* Englewood Cliffs, NJ: Prentice-Hall, 1962.

Wilson, Douglas. "Ernest Hemingway, The Nick Adams Stories." *Western Humanities Review* 27 (Fall 1973): 298.

Wilson, Edmund. "Introduction." *In Our Time.* NY: Scribner's, 1930, ix–xv.

Wylder, Delbert E. *Hemingway's Heroes.* Alburquerque: University of New Mexico Press, 1970.

Young, Philip. "'Big World Out There': The Nick Adams Stories." *Novel* 6 (1972): 11.

Acknowledgments

"Adventures of Nick Adams" by Philip Young. From *Ernest Hemingway: A Reconsideration*: 29–55. © 1966 by Philip Young. Reprinted by permission.

"Ernest Hemingway's 'The End of Something': Its Independence as a Short Story and Its Place in the 'Education of Nick Adams'" by Horst H. Kruse. From *Studies in Short Fiction* 4 (Winter 1967): 152–166. © 1966 by Newberry College. Reprinted by permission.

"Soldier Home: 'Big Two-Hearted River'" by Joseph M. Flora. From *Hemingway's Nick Adams*: 145–175. © 1982 by Louisiana State University Press. Reprinted by permission.

"Nick Adams on the Road: 'The Battler' as Hemingway's Man on the Hill" by Nicholas Gerogiannis. From *Critical Essays on Ernest Hemingway's In Our Time*, edited by Michael S. Reynolds: 176–188. © 1983 by Michael S. Reynolds. Reprinted by permission.

"'A Way You'll Never Be': A Mission of Morale" by Kenneth G. Johnston. From *Studies in Short Fiction* 23, no. 4 (Fall 1986): 429–436. © 1987 by Newberry College. Reprinted by permission.

"Hemingway's 'On Writing': A Portrait of the Artist as Nick Adams" by Lawrence Broer. From *Hemingway's Neglected Short Fiction*, edited by Susan F. Beegel: 131–140. © 1989 by Susan Field Beegel. Reprinted by permission.

"The Troubled Fisherman" by Kenneth S. Lynn. From *New Critical Approaches to the Short Stories of Ernest Hemingway*, edited by Jackson J. Benson: 149–155. © 1990 by Duke University Press. Reprinted by permission.

"Who Wrote Hemingway's *In Our Time*?" by Paul Smith. From *Hemingway Repossessed*, edited by Kenneth Rosen: 143–150. © 1994 by the Ernest Hemingway Foundation. Reprinted by permission.

"Barefoot in the Hemlocks: Nick Adams' Betrayal of Love in 'Ten Indians'" by Paul Wadden. From *The Hemingway Review* 16, no. 2 (Spring 1997): 3–18. © 1997 by the Ernest Hemingway Foundation. Reprinted by permission.

"'Scared sick looking at it': A Reading of Nick Adams in the Published Stories" by Howard L. Hannum. From *Twentieth-Century Literature* 47, no. 1 (Spring 2001): 92–113. ©2001 by Hofstra University. Reprinted by permission.

Index